INTO THE MARGINS: MIGRATION AND EXCLUSION IN SOUTHERN EUROPE

Into the Margins: Migration and Exclusion in Southern Europe

Edited by
FLOYA ANTHIAS and GABRIELLA LAZARIDIS

LONDON AND NEW YORK

First published 1999 by Ashgate Publishing

Reissued 2018 by Routledge
2 Park Square, Milton Park, Abingdon, Oxon OX14 4RN
711 Third Avenue, New York, NY 10017, USA

Routledge is an imprint of the Taylor & Francis Group, an informa business

Copyright © Floya Anthias and Gabriella Lazaridis 1999

All rights reserved. No part of this book may be reprinted or reproduced or utilised in any form or by any electronic, mechanical, or other means, now known or hereafter invented, including photocopying and recording, or in any information storage or retrieval system, without permission in writing from the publishers.

Notice:
Product or corporate names may be trademarks or registered trademarks, and are used only for identification and explanation without intent to infringe.

Publisher's Note
The publisher has gone to great lengths to ensure the quality of this reprint but points out that some imperfections in the original copies may be apparent.

Disclaimer
The publisher has made every effort to trace copyright holders and welcomes correspondence from those they have been unable to contact.

A Library of Congress record exists under LC control number : 99073318

ISBN 13: 978-1-138-32618-7 (hbk)
ISBN 13: 978-1-138-32619-4 (pbk)
ISBN 13: 978-0-429-45000-6 (ebk)

Contents

List of Contributors vii
Preface xi

1 Introduction: Into the Margins - Migration and Exclusion in Southern Europe
   Floya Anthias and Gabriella Lazaridis 1

2 The Production and Reproduction of Knowledge on International Migration in Europe: The Social Embeddedness of Social Knowledge
   Ann Singleton and Paolo Barbesino 13

3 Economic Migration and Social Exclusion: The Case of Tunisians in Italy in the 1980s and 1990s
   Faïçal Daly and Rohit Barot 35

4 Recent Immigration to Spain: The Case of Moroccans in Catalonia
   Russell King and Isabel Rodríguez-Melguizo 55

5 British Expatriates' Experience of Health and Social Services on the Costa del Sol
   Charles Betty and Michael Cahill 83

6 The Helots of the New Millennium: Ethnic-Greek Albanians and 'Other' Albanians in Greece
   Gabriella Lazaridis 105

7 The Presence of the Polish Undocumented in Greece in the Perspective of European Unification
   Krystyna Romaniszyn 123

8 Racism and New Migration to Cyprus: The
   Racialisation of Migrant Workers
   Nicos Trimikliniotis 139

9 European Union Citizenship: Exclusion, Inclusion
   and the Social Dimension
   Dora Kostakopoulou 179

Index 205

List of Contributors

Floya Anthias is Professor of Sociology and Head of Sociology at the University of Greenwich, London. She has published extensively in the area of ethnicity, gender, migration and Cypriots in Britain. Her latest book, on the Social Division of Identity, will be published by Macmillan. She is currently writing a book on young Asians and Cypriots in Britain, and researching into exclusion and citizenship in relation to self-employment practices amongst women and minorities in Britain.

Paolo Barbesino is Research Fellow at the Graduate Research Centre in Culture and Communication, University of Sussex. He is the author of articles on both communicative approaches within the social sciences and the social construction of social knowledge with a particular emphasis on the impact of information and communication technologies. He has been leading an extensive ethnographic research project on communication patterns among migrants in urban settings co-funded by the City Council of Milan.

Rohit Barot is a lecturer in Sociology at University of Bristol. He has carried out anthropological research in Uganda, India and Britain. His main area of interest is social change with respect to class, caste, ethnicity and gender. His most recent publications are *Religion and Ethnicity : Minorities and Social change in the Metropolis* (Kok Pharos 1993) and *The Racism Problematic: Contemporary Debates on Race and Ethnicity* (The Edwin Mellen Press 1997).

Charles Betty is a research student at the University of Brighton. His thesis is an exploration of the health and social issues of older British expatriates on the Cost del Sol where he now lives. After a career in teaching he became Project Director of the Social Science Research Council Action Research Project into disadvantaged children. Subsequently he became a senior educational inspector with Nottinghamshire County Council. He is the author of several children's books and a number of publications on community education.

Michael Cahill is Principal Lecturer in Social Policy at the University of Brighton. He is the author of *The New Social Policy* and his research interests encompass older people, transport and the environment.

Faiçal Daly obtained in 1990 a BSc from University of Modena in Italy and a Postgraduate Diploma and MA in European Studies in 1993-1995 from the University of West Bristol. He lived in Italy for almost ten years where he was actively involved with migrants and migration issues. As a research student in the Department of Sociology at the University of Bristol he has conducted fieldwork amongst Tunisian workers in Modena. His PhD thesis will focus on the relationship between capital and migrant labour in Middle Italy.

Russell King is Professor of Geography and Dean of the School of European Studies at the University of Sussex. He has published extensively in the field of migration in Southern Europe.

Dora Kostakopoulou is Jean Monnet lecturer in the Law and Politics of European integration at the University of East Anglia. Her research interests lie in the intersection of political theory and European integration.

Gabriella Lazaridis is a lecturer in Gender Relations and European issues at the Department of Political Science and Social Policy, University of Dundee. Her main research interests are: gender relations, human mobility from and into Southern Europe, Policies of the EU, agricultural development and women's work. She is an elected member of the ESA's executive board, has set up and is co-convenor of the European Sociological Association's (ESA) Regional Network on Southern European Societies. She is co-editor of 'Eldorado or Fortress' (Macmillan) and 'Gender and Migration in Southern Europe' (Berg). She is currently writing a book on Social Policy in Southern Europe to be published by Macmillan and researching into exclusion and citizenship in relation to self-employment practices amongst minorities in Greece (funded by the EU).

Isabel Rodríguez-Melguizo is a former postgraduate student at the Sussex European Institute, University of Sussex.

Krystyna Romaniszyn is Associate Professor at the Jagiellonian University in Krakow, Poland. She is author of two books on international migration and economic anthropology: she has also written extensively on contemporary labour migration from the East to the West. She has a background in sociology and social anthropology.

Ann Singleton worked in local government policy oriented research for several years before moving in 1992 to work in the Migration Research Unit, University College London. She has specialised in the problems of using international migration statistics and currently works with the Eurostat Migration Team in Luxembourg. She is now a member of the Centre for the Study of Social Exclusion and Injustice, School for Policy Studies at Bristol University.

Nicos Trimikliniotis is a PhD candidate at the University of Greenwich. His thesis examines the interrelation between nationalism and the state in the production, perpetuation and resolution of ethnic conflict, with Cyprus as the case study. He is a regular columnist for a Cypriot national newspaper and has been involved in various campaigns against racism, nationalism and the promotion of friendship and co-operation between the Greek Cypriots and Turkish Cypriots. He has presented numerous papers at conferences and seminars on the Cyprus problem and its resolution. He holds a BA in Law and Economics from Oxford Polytechnic, an MA in Gender and Ethnic Studies from the University of Greenwich and is qualified as a Barrister at Law.

Preface

This book is one of two volumes which arose out of a Conference jointly organised by the University of Dundee and the University of Greenwich in December 1995 at the University of Greenwich, on 'Nation and Migration in Southern Europe'. It collects together papers which provide a general overview of new forms of migration to Italy, Spain, Greece and Cyprus. The aim is to contribute to the literature in an academic field which is becoming increasingly important. Another volume is being prepared which focuses on Gender and Migration in Southern Europe (*Gender Migration in Southern Europe: women on the move*, Berg forthcoming).

We would like to acknowledge the support given by the Department of Political Science and Social Policy at the University of Dundee and the School of Social Sciences at the University of Greenwich. We would also like to thank all those who contributed to the conference, either by giving papers or participating in discussion, as well as those who gave clerical and administrative support.

Many thanks to Rose Goodwin of the Centre for Research in Ethnic Relations at the University of Warwick for producing the final manuscript.

1 Introduction: Into the Margins - Migration and Exclusion in Southern Europe

Floya Anthias and Gabriella Lazaridis

Migration is a world wide phenomenon. Transnational movements are particularly important in a global era of economic, political and social transformations. Globalisation processes have been characterised as political, economic and cultural. Globalisation has been seen as a challenge to the nation state, although also seen as generating ethnic and cultural parochialisms and localisms, or **glocalisation** in Roland Robertson's own 'hybrid' term (Robertson 1995).

It has been argued that the boundary of the nation state is traversed in the multiple ways identified by the movement of capital; the growing penetration over the globe of transnational financial capital; by the growth and penetration of new technologies; by the export and movement of communication modes including media forms and images; by the growth of transnational political and juridical groups (eg the EU and its potential); by growing international resistance and action groups (eg the Beijing Conference of Women); and by the penetration of ideologies producing a 'world system' (Wallerstein 1990) or Global Village (McLuhan 1964). One key element of globalisation theory is the identification of cultural globalisation as a core contemporary facet. Migrant groups or communities may be seen to embody the transnational principle, moving ethnic and solidary organisation from the confines of the nation state to the global arena. The nation building project of nationalism (never fully successful anywhere) of marrying the boundaries of ethnicity, the boundaries of the state and the boundaries of the nation becomes challenged. However, nation states are still with us in terms of juridical, social citizenship and cultural citizenship (Turner 1990), despite the increasing global flow of trade and communication, as well as the growth of certain forms of transnationality.

2 Into the Margins

The nation state still determines citizenship, in large part, entailing individual and group rights and entitlements, at political, juridical and social levels (an exception may be found with regard to the European Court of Human Rights). The borders of the nation state are still policed against undesirable others, in formal and informal ways, through migration controls and racism. The desire for the integration and management of minorities within, exists in the present phase of multiculturalism. At the same time there is a desire to exclude others, on the outside and the inside. Many nation states also stress the ethnic absolutist (to use Gilroy's (1993) phrase) project, of retaining the ethnic identity of their diaspora populations, and encouraging their reproduction, as well as their return to the homeland.

Social exclusion is a key term today in academic and policy discussions. Social exclusion is a term that includes within it's ambit a wide range of social relations and outcomes relating to inequality and disadvantage. At the one level, social exclusion means lack of opportunities in terms of gaining access or **inclusion** within a range of arenas in society that determine life chances. On the other hand, it also depicts a range of hurdles or boundaries that set out to prevent groups from enjoying full rights to citizenship in its fullest sense. Social exclusion may be organised around class, gender or ethnic groupings and there is always an intersection of all these dimensions and divisions for individuals. Migration is often accompanied by exclusion from social and political rights. However, men and women may experience this differently. In addition different categories of migrants will be placed differently in terms of a range of social relations; for example, economically and legally as well as in relation to the polity. Differential access to these is an important focus of contemporary discussions on new migration and new racism in Europe. Whilst current debates have depended on the experiences of migration and racism in Western Europe, there is an urgency with regard to turning our attention to the Southern European experience.

Southern Europe has a long history of transoceanic migration, that is migration to the so called 'classical countries of immigration' like the USA, Canada, Australia. It also has a long history of continental migration, that is migration to the so called 'guest worker countries' like Germany, France, Belgium, Switzerland, and the Netherlands. This came to a halt with the 'ban on recruitment' imposed by the receiving countries in the early 1970s due to the 'OPEC embargo' and the resulting economic crisis. Italy, Spain and Portugal have also long histories of colonial migration; these trends have been analysed in detail and have been intensively discussed in academic circles and in politics. In Britain, there has been a history of colonial migration, particularly from the New Commonwealth in the post-war period as well as third world migration. Economic migrants and asylum seekers have been important within these flows.

In recent years, however, a major reversal of historical patterns has developed, with the Southern European countries becoming receivers of migrants (both poor migrants and highly qualified experts) and of refugees, from non-European countries. According to Simon (1987) there were 2 million migrants in the four countries in the late 1980s, the majority of whom were clandestine or illegal migrants. For the mid-late 1990s, the number has been estimated to be around 3.5 million (King 1997: 10), 1.6 million of whom are legal migrants (King and Konjhodzic 1995: 47). The balance of legal and illegal migrants changes over time according to the pattern of arrivals, deportations and regularisations.

This quantitative growth has increased the urgency for addressing the topic because of the possible legal, social and political responses and consequences involved. The initial response to the phenomenon of migration was a *laissez faire* approach. The absence of a strategy for the development of a coherent migration policy resulted in a number of ad hoc measures. Gradually however, more rigorous controls were introduced. These were mainly the result of pressures from the Schengen partners to impose barriers on non-EU nationals seeking entry to EU member states, but also because of various internal social and political pressures to exclude non-EU nationals; the latter include xenophobia, ethnocentrism and racism. These are often couched in terms of fear of racist extremism (den Boer 1995) and of xenophobic violence 'as reactions against a growing number of immigrants (non-EU citizens)' (ibid:97). There have been a range of demonstrations, political debates, police powers and actions, press releases about the 'enemies within' in Southern European countries. Some of these countries have introduced regularisation processes which have not been fully successful in as much as many migrants have not been legalised. In addition, employers have continued to use clandestine workers, offering them no social security, job contract or decent wages.

Southern European countries may function today as the 'entrance hall' to the EU, and often serve as a 'waiting room' for many migrants who have as a destination the Northern EU countries. Moreover, there are EU nationals who migrate - both economically active people and those who have retired from full-time employment. As EU citizens they have a privileged status compared to Third-country migrants.

There are a plethora of reasons for the rapid development of migration into Southern Europe. Long coastlines, numerous islands and long mountainous borders make the clandestine entry of migrants, with the assistance of well organised smugglers, possible. In addition, many enter these countries legally as tourists, or as workers in the shipping industry and overstay, whereas others enter Southern Europe as asylum seekers. Some of these have the aim of moving on to the traditional countries of immigration in Northern Europe. The specific nature of Southern European economies yields a high demand for a flexible labour force in agriculture (harvesting of tomatoes, grapes, oranges, olives, etc.), tourism and catering, construction industries (confined to men), street hawking and domestic service (a female preserve). A large informal sector means that there is demand for migrant workers in certain low-paid, precarious jobs which are unattractive to locals. Finally there are historical reasons related to colonialism which account for migration from ex-colonial societies into the metropolitan centres.

The growth of immigration has run parallel with the trend to the flexibilisation and casualisation of Southern European labour markets. The crisis of large-scale industry affected mainly Northern European economies in the 1970s and 1980s. This was also echoed in Southern European countries, especially Italy, where it has led to a fragmentation of economic activity and the development of smaller-scale flexible units. Some of these form part of the hidden economy, and have come to rely partly on migrant workers. Side by side with these 'structural' jobs in the hidden economy are those which arise when agricultural and tourist activities are at their height, and call on seasonal foreign labour during peak periods.

One recurrent theme in much of the literature on migration relates to the ways in which 'race' and racism may be conceptualised as particular forms of social exclusion. Recent writing on 'race' and racism (eg Miles 1993, Goldberg 1993, Anthias and Yuval Davis 1993) indicates the importance of ethnic and nationalist discourses and practices. For example, the idea of a new racism (Barker 1981) embodies a shift in the central organising elements of racist discourse away from explicit biological notions to culturalist or nationalist ones. The argument is that much racist discourse is now couched in terms of cultural identity and national boundaries instead of relying on the idea of the biological inferiority of groups (Barker 1981, Gilroy 1987, Miles 1989). The 'new racism', as it has come to be called, has been the subject of much debate (eg Miles 1989). The notion of the plurality of racisms as opposed to some unitary system of representations and practices, has now become common place (Cohen 1988, Anthias 1990 and 1992).

This raises the issue of a specific European racism. Whether this form is new or not has been variously asserted or contested (eg see Miles 1992). What is clear, however, is that new forms of migration and exclusion are giving rise to particular constellations of ethnic and race based discourses and practices at a range of different societal levels. Hence it is important to begin to delineate the parameters of these in the case of Southern Europe. Goldberg (1993) gives a subtle historicised account of the extremely fluid referents of race terms. He looks at the shifting definitions and usage of the term stating that it is

> ...a fluid, transforming, historically specific concept parasitic on theoretic and social discourses for the meaning it assumes at any historical moment.
> Goldberg 1993: 74

There have been attempts to provide typologies of racism, such as those that are based on inegalitarianism and those on difference; the distinction between subordination as a form of inclusion and separation and exclusion or exploitation and extermination has been made. The recent work of Wieviorka (1991) distinguishes between prejudice, discrimination, disadvantage and violence. The problems with these typologies is that they tend to be a bit like shopping lists, and it is not clear how they begin and where they can end. It may be preferable to distinguish between the discourse of racisms and their systemic implications for action (Anthias 1990). We can designate ideological/discursive, practices/intersubjectivities, and outcomes as three different modes for identifying racisms.

Racisms are forms of ideology and practice that serve to inferiorise and exclude (or include in subordinate positions) all groups whose boundary is defined in terms of an ethnic or collective origin (Anthias 1992). The boundary does not have to be a racialised one in order for racist exclusions to operate therefore. Racism can be regarded as the most extreme form of the exclusionary face of ethnic phenomena (which can also involve practices of extermination, repatriation, exploitation, slavery as well as racial harassment and unequal social rights and denial of access to resources of different types). Other forms of the exclusionary face of ethnic phenomena are to be found in ethnocentrism (the belief in the naturalness or taken for granted superiority of the ways of being of the ethnic group) and xenophobia or the dislike of outsiders. This becomes racist when the group has power to exclude (Anthias 1992). These are probably the most common forms that racism takes in the context of new migrations in Southern Europe.

Policy makers and activists, dedicated to fighting racism in the 1990s, need to be aware of the dynamic and shifting nature of the terrain of racism and how ethnicity may be used in both the pursuit of racism and its attack. The static and reified notions of difference embodied in much multiculturalist policy in Western Europe, from education to support and funding of the voluntary sector, need to be abandoned. Attention must be paid to the complexities involved. The European framework highlights these complexities further by providing different instances of ethnic and racist practices. This book goes some way to showing the many different forms of 'otherness' implicated in the social relations of migration in Southern Europe.

The ways in which the social relation relating to migration and racism will develop in Southern Europe is difficult to predict. Much will depend on the evolution of migration and related policies in the region and within the EU. Policies towards regularisation are still in an embryonic stage, but as more and more migrants become regularised, their readiness to accept working conditions unacceptable to local citizens will diminish. At the same time, pressures from within and from the EU may push Southern European countries to move to a stricter regime of control against migration. Much will also depend on economic and broader ideological factors as well as to the political climate around 'nationalist' agendas.

This volume brings together a number of papers which provide a general overview of migration and social exclusion in some of the countries of Southern Europe. The articles collected address the phenomenon of migration in Italy, Spain, Greece and Cyprus. This collection arose out of a concern that the specificities of Southern Europe were neglected in the increasing volume of published literature in the field of migration studies. The aims of this book are multiple: first, to address the gap in the literature; second, to correct an academic agenda, which is preoccupied with the North and more recently the East; and finally, to alert us to new challenges facing the South. The book does not purport to provide a much needed analysis of the highly differentiated and gendered nature of migration. Such an enterprise would require the deployment of data and research which specifically looks at gender and other differences. Gender and migration is a theme that we address in a sister volume currently being prepared and which will be published by Berg in the near future.

The timing of the book is opportune both for the Southern countries and for the EU since it comes at a time when the South faces a massive influx of migrant labour both from the Eastern and Central European countries, from non-EU member states bordering the Mediterranean, from Africa and the Far East. The construction of marginalised 'others', the growth of new forms of xenophobia, different degrees of exclusion and the racialisation of different categories of migrants, all receive attention by the papers in this volume. These have important implications for both different groups of migrants and for the citizens of the receiving countries. The chapters in this volume address some of the themes related to exclusion, racism, stereotyping, labour market disadvantages and other forms of differential access to social and economic benefits.

Ann Singleton and Paolo Barbesino look at how methods of collection and analysis of data produces migration as an object of study and as a body of knowledge. They link this process more broadly to the question of how social knowledge is produced by the social sciences, and how this relates to the knowledge produced by public administrative bodies. The argument is that social science discourses have strengthened the selection of concepts and definitions used in the administrative processes and structures which produce statistical knowledge. They argue that there is a need to understand the study of international migration in Europe within this context. Given that many of the papers in this volume rely heavily on statistical information, this chapter is a reminder of the social construction of this knowledge. Singleton and Barbesino argue that data availability has driven much of the theoretical work in the field of migration studies. They link issues of migration to the hegemony of the nation state form within which population categories are the object of governance. Discourses on migration are shaped by policy makers, social scientists and public opinion and therefore it is problematic to work with a notion of 'objective facts' about migration. They particularly note the problem of undocumented migration in this context. They use the special case of the Italian statistical system in order to exemplify their argument.

Daly and Barot examine Tunisian migration to Italy between 1980 and 1990. The Tunisian community constitutes one of the largest migrant groups in Italy. The authors try to explore the factors that drew Tunisians to Italy, looking at economic and political changes in both countries. The paper also looks at economic stagnation and political instability in Tunisia in the late 1970s. Geographic proximity and the historical links between the two countries, the flow of information and the promotion of a consumerist culture amongst Tunisian families induced Tunisians to think that Italy was a 'paradise'. The open door policy of the Italian government until the mid-1980s also fostered in-migration. The authors look at the settlement of Tunisians in the Italian economy and the integration of Tunisians within Italian society. They argue that the regularisation processes in Italy led to 'a high level of mobilisation of Tunisians' who 'freed from the iron grip of the black economy of the South ... took advantage of the economic opportunities offered by the small and medium enterprises in the centre-north'. The authors also look at issues of racism. They examine both structural racism and discrimination in the labour market, as well as various stereotypes and the use of slogans which, as the authors argue, result in the disruption of social harmony. Immigration evokes a variety of negative reactions amongst Italians and the term migrant is a label that identifies the non-European and those with dark skins. There have been propagandist campaigns of the right wing neo-fascist parties and a growth in the marginalisation of migrant workers as well as a growth in intolerance. Anti-immigration songs and slogans in football stadiums and political meetings express particular forms of racial harassment. The race card is used by political parties in order to gain electoral power. The anti-Muslim nature of the racism is apparent. Muslims in Italy are often regarded as fundamentalists, and Arabs may be seen as potential terrorists. Citizenship is a central issue for Tunisians, for there are different rules for Europeans and non-Europeans, indicating the discriminatory nature of citizenship rules in Italy. Daly and Barot also refer to the specific role of women in migration, showing how many Tunisian women migrate to Italy to work as domestic servants. According to the authors, this allows them to escape from the traditional restrictions they face, on the one hand, but also promotes particular forms of exclusion, on the other.

King and Rodríguez-Melguizo look at recent immigration into Spain, focusing particularly on Moroccans in Catalonia. They use the notion of 'differential exclusion' to highlight the specific exclusion of Moroccans in Catalonia, a concept introduced by Castles (1995). This concept denotes that migrants may be incorporated into certain sectors but not others, and that they may be marginalised by ethnic difference and immigrant status. The links between class and ethnic background are also important. The high economic activity rates of Moroccans in Spain is typical of economic migrants more generally. In terms of labour market participation, migrants tend to be at the bottom of the labour hierarchy. Whilst migrants from Europe and Latin America are not so excluded, African groups and especially Moroccans suffer from multiple social exclusion. Ideas about the 'Moslem menace' are current in Spain, reflecting the ethnocentric and alarmist stance of the mass media towards a fear of fundamentalism and illegal migration. King and Rodríguez-Melguizo also relate the case of Moroccans in Spain to wider debates on globalisation and regionalism.

An important feature of the migration patterns to be found in Spain is retirement migration. Betty and Cahill look at retirement migration from Britain to coastal Spain, a growing and important feature of the patterns to be found in Spain. Examining the experiences of British expatriates in particular, the authors concentrate on in the use of health and social services. The issues which confront older British people in Spain are similar to those faced by their peers in the UK, but the context is different. Spain is a rudimentary welfare state and the patterns of health and social services have been influenced by a social policy which involves a greater reliance on the traditional family form as a support unit. The authors also examine the formation of exclusive expatriate clubs which, through providing voluntary social service functions, cater for the needs of the older expats. These clubs therefore fill a need for 'friendship and support', and help elderly expatriates to protect their identity. However, they also provide a form of self imposed *exclusion* from participation in the Spanish community. The inability of British expatriates to speak fluent Spanish is a deterrent to their integration of the migrant community and may indicate a failure to be oriented culturally to their country of residence. Unlike the other migrants referred to by King and Rodriguez, they have little experience of racist exclusions or xenophobia.

Lazaridis focuses on Albanian migration into Greece and analyses the processes through which the stigmatisation and social exclusion of 'other' Albanians as opposed to ethnic-Greek-Albanians, is conducted in Greek society. It also looks at differences, however subtle these may be, in the treatment these groups receive. She argues that although both these social groups are found in low-paid occupations, the ethnic-Greek Albanian is treated more favourably by the host country than 'other' Albanians. The 'other' Albanians are treated as people of a lesser human worth, and hence Lazaridis characterises these as 'helots of the new millennium'. The negative stereotyping found in media discourse stigmatises the majority of Albanians as they are frequently dealt with as an undifferentiated mass. This discourse legitimates their racialisation and functions as a mechanism of social exclusion.

Romaniszyn looks at Polish migration to Greece. Although Polish migrants, particularly the undocumented, suffer clear social disadvantages because of their legal status and social position, nonetheless they are less disadvantaged than the Albanians discussed by Lazaridis. Indeed, their personal orientation, according to Romaniszyn, is geared towards cultural integration with Greek natives. This contrasts with the British expatriates in Spain who are less motivated to acquire the language and remain aloof from the Spanish language and less oriented to Spanish culture. Polish workers in Greece try to learn the language and adopt elements of Greek culture as their own. This is similar to ethnic Greek Albanians, who according to Lazaridis, stress their Greekness as a way of becoming accepted by Greek society. Romaniszyn also charts the degree to which Polish workers in Greece are placed in the informal sector of the economy, particularly domestic service for women, and building construction for men.

Trimikliniotis considers the phenomenon of temporary migrant labour in Cyprus in order to assess the development of racism and to consider the broader impact of migration on Cypriot society. He does this by looking at official statistics and publications, and at the media, particularly newspaper reports and articles. This links to Lazaridis' illustration of the ways in which Albanians have been racialised and indeed criminalised by the media. Trimikliniotis is particularly concerned with the ways in which migration has become racialised. He also looks at the links between race and class and gender and race, exploring the different position of women migrants, particularly in their role as domestic maids and sex workers. He charts the failure of left wing groups to seriously address the problems faced by migrant workers.

In the last chapter, Kostakopoulou explores the notion of a transnational citizenship and its potential as found within the EU, whilst stressing the many facets of discrimination and exclusion in the EU framework. She sees the EU as having fruitful possibilities in terms of a post-national political arrangement, and tries to specify what these fruitful possibilities may be. She locates a central contradiction, however, which is found in the continuing ideology of nation within the parameters of the EU. She discusses some of the ways in which Southern European nations have implemented restrictive migration and citizenship policies for non-EU migrants. A central argument is the need to rethink the adequacy of the nation state category for the EU. She critiques the ethno-national approach to state formation, and opposes a notion of Europe forged through common cultural myths. However, she is in favour of treating Europe as a political community based on common political principles. Developments at the global level indicate the existence of multiple identities and loyalties crossing national borders. An alternative conception of citizenship based on domicile is advocated. This could foster, according to Kostakopoulou, the creation of a civic and inclusive European identity. She formulates a framework for developing a 'heterogeneous European public' which is inclusive and empowering.

References

Anthias, F. (1990), 'Race and Class Revisited-conceptualising Race and Racisms', *Sociological Review*, Feb. 1990, Vol. 38, 1: 19-42.
Anthias, F. (1992), 'Connecting "race" and ethnic phenomena', *Sociology, August*, Vol. 26, 3: 421-438.
Anthias, F. and Yuval-Davis, N. (1993), *Racialised Boundaries: Nation, 'race', gender, colour and class and the anti-racist struggle,* London: Routledge.
Barker, M. (1981), *The New Racism*, London: Junction Books.
Castles, S. (1995), 'How nation-states respond to immigration and ethnic diversity', *New Community*, 21: 293-308.
Cohen, P. (1988), 'The Perversions of Inheritance' in Cohen and Bains (eds.) *Multi Racist Britain*, London and Basingstoke: Macmillan.
den Boer, M. (1995), 'Moving between bogus and bona fide: the policing of inclusion and exclusion in Europe' in Miles, R. and Thranhardt, D. (eds.) *Migration and European integration: the dynamics of inclusion and exclusion*, London: Pinter.
Gilroy, P. (1987), *There Ain't no black in the Union Jack*, London: Hutchinson.
Gilroy, P. (1993), *The Black Atlantic*, London: Verso.

Goldberg, D.T. (1993), *Racist Culture: Philosophy and the Politics of meaning,* Oxford: Blackwell.
King, R. (1997), 'Southern Europe in the changing global map and typology of migration' paper presented at the conference 'Non-military aspects of security in Southern Europe: migration, employment and labour market', organised by the Institute of International Economic Relations and by the Regional Network on Southern European societies (ESA), 19-21 September, Santorini, Greece.
King, R. and Konjhodzic, I. (1995), 'Labour, employment and migration in Southern Europe' research papers in geography, University of Sussex, UK.
McLuhan, M. (1964), *Understanding Media,* London: Routledge.
Miles, R. (1989), *Racism.* London: Routledge.
Miles, R. (1992), 'Le racisme europeen dans son context historique', *Genesis* 8, Paris.
Miles, R. (1993), *Racism after 'race relations',* London: Routledge.
Robertson, R. (1995), 'Glocalisation: Time-Space and Homogeneity-Heterogeneity', in M. Featherstone, S. Lash and R. Robertson (ed.) *Global Modernities,* London: Sage.
Simon, G. (1987), 'Migration in Southern Europe: an overview' in *The Future of Migration,* Paris: OECD: 159-291.
Turner, B. (1990), 'The Two Faces of Sociology: Global or National' in M. Featherstone (ed.), *Global Culture,* London: Sage.
Wallerstein, I. (1990), 'Culture as the Ideological Battleground of the Modern World - System', in M. Featherstone (ed.) *Global Culture,* London: Sage.
Wieviorka, M. (1991), *L'Espace du racisme,* Paris: Le Seuil.

2 The Production and Reproduction of Knowledge on International Migration in Europe: The Social Embeddedness of Social Knowledge

Ann Singleton and Paolo Barbesino

1. Introduction

This chapter emerged from a series of research projects on which we have been working over a period of over four years. The research was carried out using two different broad approaches, which we then attempted to merge.

The first approach was to address the practical and conceptual problems and challenges which statistical data on international migration present to the user. For those users concerned with policy related research, these have been grouped around a number of shifting foci, moving from earlier concerns with the examination of sources, concepts and definitions, through work on the compilation and harmonisation of cross-national data-sets, to a more recent understanding of the need for qualitative data on the characteristics of migrants. This need has been well recognised in research and literature on women migrants and on the contribution of migrants to the informal economy. Future research needs are seen to drive the further development and expansion of typologies of recorded and unrecorded migrants. A central problem common to these research concerns lies in the attempts of statisticians to reduce complex and dynamically inter-related patterns and processes to the limited analytical tool of a single, common global definition of a recorded international migrant.

The second approach addresses the question of how the process of analysis, whether using qualitative or quantitative methods, produces migration as a body of knowledge and as an object of study. This relates broadly to the question as to how social knowledge produced by social sciences relates to that produced by public administrative bodies. The interaction of these two processes of knowledge production can be described as a form of ontological gerrymandering in which social science discourses have strengthened the selection of concepts and definitions used in the administrative processes and structures which produce the statistical knowledge. At the same time social scientists rely heavily on the knowledge, concepts and definitions produced within these systems. The effect is that boundaries are preserved between the conceptual and theoretical assumptions which are 'known' to be problematic and others whose status of truth is not to be questioned (Woolgar and Pawluch 1985)

We argue here that there is an academic, moral and political responsibility to understand the questions thrown up by these approaches in relation to the study of international migration in Europe. We have chosen to use a comparative approach to examine the production of statistical data in EU member states, focusing in particular on the case study of Italy.[1]

2. The paradox

Growing interest among policy-makers and statisticians in the new and emerging patterns and flows of international migrants in Europe has stimulated four broad strands of recent research, funded by Eurostat, the Statistical Office of the European Communities. Initially, the main focus was on the creation of internationally comparable datasets. This necessitated systematic analysis of the sources, methodologies, concepts and definitions used in each country (for example: Poulain, Debuisson and Eggerick 1991; Salt, Singleton and Hogarth 1994; Salt and Singleton 1993, 1994). A second, closely related area is evident in continuing concern with the production of improved, harmonised and internationally comparative statistics. A third strand is improvement of the quality of data using statistical methods. Fourthly, increasing attention is now being paid to the production of metadata which will allow the user to interpret more accurately and to manipulate statistics on recorded migrants.

The boundaries of this type of quantitative research may now, in some respects, have been reached. Further progress is likely to be restricted by the limitations arising from data sources. In this dynamic field of study, however, new and emerging flows of migrants have also stimulated demand for data which, by definition, appear impossible to obtain: quantitative and qualitative data on unrecorded migrants. In responding to this demand, it is likely that new typologies of migrants and migration flows will be developed, together with statistical models capable of identifying or quantifying flows of international migrants not currently recorded in administrative and statistical systems.

The multiplicity of sources on all recorded migrants, of methodologies, variables, concepts and definitions within and between countries present major difficulties. It is necessary to take into account the type of organisation, method of collection (for example, surveys or registers), and the type of administrative form used to record the data (for example, residence or work permit applications). In some countries there is one responsible organisation, the National Statistical Institute (Central Statistical Office). In others there may be several including the institutions or Ministries which collect the raw data and the institution which tabulates and publishes the data. Methods of collection may be direct or indirect, computerised, centralised or not. At the European level a bewildering combination may be involved. This diversity may be considered both a strength and a weakness for the purposes of research. On the one hand, it hinders attempts to obtain harmonised datasets, on the other, it allows for a wider range of migrants and migrant characteristics to be identified.

The problems above present users of international migration data with a considerable challenge: to undergo a steep learning curve in the problems of using such data and to accept their limitations whilst revising research plans accordingly. Despite efforts to harmonise definitions, the reliability of the composite cross national tables suffers from the combined limitations of all the national sources.

There are also a whole set of problems of a different nature which raise questions about the ways in which the production of statistical data construct a series of knowledges about international migration. In order to understand how these knowledges emerge, it is necessary to undertake research into the ways in which knowledge is produced and reproduced.

3. The theoretical questions

Critical sociological analysis of the types of knowledge which 'hard' sciences such as biology, physics, information technology, chemistry produce has not generally been matched by a similar reflexive approach towards the knowledge produced by the social sciences. Whereas different forms of constructivism within social studies of science and technology have questioned the standard view of science, according to which science describes the real world as it is, much more rarely has sociology cast doubts as to its alleged capacity to describe society as it is. Migration studies are no exception in this regard. In combination with a legacy of positivism and heavy reliance on statistical data, the result has often been an uncritical attitude on the part of researchers toward their own role in the production of knowledge about migration. In consequence, observations on migration and the language used to express them are usually taken to be independent of theory. The observations and statistical data are subsequently included in new theories. Hence, as in the broader fields of sociological enquiry, it is assumed that the process of theory-building consists of scrutinising a certain number of given cases and gradually producing generalisations based on their common features. Theories aim at generating 'laws' which subsequently play a crucial role in empirical research by providing a cumulative and specific cognitive background. Migration studies have not been immune to these processes and data availability has driven much of the development of theoretical work in this field (Salt and Singleton 1995).

Apart from a small number of attempts within liberal sociology (e.g. Mannheim 1936), only a few Marxist sociologists have fought this common understanding by deploying research programmes aimed at unmasking ideological presuppositions of social knowledge. Resorting to the use of concepts such as ideology or social determination of knowledge, these critiques assumed however that an ultimate access to social reality was possible. It was only by establishing such a virtual relation with something which would be the truth that they managed to distinguish between that which in a discourse depends upon truth and scientificity, and that which might depend upon other things. Yet, they still had to assume that either social knowledge or ideology were in a subordinate position towards something which should work as an economic or material determinant.

A different approach is to examine how the effects of 'truth' are historically brought about within discourses which are themselves neither true nor false (Foucault 1977:12). In this perspective, one has to approach issues of migration by relating them to the broader question of governmentality, i.e. the form of government typical of the modern nation state in which population, rather than estates or property, constitutes the object of rule. According to Foucault, this form of government is constituted by an ensemble of institutions, procedures, analyses, calculations, reflections and tactics, and it is paralleled by the invention, operationalisation and institutionalisation of specific knowledges, disciplines and technologies, which are themselves the conditions for an extension of the governing capacity (Foucault 1979: 19; Johnson 1993: 140-41). This also implies the need to investigate how contradictions and inconsistencies among the contribution of different social sciences and administrative practices are eluded or apparently reduced. Notions of scientificity and accumulation have therefore to be uncoupled, and each of them has to be given separate sociological treatment (Woolgar 1988).

As science and technology studies have shown, this has far-reaching consequences on the way that 'truth' is conceptualised. Truth now can only be regarded as an operator regulating communication among others (Luhmann 1990b: 167), or, in other words, as a set of ruled procedures for producing, sharing, circulating and functioning of statements (Foucault 1977: 27). As operator, truth has no relationship to the objectivity of reality: it only allows a distinction between true and false statements. In turn, true and false do not refer either to objects or to forms of reality. On the contrary, they are communication marks indicating which options are available when a knowledge claim is evaluated: whether to go on taking for granted what is meant to be true or to stop and think about the conditions under which a statement has been held as false. Whenever a statement is asked, on the basis of theories and methods currently at hand, whether it is true or false, this constitutes an operation of science. Standards for deciding whether a statement is true change, but in the very moment of its appearance each operation has to take them as given, without therefore being able to question and modify them. Moreover, once it is accepted that truth has an historicity, one should ask how it is possible to analyse the historicity of truth in the absence of the guarantees of truth (Dean 1994: 215).

This raises questions about the fundamental unit of analysis as well as the attitude of social sciences to transformations in the set of basic distinctions used in monitoring issues of migration and ethnicity. It becomes clear that the use of 'objective facts' about individual migrants moving in time and space and of concepts of citizenship, country of origin and nationality to classify and define migrants is a fundamentally problematic process.

4. The construction and production of migration statistics

Migration statistics are at the core of discourses around international migration at national and international levels. Any attempt to understand their relevance must address not only their cognitive dimension but also the social aspects of their production. This approach, which following Gephart can be defined as ethnostatistics, stresses concern for the actual behaviour, and the informal sub-culture, or local knowledge and activities of producers and users of statistics. This informal knowledge integrates and extends the formal and technical knowledge codified in statistics (Gephart 1988: 10; Bloor, Goldberg & Emslie 1991). In a comparative perspective the ethnostatistical study of the actual configuration of national monitoring systems in the European Union and the differences in their practices and functioning may help explain different degrees of visibility of issues of migration as well as the different forms taken by their thematisation in national discourses. As Ian Hacking (1990: 34) has pointed out, since different administrations count different things, the number that are heaped up differ from case to case. National ways of conceiving statistical data vary in the wake of the differences of different nation states as to what has to be counted and how, though this by no means implies that we should conceive of a nation state as a coherent subject. In any national context, discourses on migration are continuously shaped by policy makers, social scientists and public opinion. In this sense one could talk of a 'cultural dissemination of knowledge', whereby different sets of statements emerge, merge and re-emerge in and through the communication on migration. Such dissemination constitutes a 'discursively circular form of discourse within discourse' (Walker 1988: 55).

In the field of migration statistics in Europe, concepts and definitions used to classify and measure international migration flows have been examined and are now thoroughly documented in Poulain (1991); Salt, Singleton and Hogarth (1994); Eurostat (1993, 1994). The processes through which this knowledge is produced and legitimated are less completely understood. Inconsistent data and data sources affect the analysis of patterns and trends, identification of causes of migration, and the projection of potential future movements across Europe (Salt and Singleton 1995). This applies particularly when attempting comparison of data from more than one national source or on two or more countries of origin and/or destination. In addition, the changing composition of the EU and EEA continues to create problems and extra work annually for the statisticians in each country. Even for fully computerised databases containing fully disaggregated data on citizenship and country of origin/destination groups, resources and staffing levels do not usually allow prioritisation of the task of re-calculating the still expanding EU and EEA. Problems are most acute in attempting comparisons across the whole geographical area of Europe. They can be limited but not overcome by focusing only on the countries of the EU or EEA only. Some of these problems may be overcome by documenting existing databases and cross-national datasets. The most comprehensive cross-national data set on international migration stocks and flows in the EU and EEA is the Eurostat database. This is compiled from national sources in each member state. Other databases include those of the OECD (SOPEMI) and UNECE.[2]

Resource problems in the NSIs and Ministries have also been caused by fluctuations in actual flows. In some countries, staffing levels were increased to speed the processing of asylum applications. Reduced numbers were then followed by staff reductions in the appropriate Ministries. These fluctuations in personnel and resourcing exacerbate the problems associated with data collection and tabulation by officials who are not demographers or statisticians. In addition, despite recent changes outlined below which may help to improve the potential for data exploitation and manipulation in some countries, the problems remain in relation to data harmonisation.

The study of official statistics on migration should not, therefore, be merely concerned with showing that data derived from official sources may be to some extent inadequate. In fact, social scientists have for long complained that official statistics may suffer from bias and distortion, or that the practical concerns of bureaucracies may prevent data from being formulated according to social science standards (Hammersley & Atkinson 1995: 168-69).

5. Documenting the undocumented

Given the current growth of interest in 'undocumented' and 'illegal' migration, there is a new additional onus on researchers to understand the processes of knowledge production described above. It is now clear that in addition to tackling the data problems connected with recorded migration, academics and policy-makers increasingly are attempting to grasp the nettle of measuring and/or estimating the stocks and flows of unrecorded or inadequately recorded migrants. These are migrants who are not recorded in official administrative or statistical systems. Existing sources on labour migrants do not cover new types of labour migrants - those manifested in flows of tourist workers, suitcase traders and many forms of temporary employment, including legal and illegal employment in the informal economy. But the question is not straightforward. Categories of unrecorded, or inadequately recorded, labour migrants include EU nationals such as posted workers, transit migrants of all nationalities, suitcase traders from different countries of origin, the self-employed, 'forced' migrants and hidden migration including clandestine movements. Additional statistical definitional problems arise from the equation of unrecorded as illegal, and with the many outstanding areas of unharmonised legislation on migration across Europe. 'Category-switching', the movement of an individual over time between different administrative categories and legal statuses, further complicates the question of obtaining up-to-date data on recorded migration.

Consequently, problems associated with using data on recorded migrants appear minimal when set beside those on unrecorded migrants although they may be categorised as being related to three broad areas: sources, definitions and concepts.

Firstly, there are few sources other than estimates, border head-counts and statistics on persons removed or deported. The data from Ministries of the Interior are universally partial, covering only certain categories of unrecorded migrants when they have become known to the authorities. In considering unrecorded migration, the use of estimates of total numbers does nothing to indicate the complexity of these flows and the range of characteristics of unrecorded migrants. The estimates may be to a greater or lesser extent accurate depending on the method of estimation. Where they are produced by statistical modelling techniques and influenced by a relationship with data on recorded migrants, their accuracy will be influenced by the factors relevant to the sources on recorded migrants.

Secondly, the definition of unrecorded migrants is often taken to be synonymous with 'illegal' migrants. The two are not equivalent, as recorded migrants may be in an illegal situation of one kind or another, and unrecorded migrants may be legally present in a country. In addition, there is often an overlap between categories of migrants who are temporary, in irregular employment and those who are unrecorded. The overlapping categories create problems of 'double-estimates'.

Thirdly, there are complex and significant conceptual problems arising from the attempt to use cross-national estimates of stocks and flows of unrecorded international migrants in Europe. Comparison is hindered by the differing populations captured in each statistical system and by the different legal systems in each country.

In addition to these three broad areas, remains the question raised above, about the production of knowledge. Of course, it is important for researchers to obtain as full an understanding as possible of the internal inconsistencies of international data-sets. One of the authors has spent almost four years engaged in such tasks. It is not sufficient, however, to document limitations produced by incompatibility of sources, concepts and definitions and the internal inconsistencies of data sets. If we do not tackle the question of the need to understand the character of statistics as a social product we are suggesting that it is possible to identify something close to a truth about migration or illegal migration.

The crucial issue is to investigate under which conditions the construction of statistical data occurs. Cicourel made this point clear by remarking, for instance, that 'the basic assumption of conventional research on crime, delinquency and law is to view compliance and deviance as having their own ontological significance, and the measuring rod is some set of presumably "clear" rules whose meaning is also "ontologically" and epistemologically clear' (Cicourel 1967: 331). Moreover, even in the study of social problems, language is widely misperceived as transparent. The social 'work' performed by language in selecting, varying or retaining forms of construction of social problems is routinely overlooked (Fairclough 1992: 211). An example of Italian research on migration may help to explain this point. In a paper presented to a plenary session of the Italian Statistical Society, on Foreigners in Italian Society commenting on the impacts of a new (1992) citizenship law the author states:

> in the future it will become impossible to determine the size of the foreign immigrant population and their descendants in the country by referring to their nationality, for such a category does not enable us to distinguish and to monitor the ever increasing numbers of people who *have become* or who *are held to be* Italians.
>
> Strozza 1995: 3, emphasis added

This statement enacts a paradox. It is suggested that people who *have become* or *are held to be* Italians under the law on citizenship should not be counted as Italians because they *have become* or *are held to be* Italians under the citizenship law. Such a paradox cannot be unfolded by appealing to any set of presumably 'clear' rules whose meaning is also ontologically and epistemologically clear. On the contrary, it can be unfolded by interpretation and negotiation processes which occur in the creation of knowledge. For instance in Norway, the foreign population is been redefined and categorised to produce new tabulation of statistical data which will include as foreigners children who are Norwegian citizens if their parents were foreign-born. In the UK, an 'ethnic question' which was not solely about 'ethnicity' was introduced in the 1991 Census. In the classification nine identifiable groups were used: Black African, Black Caribbean, Black other, Indian, Pakistani, Bangladeshi, Chinese, White, Asian, and Other, thus combining concepts of ethnicity, nationality and citizenship (Johnson 1993). Social sciences play a crucial role in preserving the outcome of such processes by enacting practices to keep the boundaries between what is meant to be problematic and that whose status of truth is not to be questioned (Woolgar & Pawluch 1985).

6. Studying the statistical systems - the use of ethnographic approaches

International migration statistics, by definition, record only those migrants known to the civil, administrative or police authorities (depending on the source). These statistics are forms of hard data. Ethnographic fieldwork in situations where hard data are routinely produced provides precious insights into the production of knowledge about international migration. By focusing on the role played by contingencies, interpretation and negotiation in the creation of knowledge (Knorr-Cetina 1993: 258-59), ethnography helps understand the organisational culture of each agency as well as processes whereby variables are constructed and final statistics produced.

In order to lead an ethnostatistical analysis of a national system producing statistical data all agencies involved in monitoring activities have to be preliminarily sorted out. It is necessary to distinguish between the territorial and the functional segmentation of agencies.

One has then to distinguish between the system integration and its articulation. Integration is understood as systematic continuity in the collection of data together with its capacity for intertwining among different databases and the linkage among agencies. Analysis focuses on a) gathering procedures, b) organisational dynamics of single agencies, and c) interorganisational dynamics shaping the overall configuration of the monitoring system. Assessment of the performance of such a system entails considering lack of synchronicity in the gathering of data by different agencies and dishomogeneity in the structure and quality of data.

Articulation refers to both the total extension of monitored variables and the degree of internal differentiation of each variable. Here the analysis aims at mapping the variables monitored by the system and assessing the degree of precision and accuracy of the implemented devices when compared to the distinctions whereby variables are set.

Administrative agencies have to be carefully distinguished from other non-administrative statistical sources, whether they belong to the state or not. By so doing one can draw the actual map of the monitoring system and define its structure. Particular attention should be paid to likely networks of formal communication among different agencies. A further step is to collect the set of monitoring devices used in day-to-day activities so to find out which are the variables included and the way in which they are shaped (e.g. forms, questionnaires). This eventually leads to the analysis of published statistics and the rhetoric that accomplishes the meanings in reports displaying those statistics.

Interviews with experts within given agencies who are in charge of selecting methodological options and data-collecting procedures may be useful provided that the peculiar situation arising from the interviewer and the respondent having a common background knowledge and shared understandings is attentively considered (Platt 1981). At this stage the structure of computer software used has to be analysed in order to find out whether a loss of information occurs when transferring data from paper forms to computer-aided storage and processing. Ethnography also allows us to detect networks of informal communication among agencies which may help the system cope with low levels of integration.

Building on this research program, since late 1994 we have been investigating the structure and functioning of the Italian statistical system releasing data on migration. The analysis of the set of monitoring devices, the way in which they were originally established, and the kind of transformation they underwent, provides useful insights into the way in which the discourse on migration is framed in the country and how it has changed since the late 80s. The Ministry of Interior has been releasing official statistics on refugees since

1954 and on legal immigration since 1968. In the late 1960s the Ministry of Justice started to collect data on criminality among foreign people but so far statistics refer to the total number of crime and punishment sentences without providing any information on recidivism (Palidda 1994). In 1984 the National Statistical Bureau (Istat) introduced the item on citizenship in records for births, deaths and weddings, whereas since 1986 it has been publishing data on foreign people residing in the country. But it was only in the early 1990s that efforts were made to establish a national monitoring system in the wake of the new Italian migration policy fostered by law 39/1990 (Natale 1990). An expert at the Statistical Bureau described the situation by saying:

> Before 1990 we were well aware that there were lots of people around. We saw them on buses and trains or walking in the street. Sometimes visiting friends at their place we came across a foreigner serving there. But then when we went back to work we were unable to find any trace of all these people. It was a rather uncomfortable situation indeed.

An influential civil servant at the Ministry of Interior commented:

> During the early 1980s police-headquarters had been continuously reporting about the burgeoning growth of immigrants in the country. We informed policy makers and asked them for responses in terms of policy. But we were left devoid of any real device to monitor what was happening around us. In a sense we have been for long relying upon informal communication. All records on immigrants were hand-written or typewritten. It was only later that we stored them in our computer system.

Yet no data were available on the labour market before 1990 and on social security before 1991 (published in 1994), though the Ministry of Labour led an ad hoc survey on regularisations in 1986. In the same year the Statistical Bureau started to introduce the item on citizenship in forms used in the national health system but no statistics were produced for health policy purpose. So far the item on citizenship is still the only one monitored by the NHS, despite the fact that NGOs providing medical assistance to those not entitled to the public service warned that issues such as ethnicity and religion were relevant to the improvement of the quality of health. So far systematic data on schooling on a national basis are still missing, whereas some local administrations led small area studies.

Since 1990 an increased sensitivity towards immigration prompted an improvement in the monitoring capacity of different agencies. In 1992 the law establishing the National Statistical System promoted higher levels of integration and articulation. Yet the current situation can be still described in terms of emergency (Campani 1993). As a policy expert states:

> we were always thinking that immigration would be a temporary process. Public and private needs arising from rapid migration were not foreseen, even though the forecast predicted a rapid increase in migration. This is because, still, in this country, a foreign person is seen either as a worker and/or as a threat to public order. The perception remains that after we address these two problems of foreigner as worker and foreigner as threat, that will be sufficient. We build policies to address an extraordinary situation. However, we need to change our starting point, to see migration as not an extraordinary occurrence, but rather as an ordinary fact of life in Italy.

The monitoring system is shaped and functions according to such an understanding which stresses the need to frame different dimensions of migration in mechanisms of security (Mitchell 1994: 191). Often this is evident in the very name and position within administrative agencies of units in charge of dealing with foreign people and releasing statistics. For example, at the Ministry of Interior the Foreign Citizens Office is a branch of the Public Security Department, whilst at the City Council in Milan, the Foreign Citizens Office is a branch of the Hygiene, Health & Marginality Department.

Whereas most administrative and state agencies release statistics, the National Statistical Bureau is still far from acting as the agency in charge of publishing all available data in a single report (ISTAT 1993).

Within the Statistical Bureau, transfer of relevant information on international migration often occurs by informal communication. No special unit has been established and collaboration among different experts occurs only on an occasional basis. For example, any attempt to assess the global amount of immigrants has only taken place so far as a by-product of calculations to assess the GNP of a given year which indeed requires assessment of the hidden segment of the labour market in which undocumented immigrants are employed. Often statistics on migration are produced only as part of the overall monitoring activities of population and by using customary monitoring devices. This helps explain why, though the 1991 Census form for foreigners contained instructions in six languages other than Italian, the relevance of data on language has been perceived only after starting the data-entry and no field for language was inserted in the database. Since the early 1990s an annual report on immigration in the country is released by an NGO which acts as a proxy supplying policy makers, social scientists and the media with statistics mostly produced by administrative and state agencies. In turn policy makers, social scientists and the media heavily rely upon such a report in shaping the discourse on migration, turning the report itself into a highly influential and almost official publication. But in order to keep access to the latest available first-hand data and to preserve good informal relations with institutions, this NGO eschews any in-depth secondary qualitative analysis of database construction in administrative and state agencies.

This strengthens the crucial role played by statistics on permits of stay. Such statistics are usually released twice a year by the Ministry of Interior. Permits of stay are issued by police-headquarters. Before approval, applications are stored in computers on a local level. Since late 1991, along with a top-down standardisation of procedures, an electronic network connecting local police-headquarters to the national database has been introduced, though there were local differences in the timing of implementation. But the system does not allow any connection between different police-headquarters. To issue or extend a permit of stay data have to be transferred to the national database where checking procedures are automatically implemented. If an application is accepted data are stored.

Analysts usually stress that data do not count young people who, not holding a personal permit of stay, are enlisted in their parents' or relatives' document. They also note that duplications as well as a small amount of expired permits may be included in the released data. These features can be fully understood once one recognises that the structure of the Ministry of Interior's database has been shaped in order to meet security requirements aimed at keeping track of the actual position of each foreign person before the law.

These statistics refer to the total number of permits of stay whose records are still writable in the database. This implies not only that a certain amount of permits referring to the same person may be included in the database at a given date, but also that expired but not yet write-protected records may be counted. The decision to write-protect a record is made by local police-headquarters according to different rationales, though it has to be implemented at the national database level. Indeed, after the expiry of a permit of stay police officers may decide not to write-protect a record in order either to allow its holder to safely apply for extension, or to keep track of a lack of information as to the holder leaving the country. But the time span before write-protection is set only at the local level. Different police-headquarters have different timing for implementing such an option, and sometimes write-protection is implemented within a two-year time frame.

If the national database is asked about a single person all information available will be immediately to hand, including the number of renewals, different ways of spelling her name and, in particular cases, any aliases used. Criminal information is also supplied. If the database is asked about the total amount of stored records it will simply provide the actual number of records referring to permits of stay which are either still valid or expired but not write-protected. These data by no means have to be on the actual numbers of people legally entitled to stay in the country.

In the cognitive frame of the Ministry of Interior the national database is first and foremost conceived of as a device for supplying individual information. This is why according to an influential civil servant at the Ministry:

> the overall reliability of our database is unquestioned. In our records one can read the story of an individual in the country. The only problems we have are when a foreign person leaves the country or dies. For the time being our main concern will be to increase the level of security.

Only recently the National Statistical Bureau has released statistics on permits of stay which are free of duplicate and expired permits (Istat 1995) but when asked the Ministry replied that they have not been yet informed about that.

Statistics on the labour market issued every three months by the Ministry of Labour are the second most important source on immigration in the country. These data refer to unemployed and recently employed workers. The former are arranged so as to count the stock of unemployed workers applying for a job at employment bureau. The latter refers to the amount of placements per term and therefore count positions. The way in which data are aggregated does not allow any cross-tabulation, and no evidence can be supplied in terms of historical trends, as data on an individual's employment history are not monitored.

Data are collected locally and aggregated to be sent later to the Ministry, mostly on paper sheets following a standardised form. At the Ministry no ad hoc unit has been established. At the office in charge for monitoring overall trends in the Italian labour market, two people collect the forms and enter data in a standard spreadsheet. Checking procedures are limited to assessing the face value consistency of new data with previous series, for no raw data transfer occurs. So far no national database has been established, though several local offices store data in computer systems. The software is provided by the Ministry but on a local level the program has been customised to fit local needs. Computer records contain an extensive range of information on individual workers. A hand-written or typewritten record with less information is also arranged, and data are collected drawing on this archive. Sometimes there are misunderstandings between the Ministry and local units as to how to fill in tables correctly, and quite often the existence of such misunderstanding is hardly perceived by the actors involved.

The Ministry of Labour and the Ministry of the Interior use different lists of 'nationality' categories. In its current version the standardised form issued by the Ministry of Labour allows data entry of as many as 26 different nationalities, others being grouped under the heading 'Other countries'. When published, the statistics list only 23 nationalities. Such a list is extremely poor if compared with guidelines issued by the National Statistical Bureau and used by other Ministries which list as many as 134 countries. Moreover, the list itself is the outcome of the combination of a first list which is alphabetically ordered and two later sets of items not following any ordering criterion. If one compares this ranking with that supplied by the Ministry of Interior one can see that nationalities which in the latter are within the top thirty (such as those referring to Romania, CIS, Peru, Colombia, and Dominican Republic) are not monitored by the former. On the contrary, quantitatively less important nationalities in terms of permits of stay (such as those referring to Algeria, Turkey, Japan, Chile, Lebanon, Mauritius, and Nigeria) are considered.

Statistics on labour are one of the outcomes of the way in which issues of migration are shaped within the Ministry of Labour. This frame is depicted in the following statement by a civil servant at the Ministry:

> if you are a good worker in the workplace you will not have problems. A policy which is particularly geared towards foreigners, in my opinion, should not be geared towards special laws. The less you distinguish, the less you discriminate.

The same idea is expressed when commenting on the educational policies promoted by the Ministry of Education on the basis of a detailed monitoring of foreign pupils in schools. Indeed he adds 'In terms of multicultural education, I think there is far too much emphasis on difference'. As a leading principle, de-emphasising difference entails reducing the total number of distinctions whereby the labour market is monitored and affirming that the only distinction worth considering is that between 'good' and 'bad' workers.

So far examples as to how ethnostatistical research can help understand the social construction of statistics within single agencies have been supplied. This approach, applied to the overall structure and functioning of a monitoring system may provide precious insight into the ways in which technologies of government intermingle with techniques of government and shape the discourse on migration. A monitoring system is the field in which intellectual technologies, such as the use of statistical tables, graphs, reports, and forms, are at work to elicit, record, memorise and transfer information. It therefore constitutes an indispensable mechanism whereby specific aspects of governed reality are shaped as knowable entities amenable to governing (Mitchell 1994: 187-88). Different forms of coping with needs of integration and articulation in a monitoring system constitute therefore a further outcome of the intermingling of these techniques and technologies.

In Western liberal democracies integration can be achieved by formal exchange of information among different agencies and by providing different databases with adequate linkages, without therefore even inadvertently disclosing information about identifiable individuals and households. This also requires guidelines to be issued in order to set the timing of monitoring activities and to define compatible and standardised procedures on both the national and local level. But integration can also be achieved in the absence of such a framework if some agencies are in a position to gain access to information collected by other units in the system, whereas others are not. Such privileged positions have far-reaching impacts on the ways in which issues at stake are socially constructed. Conversely they represents outcomes of this very construction. Articulation depends upon the number of dimensions whereby representation is enacted under localised conditions. By the very construction of a social problem, methods 'for producing a connection between representation and a transcendental reality which supposedly resides beyond the outside of representing agent' are supplied (Woolgar 1989: 202).

In Italy, 11 agencies are responsible for producing 14 main kinds of data on immigration. Yet integration has not been systematically achieved. Data storing and processing procedures diverge too much, whereas in the absence of a overall monitoring policy interorganisational communication and interaction mostly occurs by resorting to informal networks. So far any linkage among different databases is still missing but agencies in charge of implementing public security policies have a privileged access to information collected by other units. Proposals to give permits of stay an alphanumeric code to be reported on any single act involving a foreign person have been rejected, whereas the use of the national social security and fiscal code is still scarcely implemented unlike in the case of Italians. Lack of synchronicity among different statistics is therefore increased. Data referring to diverse but partly overlapping dimensions are not made available within the same time span. Some agencies process and release data with more than a year's delay, though no real technical difficulty seems to justify such a delay. Rather than being systematic and periodical, checking procedures mostly respond to internal organisational dynamics of administrative and state agencies. Therefore, any chance of fully analysing not only structural features but also developmental trends in migration is seriously affected.

The discourse on migration has only in recent years portrayed it as not an extraordinary occurrence, but rather as an ordinary fact of life in Italy. Basic monitoring devices are only slowly being worked out to understand characteristics, needs, and expectations of migrants. At this level, non-governmental actors play a crucial role in increasing the articulation of the monitoring system. So far that occurs through informal networks of communication rather than by reaching actual agreements among state agencies and NGOs. Nevertheless, information of use to those concerned with service delivery issues, particularly in the welfare field, are only occasionally monitored, and their meaning is often misperceived. For instance, whereas only refugees are asked about religion and ethnicity, the latter is still often confused with the question on nationality. This is exemplified in the following statement by a civil servant promoting educational policies:

> I appreciated very much your asking the question of terminology - it is important that we understand one another. From a cultural point of view, there is a modern interpretation towards migrants which involves the mutual enrichment of cultures. An educational agency should have this as its goal. Our laws and circular letters accept integration and interaction; foreign pupils and students, even illegal ones, must be encouraged to learn their original language and culture, and we also promote common activities. We face many practical problems however. We have 134 dispersed ethnic communities.

Conclusion

We regard the issues raised in this paper as crucial for tackling current limitations in the analysis and understanding of international migration and progressing the sociology of knowledge and power. International migration is at the core of discourses in Europe around external borders, citizenship, population change. It is also central to policy debates and inter-governmental agreements on crime, terrorism and policing. The dissemination of these knowledges and the role of the media as well as the academic community informs public opinion, politicians and the demand for data, which in turn drives academic research and policy development. The example of Italy shows how these processes of knowledge production serve to legitimate each other. It is only by unpicking all the processes and discourses involved that we can understand where our knowledge on international migration comes from.

Research into migration as a gendered phenomenon in Europe should also not be excluded from the questions raised here, if it is not to be limited to the research agenda determined by the demands of policy makers. It now appears more important than ever to examine which questions are being asked than to refine answers to existing questions in the field of migration studies. The production and reproduction of knowledge on male and female migrants presents an opportunity for the development of methodologies which could transcend those limitations imposed by national monitoring systems and measures which are the products of administrative statistical systems. The academic understanding of migration patterns and processes can only be enhanced alongside such a development.

References

Beer, J. de, Kuijper, H., Noordam, R., Prins, K. and Sprangers, A. (1993) 'The linking of immigrant flow and stock data in the Netherlands; present and future possibilities', *Statistical Journal of the United Nations Economic Commission for Europe*, Vol. 10, No. 4: 321-334, cited in Prins and Harmsen (1994).

Bloor, M., Goldberg, D. & Emslie, J. (1991) 'Ethnostatistics and the AIDS epidemic', *British Journal of Sociology*, 42(1): 131-38.

Campani, G. (1993) 'Immigration and racism in southern Europe: the Italian case', *Ethnic and Racial Studies*, 16(3): 507:35.

Cicourel, A. (1967) *The Social Organization of Juvenile Justice*, London: Heinemann.

EUROSTAT (1994a) *Asylum-seekers and refugees, a statistical report. Volume 1: EC Member States*. Luxembourg, Office for official publications of the European Communities.

EUROSTAT (1994b) *Asylum-seekers and refugees. A statistical report. Volume 2: EFTA countries*. Report compiled by the Netherlands Interdisciplinary Demographic Institute at the request of the EFTA Secretariat in Luxembourg.

Fairclough, N. (1992) 'Discourse and text: linguistic and intertextual analysis within discourse analysis', *Discourse & Society*, 3(2): 193-217.

Foucault, M. (1979) *Metafisica del potere*, Torino: Einaudi.

Gephart, R.P. (1988) *Ethnostatistics*, London-Beverly Hills: Sage.

Hacking, I. (1990) *The Taming of Chance*, Cambridge: Cambridge University Press.

Hammersley, M. & Atkinson, P. (1995) *Ethnography: Principles in Practice*, London: Routledge.

ISTAT (1993) 'La presenza straniera in Italia', *Notiziario Istat*, 14(11).

ISTAT (1995) *Rapporto annuale*, Rome: Istat.

Johnson, M.R.D. (1993) 'A question of ethnic origin in the 1991 Census', *New Community*, 19(2): 281-89.

Johnson, T. (1993) 'Expertise and the state', in M. Gane & T. Johnson, *Foucault's New Domains*, London: Routledge: 139-52.

Knorr-Cetina, K. (1993) 'Liminal and Referent Epistemologies in Contemporary Science: An Ethnography of the Empirical in Two Studies', *Teoria sociologica*, 2: 258-82.

Mitchell, D. (1994) *Critical and Effective Histories. Foucault's Methods and Historical Sociology*, London: Routledge.

Natale, M. (1990) 'L'immigrazione straniera in Italia: consistenza, caratteristiche, prospettive', *Polis*, 5(1): 5-40.

Palidda, S. (1994) *Devianza e criminalità tra gli immigrati*, ISMU Working Paper.

Platt, J. (1981) 'On interviewing one's peers', *British Journal of Sociology*, 32(1): 75-91.

Poulain, M., Debuisson, M., and Eggerickx, T. (1991) *Projet d'harmonisation des statistiques de migration internationale au sein de la Communaute Europeenne. 5pt*. Louvain.

Prins, K. and Harmsen, C. (1994) 'A new system to collect demographic data', *Netherlands Official Statistics* Winter: 46-47.

Salt, J. and Singleton, A. (1993) Comparison and evaluation of the Labour Force Survey and Regulation 311/76 data as sources on the foreign employed population in the EC. Report to the Migration Statistics Working Party, Eurostat, December.

Salt, J. and Singleton, A. (1994) Report on the extension of the historical series of statistics on international migration held in the MIGRAT database. Report to the Migration Statistics Working Party, Eurostat, November.

Salt, J. and Singleton, A. (1995) Analysis and forecasting of international migration by major groups. Report to Eurostat, February.

Salt, J., Singleton, A., and Hogarth, J. (1994) *Europe's International Migrants. Data sources patterns and trends*, London: HMSO.

Singleton, A. (1995) 'International migration in Europe. Data sources and data availability. Recent developments, problems and possibilities'. Paper presented to the EAPS/IUSSP European Population Conference, Milan, 4-8 September 1995.

Strozza, S. (1995) 'Possibilità di quantificazione della presenza straniera in Italia: il punto della situazione', mimeo.

Walker, T. (1988) 'Whose Discourse', in S. Woolgar (ed.), *Knowledge and Reflexivity*, in S. Woolgar (ed.) *Knowledge and Reflexivity. New Frontiers in the Sociology of Knowledge*, London-Beverly Hills: Sage: 55-79.

Woolgar, S. (1989) 'Representation, cognition and self: what hope for an integration of psychology and sociology?', in S. Fuller (ed.) *The Cognitive Turn*, Dordrecht: Kluwer: 201-24.

Woolgar, S. & Pawluch, D. (1985) 'Ontological Gerrymandering: The Anatomy of Social Problems Explanations', *Social Problems*, 32: 214-227.

Notes

[1] The chapter is based on research carried out in Italy by Paolo Barbesino of ISMU, Milan and in the EU member states by Ann Singleton of the Migration Research Unit, UCL.

[2] There is considerable scope for improved documentation of existing databases, such as is currently taking place in a joint project between the MRU and NIDI to document Eurostat's database on international migration flows. Country by country inventories and evaluations of data sources for each of the European countries are also being revised with the help of official contacts. The work will include updating relevant sections of a report to the UK Home Office published in Salt, Singleton and Hogarth (1994) to which the reader is referred for full background information.

3 Economic Migration and Social Exclusion: The Case of Tunisians in Italy in the 1980s and 1990s

Faïçal Daly and Rohit Barot

Introduction

The purpose of this chapter is to explain Tunisian migration to Italy in the 1980s and 1990s in the context of economic and political changes which have taken place both in Italy and Tunisia. It will examine the demographic characteristics of migrants in Tunisia and consider the economic and political factors which have made Italy an attractive destination for work and settlement by Tunisian workers. This account will also focus on Tunisian settlement and location within the Italian economy. A number of European states like Germany and Switzerland have implemented policies which recognise the need for the presence of temporary workers with minimum possible social cost to the receiving society. The case of Tunisian migrant workers in Italy clearly shows the contradiction between the need for labour power and the unwillingness of the state to make proper social provision for migrants. It is this contradiction between economic inclusion and social exclusion which is a central theme of this chapter.

Recent history of international migration clearly shows that Italy, even before its unification as a nation state, has sent out millions of Italians round the world from Argentina to Australia. The presence of Italian communities in these far flung locations is equally matched by Italian migration to North America as well as to various states in Europe. Out-migration from Italy in the past two centuries has played an important part in modern Italian history and Italy's economic development. The Italian state has consistently defended and promoted civil rights for Italian settlers everywhere. While in-migration from the Third World countries to Britain, Germany and France occurred between 1950s and 1980s, in migration to Italy on a similar scale took place mainly in 1980s and 1990s and it is this period which constitutes the focus of discussion in this chapter.

In this chapter the authors focus on Tunisian migration to Italy and its economic and social consequences. The first part of the chapter concentrates on the factors which account for Tunisian migration to Italy. An examination of some of the features of Tunisian migrants and their settlement in Italy forms the second part of this narrative. One of the central arguments in this chapter concerns racism and social exclusion. This forms the third section. The conclusion analyses the dynamic between the integration of Tunisian migrants in the Italian political economy and their exclusion from some dimensions of civil society.

What drove Tunisian migrants to Italy?

Since 1973, for the first time in its modern history, Italy ceased to be Europe's largest supplier of migrant labour. Instead, the country began importing cheap labour from its previous African colonies (Eritrea, Ethiopia and Somalia) and from its neighbouring countries, in particular, North Africa (Algeria, Egypt, Morocco and Tunisia). Although Tunisia was the first Roman colony after the defeat of Carthage in 146 BC in the Third Punic War with Rome, in modern times it was the French who ruled Tunisia from 1881 to 1956. However, both countries belong to the same Mediterranean Region, and are geographically so proximate that Pantelleria Island is just about sixty miles from the Tunisian coast. The historical relationship between Italy and Tunisia has developed and evolved over centuries and movements of population between the two countries has always existed. This historical context (Zolberg 1994) is crucial for an understanding of Tunisian migration to Italy. However, in more recent period, since the change of political leadership in Tunisia in 1987, the Tunisian regime has sought to forge closer economic and political ties with Italy as a strategy to reduce the significance of the old colonial relationship with France.

Besides the broad sweep of economic and political connection between Tunisia and Italy, the following factors are crucial for explaining the nature of recent Tunisian migration to Italy.

a) The economic stagnation and political instability in Tunisia in the late 1970s and mid 1980s.
b) Geographical proximity and historical links.
c) Demographic growth in Tunisia.
d) The mass media, information and transport influences.
e) The open door policy adopted by the Italian government.
f) Settlement and location of Tunisians in the Italian economy.

Economic stagnation and political instability

Most Tunisian migration to Italy could be explained by an analysis of the economic, political and social situation in Tunisia between 1978 and 1987. During this period, Tunisia entered a phase of economic stagnation, political instability and social conflict. In this phase, it can be argued that poor management, corruption, and those practices which depended on nepotism rather than merits had paralysed the development of the country and driven the population into poverty. Sporadic uprisings and riots occurred everywhere and the starving population expressed its anger with a general strike in 1978. There was a bread riot in 1984 and various protests some of which ended in killing and bloodshed. Regional discrimination and imbalance in the distribution of resources and industries (75% of Tunisian industries are located in the capital and in the coastal areas) caused the rise of unemployment in the interior regions. As Bel Hadj Amor (1992:2) has noted,

> Since the earliest plans (referring to economic development plans) the Tunisian authorities relied on emigration to provide work for all or part of the excess labour that economic development was unable to absorb.

In addition, the Government had to confront the Islamic opposition by El Nahdah (the Renaissance Party) which was leading the country into civil war. The economy was placed into an impasse. Furthermore, restrictions imposed by the European Community on textile, leather and olive oil exports (75% of Tunisian exports and 80% of its imports) made the economy more vulnerable to external factors and increased the suffering of the population. Several years of drought, natural calamities, the loss of fertile land due to the desertification and erosion caused serious difficulties to the main sector of the economy. A large number of peasants left their land to settle temporarily in cities and to prepare for later emigration. The rural exodus rose during a period of inadequate rainfall and drought. The wage gap between Italy and Tunisia was one to fifteen. The Tunisian purchasing power declined by almost 20 per cent between 1978 and 1987. In this connection, as Bel Hadj Amor (1992) has noted, the gap between job-creation and demand for jobs has become much wider than before and has produced a significant level of unemployment which has further contributed to impetus for migration.

In 1987, Zine El Abedine Ben Ali assumed the office of the President ending the thirty years of the Habib Bourguiba regime and its strong grip on political and economical reforms. A new political and economic era opened with growing co-operation between Italy and Tunisia. By 1990, Italy became Tunisia's second most important economic partner. The new government began implementing a programme of economic reform and liberalisation under the supervision of the World Bank. Privatisation, restructuring of the companies' deficit and even closure of non-profitable ones had temporarily caused further rise of the unemployment rate and job losses. For instance, in the Societé Tunisienne Industrial Automobile, 2,200 workers were made redundant (Ghiles 1990:6). About a quarter of Tunisian young labour force was unemployed and the economy could not create the 60,000 jobs needed annually to absorb this growing demand for work. People were forced to migrate because migration was the only possible alternative. Furthermore, approximately 40 per cent devaluation of the Tunisian currency in 1990 also accelerated Tunisian migration (Field 1990:4).

Geographical proximity and historical links

Tunisia is the nearest country to the Italian coast (Pantelleria, Lampedusa, Trapani and Palermo in the south are reached between 2 to 8 hours depending on the kind of the boat used). Contact between fishermen's boats from both countries is common on a daily and even hourly basis. Therefore migratory movement from Tunisia to Italy and vice versa, although relatively small, has always existed, particularly between southern Italy and northern Tunisia. Furthermore, soon after the petrol crisis of 1973, most European countries like France, Germany and the UK began to adopt restrictive immigration policies. To overcome these restrictions, Algerians, Moroccans and even Sub-Saharan African migrants have used Tunisian borders as the main route for their entrance to Italy and France. It is easy for a Tunisian, especially if he or she lives in a coastline city to find a passage to Italy as Tunisian migrants interviewed by Daly emphasised (Daly 1990). Benefits for smugglers, as Susie

Morgan reports, are huge. The passage from Tunis to Italy costs between US $500 and $2,000, and vessels can accommodate up to 50 passengers at a time. Elsewhere in Europe, a passage can cost up to US $25,000 (Morgan 1995: 1-2). The sophisticated Mafia organisation, some custom officials and police authorities have further played a major part in the smuggling of illegal migrants to Italy.

Demographic growth

There was a substantial differential between demographic growth and economic development in Tunisia during the 1980s and early 1990s (Bruni & Francia 1990: 129-130). Tunisia had an average population growth of 2.6 per cent between 1980 and 1987 compared to 0.2 per cent in the same period in Italy (Popovic 1992: 302). Although the Tunisian authorities estimated 1.76 per cent growth in 1994, according to the UN estimate the population increased by 2.3 per cent (Khalaf 1995: 5).

The differences in the GDP per capita in both countries are even more marked. The average annual income for a Tunisian is US $1,180 in contrast to US $10,350 for Italians (World Bank Annex: 1982, 1988). Unemployment has stricken 25 per cent of its 2.25 million active young work force. 56.5 per cent of the 8.5 million of Tunisian population is under 20. Before the school reforms[1] in 1994, compulsory education was limited to primary school. Therefore the level of illiteracy is 35 per cent among the population. Early school leavers provided a cheap child labour for the underground economy and increased the adult unemployment rate. Therefore adults were pushed out of the labour market and were compelled to emigrate.

The effect of mass media, information and the ease of transportation

The tendency of Tunisians to migrate to Italy was further boosted when the 'Habib' boat started operating between the ports of Tunis and Genoa. The cost and speed of transport was reduced and the links between the two countries increased (i.e. a return ticket costs less than a month's wages for an ordinary worker) which encouraged more young people to play the migration card to improve their living standards (Hatton & Williamson 1994: 547).

The diffusion of Italian television programmes in Tunisia had firstly made Italy more culturally close, and promoted a consumerist culture amongst Tunisian families. 'Made in Italy' became a life style. Families who were previously suspicious and feared Mafia criminality, now supported the migration of their sons and daughters to Italy. Secondly, the improved quality of information helped many young Tunisians to learn the Italian language which would facilitate their migration. Thirdly, the transmission of television programme promoting Italy's wealth and welfare induced many people to think that the neighbouring country was 'the promised paradise'.

During the 1980s young Tunisians faced a difficult choice between the Arabic Islamic culture promoted by the Islamic opposition and the westernisation transmitted by Italian and French television and sponsored by the old Tunisian regime. The attraction to the West had already become a powerful force and had already drawn many Tunisians to Italy. Moreover, relatives and friends and the network of those who had already settled had further influenced the migration flow. First of all, they confirmed in their letters and stories what was transmitted in the *Domenica In* (Sunday In) television programme received on Tunisian television screens. Some enthusiastic Tunisian migrants even conveyed that there was money everywhere and Italians were *brava gente* (kind people). Some of them even offered hospitality and generous financial help to the future migrants. This sort of information, although misleading at times, had influenced a large number Tunisians to leave their homeland for what they regarded as better material conditions in Italy. This contributed to the rise of the migration flow in the late 1980s and early 1990s.

From an open door policy to a restrictive immigration legislation

The Italian open door policy was in contrast to the 'Stop recruitment' strategy adopted by Germany in 1973, France in 1974 and most countries in Europe during the economic recession and the petrol crisis of the early 1970s (Rogers 1985: 2). This ban on migrant labour mostly affected non-European workers. In this context, Tunisian migrants were still able to enter Italy without visa requirements. This was because Italy did not join the Schengen agreement until 1990. If it had, it would have implemented a restrictive immigration policy - especially the visa requirement. Under the pressure of leading European nations, the Italian Government was compelled to abandon its open door policy. The Italians began to implement restrictions after they applied to join Schengen. Till then, the Tunisians were able to use non-restriction to their benefit. In any event, other European countries did not allow them access to their labour markets. Tunisians also regarded Italy as a temporary bridge to settlement in other European countries and for possible illegal infiltration through the Italian borders.

Before 1986, the Italian state pursued an open door policy in response to migration. International conventions and discretion of the police sometimes depended on earlier Fascist laws No 773 (1931) and No 635 (1940) which dealt with entry of foreigners to Italy with respect to security and public order. The first immigration legislation was in 1986 with Act No. 943. It legalised the status of immigrants by regulating entry, residence, working conditions and family reunion. It also provided consultative bodies which took up immigration issues. The Act also recognised Italy as a country of immigration and almost ended the open door policy. It also regularised the position of 115,000 illegal immigrants who constituted only a small proportion of the total. As the implementation of this act was more concerned with law and order rather than the welfare of immigrants, migrants feared that the purpose of the Act and the amnesty was to establish their identity for eventual deportation. The Act also excluded non-European asylum seekers.

In 1990, the Italians approved a new legal measure, the so-called Law Martelli (referring to the socialist Deputy Prime Minister and Justice Minister Claudio Martelli), to comply with the European Union's demand for strict immigration controls in conformity with the Schengen agreement. In addition, this legislation provided funding for vocational training, language courses, dormitories and reception centres and also recognised professional rights and self-employment of the migrants. The Act also extended the refugee status on a more universal basis and set up a quota system for future immigrants. Since the quota system has not been put into practice, illegal immigrants continue to come to Italy through the Mafia and corrupt embassy officials in some sending societies such as Albania and Nigeria. In November 1995 the Italian Parliament discussed the possibility of granting amnesty to irregular migrants. In 1995, the Dini Government passed a decree yet again to provide legal status to clandestine migrants but trade unions, migrant associations and voluntary organisations regarded this measure as being against the welfare rights of the migrants, especially in relation to deportation without a fair trial. Subsequently in March 1996, the Italian Government implemented those measures which modify the Law Martelli and provide amnesty to many migrants whose status was uncertain. As these legislative measures have proved to be inadequate, the present Italian centre-left is currently debating a comprehensive immigration bill. Whether this measure provides a just and proper policy for the migrants remains to be seen.

Settlement and location of Tunisian migrants in Italy

Tunisian migration to Italy has distinctive features which have roughly evolved in the following two phases:

a) Migration before 1986:

Tunisian migrants were attracted to Italy by economic opportunities offered in Sicily and southern Italy in the fishing industry, in intensive agriculture (Ascoli 1985: 202), the underground economy which flourished in the Campania region and the services sector in the Lombardy region. Tunisian migrants employed in the fishing industry in Sicily were estimated to be a third of the work force (Di Comite 1986: 224; Vizzini 1983: 363-364). They constituted a third of the fishermen in Mazzara del Vallo (Vaccina, 1983: 323). This estimate would be higher if the illegal Tunisian migrants were accounted for. These migrants are professional and skilled fishermen who were trained in their homeland and were relatively highly paid. In contrast to the type of seasonal migrants employed in agriculture, those employed in fishing industry enjoyed stable and permanent work and settlement. Most of these people came from the coastal cities. A survey conducted in 1983 in Mazzara del Vallo (Sicily) found that the Tunisian community accounted for 20 per cent of the local population and 80 per cent of the Tunisian migrants came from two coastal towns: Mehdia and Shebba in East central Tunisia (Vaccina 1983: 322). During harvesting and crop-picking, seasonal and clandestine Tunisian migrants are recruited by local Mafia through the so-called *i caporali* (Mafia intermediates) in the local square and transported to the camps where they work for 10 to 15 hours for a modest salary of 10 to 15 pounds or about 50 pence for every box of tomatoes or grapes they pick up. In this sector, Tunisian migrants were unskilled, underpaid, highly exploited and because of their illegal status unprotected. Besides these seasonal migrants, students also came from inland towns. They accepted harsh conditions in order to save some money and return home as soon as the harvesting season had ended. Tunisian migrants were easily integrated in the *sapere arrangiarsi* (literally 'know how to cope', meaning those who know how to survive in severe conditions) life style widespread in the southern region. The development in the Campania region, particularly in Naples, of the black economy has favoured the inclusion of illegal Tunisian migrants and prolonged the permanence of seasonal workers. Brunetta and Turatto (1996: 199) observe, 'The real problem with the Italian labour market is not that there are too many unemployed but that there are too few people employed in the official economy...'. In fact, the prosperity of this form of 'underground economy' is linked to the supply of cheap, flexible and unprotected labour force. As Weiss (1988: 219) has noted, 'compared with Italy, most countries have a relatively small underground economy - usually under 10 per cent of the labour force'. The employers, therefore, intimidate, exploit and underpay migrant men, women and children and ignore social provision for them. In the Lombardy region, for instance, owners of restaurants and bars informally employ some Tunisian workers as cleaners. Similarly small businesses and factories employ Tunisians in precarious jobs in the industry scorned by the local people.

b) Migration after 1986:

This phase is characterised by an acceleration of Tunisian migration due to the intolerable living situation in their homeland as explained at the beginning. In 1986 and 1990 the Italian government promulgated two Immigration Acts to promote the regularisation of illegal migrants. After these amnesties the number of Tunisian migrants rose to 42,223 (Italian Interior Ministry in Caritas 1995: 90). However, rigid eligibility conditions, (housing and work requirements) discretional practices and the fear that they may lose their jobs if they were reported to the authorities, prevented many Tunisians from obtaining the permit needed for working legally. The regularisation has created a high level of mobilisation amongst Tunisian migrants who are freed from the iron grip of the black economy in the south. Tunisians took advantage of the economic opportunities offered by the small and medium enterprises in the centre-north. The newcomers were regularly recruited in those sectors where there was a shortage of labour power. They found work in foundries, steel, ceramic, building and paper industries and on farms in Tuscany, Emilia-Romagna, Lombardy and Piedmont regions (Barsotti & Lecchini 1992: 11). These jobs are located in what Pugliese called the 'secondary labour market' in the 'informal economy' (Pugliese 1992: 170). Many of these jobs are precarious, heavy, dirty and risky. The indigenous population who saw their living standards, education and skills improve had rejected these jobs. In fact, the local Italian workers no longer accept the regime of flexibility, shift work, long and unsociable working hours above the terms and conditions of their employment. This suggests that Tunisian migrants in Italy did not compete with the local workers. Furthermore, even the skilled fishermen in Sicily have only filled a shortage in the labour force and replaced southern Italians who emigrated in the post-war period to Northern Europe or to Northern Italy.

Tunisian migrants and some features of their settlement in Italy

As we have just mentioned, the first phase of Tunisian migration to Italy was mostly dominated by migrants from the north and coastal cities, while the second phase has been mostly from interior areas. The following characteristics refer to migrants from both phases with relatively different experiences according to the areas where the migrants came from:

a) Seasonal and temporary migration dominated by individual young workers, students and traders who migrated to work for a short period in intensive agriculture during harvesting in the summer time. This excluded the few legal migrants in the fishing industry who were better organised and almost settled in Italy.

b) Increasing contact and co-operation between Italy and Tunisia has aided the Tunisian migrants to settle with much greater a degree of ease. Development of their own associations and cultural facilities along with their own restaurants and shops has enabled them to reproduce their own cultural surroundings. Over a period of time, there has been some improvement in the relationship between the Italians and Tunisians. Some Italians who have close contact with Tunisians accept them and respect their culture. However this process has to go a long way before the tensions between the Italians and Tunisians go down for the Italians to trust the newcomers and appreciate aspects of their culture.

c) As more and more Tunisians acquire legal rights to stay in Italy, this process has stimulated a desire for long term settlement. At the same time, this has increased the formation of homogenous groups of friends and relatives who come from the same Tunisian towns. For instance, families like Neheri, Haddaji, and M'tiri brought more than 100 men, women and children from Kairouan in Tunisia to settle in Modena. The pressure for family reunification has brought more men and women to Modena.

d) Earlier Tunisian migrants who came to Italy before 1986 have tended to settle more permanently than recent migrants. Through their close contact with the local Italian communities, their integration has been effective. Many Tunisian men and women from this phase of migration have intermarried with local Italians and their identification with the Italian society is an indication of their successful integration. However, the rise of right-wing political parties creates some uncertainties. The resentment of the right wing groups towards migrants is a source of deep anxiety for all non-European workers in Italy. For this resentment can threaten the process of social integration and possibly increase the prospects of social exclusion for the migrants.

Although men tended to dominate the pattern of Tunisian migration to Italy, it is important to note the part which women began to play in migration and settlement. It must be noted that Tunisian women did not emigrate as independent individuals as their Islamic tradition and patriarchal dependence on men did not allow their self-reliant migration. However, they began to join their husbands and relatives from an earlier stage. Before recent waves of male migration, in Sicily women were already joining their relatives for family reunification. This pattern is consistent with recent Tunisian migration. Men emigrate first, find employment and housing and then call their wives and other dependants to join them. Despite some legal and bureaucratic constraints, now more women join their husbands in Italy.

As the Italian immigration controls become more restrictive, opportunities for men and women to emigrate to Italy are correspondingly reduced. However, immigration legislation does allow recruitment of domestic workers. As a consequence, many Tunisian women have applied to do domestic work in Italy. This venue enables women to escape from some of the traditional restrictions and to find freedom and educational opportunity. This particular theme is clearly demonstrated in the decision which Nadia had made in order to find domestic work in Modena to start with. However, she did not see working as a domestic as her long-term destiny. As she said to us,

> When I was in Tunisia, I worked as a senior administrator in the public sector. Although my work was interesting, I was very keen to study for a university degree in Europe. Therefore, I accepted a domestic work contract with an Italian family in Modena. While I worked as a domestic servant, I did manage to learn the Italian language in order to fulfil my ambition. As soon as I was able to use the language effectively, first of all, I managed to pass the Italian language test to enter the Faculty of Political Science in Bologna where I am a student at the moment.

It is not uncommon for some young Tunisian women to have a friendly relationship with Italians visiting their country. Such friendships can develop into long term contact that can often lead to marriage and settlement in Italy. As young and educated women become more and more aware of rewards of migration to Europe, it is perfectly possible that they will use this opportunity to improve their condition. As far as the legal migration to Italy is concerned, now there are more Tunisian women going to Italy than Tunisian men. With the increasing number of Tunisian women going to Italy for work in the 1990s, the imbalance between male and female immigration is being redressed.

To sum up, the bulk of Tunisian migration has developed in the second half of the 1980s. The early Tunisian migration in Sicily has been responsive to labour market shortage while the later one was due to the fact that Tunisia, the old granary of Rome, was unable to feed its population. What is abundantly clear is that poverty, deprivation, economic stagnation and the labour crisis in Tunisia drove both men and eventually women, to find employment, security and a better standard of living in Italy.

Racism, citizenship and integration

Generally speaking, racism has referred to unequal treatment of groups on the basis of some conception of biologically determined cultural differences (Banton 1983, Rex 1973, Miles 1989, Solomos 1993, Anthias & Yuval-Davis 1992). However, as most academics have increasingly rejected biological racism in recent years, it has become a common practice among the social scientists to use the concept of racism as a system of ideas that justifies discrimination, exclusion, intimidation, harassment and violence against particular groups of people with reference to their ethnicity and culture. It is in this broad sense that the expression racism is used here to describe and analyse the situation of Tunisian migrants in Italy.

The expression of racism against non-European migrants in general and Tunisian migrants in particular takes personal and individual as well as institutional form. However, it is not merely the presence of migrants that has brought about the discourse of race in Italy. For, the division of the Italian society between North and South has been expressed not only in economic and social terms but also in terms of physical and cultural differences between the Northerners and Southerners.

As Northern Italy has advanced economically much more than Southern Italy, throughout the 1960s and 1970s a large number of poor southerners have emigrated to the rich north of the industrial triangle of Turin, Milan and Genoa. What is worth noting is that the Northerners have often used offensive and abusive language to identify and stigmatise Southerners. Northerners use slogans such as *da Roma in giù l'Italia non c'é più* (beyond Rome, Italy does not exist) or *prima i Meridionali e adesso gli Africani* (Southerners before Africans now) in streets and inscribe these on the walls. Institutional racism (Castles & Miller 1993: 30) and discrimination against migrants in the labour market and in welfare provision is still predominant. Immigration evokes a variety of negative reactions among the Italians. They use the term migrant to identify the non-Europeans, above all, those with dark skin such as Moroccans and Tunisians. Deviant behaviour becomes significant when related to ethnic and racial stereotyping as Sciortino (1991: 95) has pointed out. Just to quote a few examples of Italian cultural stereotypes *Marocchino* (Moroccan), *Vùcomprà* (hawker) and *Spacciatore* (drug dealer) are abusive terms applied indiscriminately to Tunisians as well as to Moroccan migrants. Such general stereotypes and their consequences have always created tensions. For example, in Bologna and Bolzano, waiters refused to serve Tunisians or overcharged them. Anti-immigrant resentment, violence (a racially motivated attack by 70 to 80 Nazi skinheads on a Tunisian migrant in Ostia in February 1994) and aggression have been recently ideologically promoted by propagandist campaign of the right-wing, neo-fascist parties and comments of some government officials. Sciortino (1991: 96) argues,

> policies claiming to control racial tensions actually encouraged the perception of immigrant as 'illegal' and favoured racial justification for social conflict.

Marginalisation, intolerance and political indifference have further increased the segregation and isolation of the migrants and created possibilities of social conflicts. Italy is no longer in a pre-racism phase as some authors have argued. Racism has existed in Italy in the distinctions between the North and the South as well as in representations of the incoming non-European migrants. In fact the expression of racism is visible in every region and town from Villa Literno to Bolzano. Recent racism in Italy is ideologically motivated. Anti-immigrant songs and slogans are shocking in the football stadium and during political meetings. Like in France, the race card and immigration issues are being subject of trade between political parties, a winning horse and prosperity for right-wing parties during the elections (i.e. bargaining between political parties to introduce the law to expel migrants). Integration and social harmony have been further disturbed by the provocative proposal of three Senators of the Lega Lombarda (Lombardy League). Two of these Senators would like to introduce footprinting the migrants. What they imply is that the migrants are so low that they should not be fingerprinted. The third Senator also wants to equip the police with rubber bullets to fight the crime by migrants. Migrants have faced this challenge with hunger strikes, sit-ins, and the occupation of council buildings in Milan, Modena, Florence and Rome.

Besides their racist attitude to non-European migrants, as in other European countries like France and Britain, Italians have also stereotyped Muslims as fundamentalists and Arabs as potential terrorists. During the Gulf War, some Italian employers dismissed their Tunisian workers simply because Tunisia had expressed some sympathy for the Iraqi people. Some employers are also known to have asked their workers to go to Saddam Hussein to get jobs. Such anti-Muslim feelings have surfaced in large Italian cities from time to time. Such stereotyping has been discriminatory in specific situations where local Muslim groups have often failed, for instance in Modena, for more than ten years to find space for building their mosque. As far as it is known, the authorities have also failed to provide land for a proper Muslim cemetery. As for the performance of funerary rites for Muslims, the Italian medical establishment has been generally insensitive to such a crucial religious and cultural need that affects all Muslims who live in Italy. As different Muslim groups become more and more organised, they will, no doubt, bring pressures on the local authorities for the fulfilment of their civil rights.

As Tunisian and other migrants continue to face both personal and institutional racism, the question of their right to become Italian citizens and to enjoy their civil liberties like other Italians is a matter of great importance. Full-citizenship would facilitate the participation of migrant communities in civil and community life of Italian towns and cities where they live. Although Enrico Pugliese (1996) has argued that citizenship does not constitute a pressing issue because of recency of migration to Italy, it is evidently clear that the number of migrant men and women who qualify for Italian citizenship, for instance, through inter-marriages, is an indication of their willingness to participate fully in Italian social and political life. Until 1993, anyone who wanted to become an Italian citizen had to be resident in Italy for a minimum period of five years. However, the Italian Government has recently amended the citizenship law. According to this amendment (Citizenship Act No. 572/1993), the European migrants to Italy can acquire citizenship after four years residence rather than five years as before. However, non-European migrants have to satisfy this residential requirement for 10 years. This unequal distinction between Europeans and non-Europeans is patently discriminatory. Such unfair and unjust measures are unlikely to inspire confidence in Italian citizenship. The perception of this inequality and inequity in law will not facilitate the process of migrants' full participation in economic and political institutions of the Italian society.

Concentration of migrants constitutes another barrier for their integration. Besides dormitories, old building and collapsing factories without water, electricity and any decent sanitation are the migrant's refuge and dormitories. Migrants are vulnerable and the first to be made redundant during bad economic situations. Homelessness and joblessness have exposed migrant workers to the exploitation of organised gangs who deal in the distribution of drugs. Nevertheless, serious efforts are being made to improve 'race relations' in Turin, and more recently in Modena, where the Mayors have sponsored the election of a consultative migrant body where migration issues are raised (Hooper 1995). It is paramount that social and welfare support for migrants and their families is an essential condition for their successful integration in local communities. Therefore, it is vital that such elected consultative bodies provide the leaders of the migrant communities a real measure of influence to improve their life chances.

Conclusion

Given the industrial restructuring and economic development which marks modern Tunisia, it is likely that Tunisian migration to Italy will continue as a 'safety valve' for the demographic and economic imbalance in Tunisia. The future of migration depends on economic progress and foreign investment in Tunisia, particularly from France and Italy. The strict economic austerity adopted by the new Tunisian government after 1987 has curtailed the budget deficit from 5.2 per cent on average in the mid-1980s of the GDP to 3.3 per cent in 1993 and is expected to fall to 1.9 per cent this year (Ghiles 1994: II). The tremendous effort that Tunisia has made to control and reduce its demographic growth, the implementation of radical change in economic strategy should be supported. Rapid strides have been made to transform the protectionist old regime by the capitalist market economy. Privatisation and liberalisation are reshaping the structure of the economy. However, the economy remains vulnerable to weather conditions although good rains can also bring bumper harvests. Market diversification and financial injections are urgently needed. Because of its successful structural adjustment and of a GDP growth rate of 8.6 per cent in 1992, Tunisia was described as 'the Singapore of the Mediterranean' and described by the IMF managing director Michel Camdessus as 'the most beautiful present I have ever been given' (Marks 1993: XIII). This economic recovery should be sustained by an effective co-operation and partnership between Italy, Europe and Tunisia. The European Union should tie the knot and strengthen its relationship with Tunisia. The peripheral policy adopted recently by the European Union to create the so called 'Free Trade Zone' in North Africa to stop immigration flows is economically motivated and not based on fair trade or as an aid to development. However, the political stability that has characterised Tunisia in the past eight years is crucially linked to economic recovery and better performance. Consolidation of this process is vital to reduce the imbalance between demographic and economic growth. The Tunisian government is ambitious to achieve an export-led growth so that new jobs will be created and migration brought under control.

As this chapter has demonstrated, Tunisians now form an important part of Italian society. More than forty thousand Tunisians now work and live in Italy. They are increasingly joined by their families. In view of this distinctive change in the pattern of their settlement, the Italian authorities need to respond to their long-term settlement rather than regarding them as temporary migrants. For Tunisians, like other non-European migrants in Italy, are there to stay. Therefore, the question of their civil rights and the fair allocation of resources for them is crucial so that they do not form a marginalised and disadvantaged underclass that can only live on the periphery of the Italian society. In this process of integration, it is absolutely vital that all migrants to Italy, irrespective of their ethnic and cultural background, should have fair and equal access to citizenship and civil liberties. It is this full civil incorporation which is likely to reduce the exploitation of migrants as a source of cheap labour for Italian employers, and give them some political influence through their vote. Recently, the Albanians who came to Italy in utter desperation as refugees received rather harsh treatment from the Italian authorities after they were rounded up in a stadium and transported back to Albania. It is unlikely that the Italian authorities will respond to the need of migrants without a great deal of political pressure, however.

Acknowledgements

Faïçal Daly is a Research Student in the Department of Sociology at University of Bristol where he is conducting a project to investigate the impact of Tunisian migration on the small and medium firms in middle Italy. He acknowledges the support of a University of Bristol Scholarship (1995) that has made this study possible. He is being jointly supervised by Professor Theo Nichols and Dr Rohit Barot. This paper was presented at Nation and Migration in Southern Europe Conference at the University of Greenwich on 18-20 December 1995. Faïçal Daly is grateful to the conference participants for their helpful and constructive comments on his findings. Both Faïçal Daly and Rohit Barot thank Professor Floya Anthias and Dr Gabriella Lazaridis for their constructive editorial assistance.

References

Anthias, F. & Yuval-Davis, N. (1992) *Racialized boundaries: race, nation, gender, colour and class and anti-racist struggle*, London, Routledge.

Ascoli, U. (1985) 'Migration of workers and labor market: is Italy becoming a country of immigration?,' (ed.) Rogers, M., London, Westview Press.

Banton, M.P. (1983) *Racial and ethnic competition*, Cambridge: Cambridge University Press.

Barsotti, O. & Lecchini, L. (1992) *Social and Economic Aspects of Foreign Immigration into Italy*, Università di Pisa paper (unpublished).

Bel Hadj Amor, M. (1992) 'International aid to reduce the need for emigration: The Tunisian case,' World Employment Programme Research Working Paper, Geneva, International Labour Organisation.

Brunetta, R. & Turatto, R. (1996) 'The Italian labour market and European convergence' *Review of Economic Conditions in Italy*, No. 2 (July/December), 199-214.

Bruni, M. & Francia, A. (1990) 'Squilibri Demografici, Crescita Economica e Fabbisogno Occupazionale nei Paesi del Mediterraneo dal 1950 al 2000', *Affari Sociali Internazionali*, 1, 119-141.

Caritas, di Roma (1995) *Immigrazione Dossier Statistico '95: il fenomeno migratorio negli anni '90*, Rome, Anterem Snc.

Castles, S. & Miller, M.J. (1993) *The Age of Migration: International population Movement in the Modern world*, Basingstoke: Macmillan Press Ltd.

Daly, F. (1990) *Indagine sulle condizioni lavorative degli Extracommunitari a Modena*, Unpublished Thesis, Università degli studi di Modena, Facoltà di Economia e Commercio.

Di Comite, L. (1986) 'L'immigration tunisienne en Italie: quelques données censitaires', *Studi Emigrazione*, 82/83, 217-227 Centro Studi Emigrazione, Roma.

Field, M. (1990) 'The Changes are in place, but Tunisia's bureaucratic past lives on' *Financial Times* (30 January 1990), 4.

Ghiles, F. (1990) 'Unbundling the State: Drought-Struck Tunisia slow to dismantle ailing state sector' *Financial Times* (19 April 1990) 6.

Ghiles, F. (1994), 'The gods are still smiling', *Financial Times Survey of Tunisia,* 27 July 1994:II.

Hatton, T.J. & Williamson, J. (1994) 'What drove the Mass Migration from Europe in the late Nineteeth Century?,' *Population and Development Review,* 20 (3), 533-558.

Hooper, J. (1995) 'Migrants get hint of power in Turin's mini-parliament', *The Guardian,* 5 August 1995.

Khalaf, R. (1995) 'Politics mask N. African population successes : European fears of migration from the Maghreb are exaggerated', *Financial Times* (15 February 1995) 5.

Marks, J. (1993) 'Problems but full of promise', *Financial Times* 13 October 1993:XIII.

Miles, R. (1989) *Racism,* London, Routledge.

Morgan, S. (1995) 'Mafia makes a killing on human cargo', *Gemini News Service* (Netscape http://www.oneworld.org/gemini/gemini-mafia.html).

Popovic, B. (1992) 'Employment growth and change in the Mediterranean basin during the 1980s', *International Labour Review, 297-311.*

Pugliese, E. (1992) 'The new International Migrations and the Changes in the Labour Market', *Labour* 6(1), 165-179.

Pugliese, E. (1996) *Italy between Emigration and Immigration and the problems of Citizenship,* London: Routledge.

Rex, J. (1973) Race, Colonialism and the City, London, Routledge & Kegan Paul.

Rogers, R. (1985) *Guests come to stay: The Effects of European Labour Migration on Sending and Receiving Countries,* Boulder, Colorado: Westview Special Studies in International Migration.

Sciortino, G. (1991) 'Immigration into Europe and public policy: do stops really work?', *New Community* 18 (1) 89-99.

Solomos, J. (1993) *Race and Racism in Britain,* London: The Macmillan Press Ltd.

Vaccina, F. (1983) 'Alcuni aspetti dell'immigrazione tunisina a Mazzara del Vallo', *Studi emigrazione,* 71, 319-326, Centro Studi Emigrazione Roma.

Vizzini, S. (1983) 'Su talunni aspetti demografici ed economici dell'immigrazione araba a Mazzara del Vallo', *Studi emigrazione,* 71, 362-366, Centro Studi Emigrazione Roma.

Weiss, L. (1988) 'Explaining the underground economy: state and social structure' *The British Journal of Sociology,* 38 (2) 216-234.

World Bank, Annex 1982 & 1988.

Zolberg, A.R. (1994) 'Changing Games and International Migration', *Indiana Journal of Global Legal Studies*, 2(1).
http://www.law.indiana.edu/glsj/vol2/tocv2i1.html).

Note

[1] Prior to School Reforms, primary school education was compulsory for first six years. After the School Reforms, the schooling period was extended from six to nine years for all Tunisian pupils.

4 Recent Immigration to Spain: The Case of Moroccans in Catalonia

Russell King and Isabel Rodríguez-Melguizo

> If I were a 20-year-old North African, I would be in one of those boats, and even if I was deported, I would try to cross the Strait again.
>
> Felipe González, 1992

This statement by Spain's former prime minister reveals, if not an open endorsement, at least an appreciation of the rationality and inevitability of Moroccan migration to Spain. A few kilometres of sea which, on most days of the year, sparkles in the sunlight and is dotted with the bright sails of pleasure yachts and windsurfers, is also Europe's migration frontier: the invisible rampart of fortress Europe where the European continent and the 'Third World' of Africa draw close and almost touch each other. Economic and demographic gradients across this narrow strait are amongst the sharpest anywhere in the world. On the one side Spain has a GNP per capita of $13,590 and the lowest fertility rate of any country in Europe - just 1.2 children per woman. On the other side Morocco's per capita GNP is, at $1,040, just 7.6 per cent of Spain's, yet its fertility figure of 3.6 is three times as high (UNDP 1996).

The causal factors propelling Moroccan migration to Spain could hardly be clearer. They recall two of Ravenstein's famous 'laws' of migration enunciated over a hundred years ago: most people migrate for economic reasons; and people are more likely to migrate over short distances (Grigg 1977). For Moroccans the lure of the 'West' is so close they can almost swim to it, or try to bob across in a flimsy boat. Since Spain has been obliged by its EU partners to tighten the southern frontier of the fortress to satisfy Schengen criteria, many would-be migrants do not make it. Some are picked up by police patrol boats; others, increasingly desperate to cross the Mediterranean 'Rio Grande' by whatever means, pay the ultimate price, their bodies eventually washed up on the sandy shores. Even for those who do make it, and become either legalised or undocumented migrants in Spain, life is far from easy, and this chapter explores some aspects of their difficult relationship to Spanish, and Catalan, society.

The chapter will be in two main parts, as indicated by its title. The first part will be a general account of the circumstances surrounding recent immigration to Spain from various developing countries, of which Morocco is the most important. Within this general account, the following points will be highlighted: Spain's position within the southern flank of the EU; the link between recent immigration and the specific character and restructuring of the Spanish economy; the general attitude of the Spanish population and authorities towards migrants, and towards specific groups of migrants; and the evolution of Spanish migration policy towards non-EU migrants.

The second half of the chapter will focus on Moroccans in Catalonia. Catalonia has a longer history of incorporating labour migrants than other parts of Spain because of its economic primacy and the tradition of immigration from Andalusia and elsewhere. The notion of differential exclusion will be used to examine the treatment of migrants coming from different source areas. The specific experiences of Moroccans in Catalonia - housing, employment, social relations with the host population, media treatment etc. - are explored as various dimensions of their social exclusion.

The conclusion will relate to the case of Moroccans in Spain to wider debates about the globalisation and regionalisation of international migration and labour markets, and to the situation in other European, especially south European, countries.

Spain as a new country of immigration

Over the past twenty years Spain has become a country of immigration, thus reversing its previous long-term role as a country of emigration. Although the data available tend to indicate that Spain has been proportionately less affected by recent immigration than Italy and Greece (cf. King and Konjhodzic 1995; King and Rybaczuk 1993), there is no doubt that Spain, along with the rest of the southern EU, has joined the ranks of European countries which are seen as 'desirable' by potential migrants from various world areas. As in Portugal, Italy and Greece, the 'migration turnaround' in Spain in the 1970s and 1980s resulted from a phased interplay of three distinct migration trends: the sharp decline in emigration after the mid-1970s; increased numbers of returning emigrants during the late 1970s and early 1980s; and the sharply rising influx of immigrants after the mid-1980s. According to Izquierdo (1994), Spain's transformation from a labour-exporting to a labour-importing country took place in just one decade and was especially concentrated in the years between 1985 and 1991.

The rapid growth in migrant numbers - especially of those coming from North Africa and other countries of the developing world - can be largely explained by reference to the following factors:

- the closing-off of entry possibilities into the traditional immigration countries of North-West Europe during the second half of the 1970s, which left Spain with a 'waiting room' function for migrants on their way north;

- Spain's geographical position as a 'frontier country' between Western Europe and Africa, combined with the permeability of its borders and the laxity of formal entry control procedures (a problem partly related to the need to facilitate the mass entry of tourists);

- the country's growing prosperity, paralleled by increasing living standards, especially after EU entry in 1986;

- the expansion of the underground economy, which has become especially attractive to, and reliant upon, migrant workers.

The last of these factors needs a little more explanation. The special character of the Spanish economy, with its reliance on intensive agriculture, tourism, the construction trades and small industry, creates a widespread demand for flexible, casual and often seasonal labour. Much of this demand is spatially concentrated in tourist resorts, areas of specialised farming and big cities. Local labour markets often cannot respond to these labour needs which are highly concentrated in time and space; moreover the types of jobs involved - hard manual labour or low-status work in the service sector - are increasingly rejected by a Spanish population with ever-more bourgeois characteristics.

In one of the very few English-language accounts of recent immigration to Spain, Cornelius (1994: 332) sums up both the economic role of migrants and provides an introductory perspective on the policy dilemmas of the Spanish government which faces a trade-off between the perceived socio-cultural costs of admitting more foreigners and the economic costs of not exploiting this source of cheap labour.

> Government, business and most members of the public want access to cheap, flexible, disposable labour for certain sectors of the economy, such as agriculture, construction, and domestic service. It is also widely recognised that the vitality of the country's very large and diversified underground economy, which supplies and otherwise supports many firms in the mainstream economy, depends on continued access to immigrant labour...
> (T)he Spanish welfare state provides generous benefits (mainly unemployment compensation and other transfer payments) that reward native-born Spaniards for *not* working, at least in the formal economy. Whenever the government seeks to curtail these benefits, partly to force native-born workers back into immigrant-dominated labour markets, it meets stiff resistance.
>
> Cornelius 1994: 332

We shall examine these and other policy questions at various points in the rest of this chapter.

Regularisation and the question of numbers

One of the more pragmatic aspects of Spanish immigration policy has been the two regularisation programmes carried out in 1985 and 1991. The first regularisation resulted in the legalisation of some 58,000 illegal migrants. The main nationalities to take advantage of this amnesty were Moroccans (18.1% of the total), Portuguese (8.8%), Senegalese (8.2%), Argentineans (6.6%) and Gambians (6.1%). The vast majority were engaged in service sector activities (70.4%), with 17.0 per cent involved in agriculture and much smaller numbers employed in construction (6.8%) and industry (5.8%). The provinces which registered the main concentrations of these regularisations reflected the map of seasonal and casual labour demand in agricultural work, tourism, construction and urban low-grade services. Hence Barcelona accounted for 21.2 per cent of the 1985 regularisations, Madrid for 14.0 per cent, Baleares 8.4 per cent, Málaga 7.8 per cent, Las Palmas 7.3 per cent, Girona 5.2 per cent and Alicante 4.0 per cent (data from SOPEMI 1990: 96-100).

The regularisation data from 1985 confirmed certain characteristics of Spain's immigrant population which had been suggested by other partial surveys, but the programme also had its limitations. The biggest shortcoming was that it only drew forth a small minority (maybe as little as 10-15%) of the total estimated number of 'illegals'. The majority avoided the regularisation through suspicion or for fear of losing their jobs with their employers who preferred to hire illegal (and hence vulnerable and exploitable) migrants. What the data did confirm was the clear tendency for illegal migrants to enter those employment sectors which already contained foreign labour, including legally established migrant workers. This continuity reflects the fact that illegal migrants are an integral part of the wider migration process and are therefore able to take advantage of established ethnic communities to help them find employment and accommodation.

The second regularisation, held in 1991, resulted in about twice as many legalisations as the first. There were about 133,000 applications, of which 109,000 were granted legal status. The 1991 programme reinforced the realisation that Spain's foreign population was no longer mainly European, made up of Portuguese workers and British and other North European retirement migrants, but had become predominantly 'Third World', made up of Africans (55.4% of the legalisations), Latin Americans (26.3%) and Asians (9.1%); only 7.5 per cent of the regularisations were Europeans and 1.5 per cent North Americans. Moroccans were far and away the largest single group to regularise, accounting for 44.5 per cent of the total.

According to Izquierdo (1994), the 1991 regularisation changed not only the demographic and social composition of the migrant population in Spain, weighting it more to young males, but also 'normalised' it in the sense of the statistics bearing a closer resemblance to the reality of immigration. The programme increased the proportion of workers in the total immigrant stock from 28 per cent in 1989 to 45 per cent in 1992 - with much higher rates for the non-European groups. Agriculture, construction and, above all, low-skilled services continued to be the main employment sectors, but with strong differentiation on the basis of both nationality and gender. For example the predominantly female Filipinos were mainly engaged as domestic helpers in wealthy urban households, whereas the overwhelmingly male Senegalese were street-hawkers in the main towns and tourist resorts. The numerically-dominant Moroccans, also a mainly male group, were (and are) found in a variety of employment niches as construction workers, seasonal farm labourers, waiters, market-traders and craftsmen.

The regionally specialised nature of the Spanish economy combines with the specific linkage of migrant nationalities to distinct labour market niches to produce a clearly-patterned geography of migrant groups. The two major concentrations of economic migrants are found in Madrid and Barcelona, the dominant poles of the national economy. Here is found the greatest variety of migrant nationalities, reflecting the variety of types of work obtainable. Migrants from Latin American countries, who tend to be well-qualified and have few linguistic or cultural problems, are over-represented in the big cities. Asian migrants are also predominantly urban. The most distinctive Asian group are the Filipino domestic workers - almost entirely females. Indians, Chinese and Iranians are the other important Asian nationalities: these groups are often involved in small enterprises such as restaurants, grocery stores and trading concerns. From Black Africa the main groups are from Gambia, Senegal and Cape Verde. As elsewhere in Southern Europe, the Senegalese have a penchant for working as hawkers. Other Africans, including Moroccans, take up seasonal and precarious jobs in the informal economy - especially in agriculture, tourism and the textile industry. The major concentrations of temporary farm labour are found along the intensively cultivated coastal plains and basins of Mediterranean Spain: Maresme in Catalonia, Valencia, Alicante, Murcia and Andalusia. The Mediterranean coast, along with the Balearic and Canary Islands, represent the main foci of attraction for seasonal work in the tourist sector. Finally, in north-east Spain, there is an important and longer-established concentration of Portuguese who have working links to the mining and industrial activities in Galicia, León, Asturias and the Basque Country.

We close this section with a brief note on numbers. The most recent SOPEMI data (for 31 December 1993) give a total legally resident foreign population of 430,400 (SOPEMI 1995:208). The ten largest groups are Moroccans (61,300), UK nationals (58,200), Germans (34,100), Portuguese (32,300), French (25,500), Argentineans (21,600), Italians (15,900), citizens of the USA (14,300), Dutch (11,100) and Peruvians (10,000). This list reveals the still-large numbers of Europeans, although the next biggest ten includes a preponderance of non-Europeans (Dominicans, Filipinos, Chinese, Belgians, Venezuelans, Colombians, Chileans, Swiss, Indians, Swedes). What these figures do not tell us, of course, is the quantity of illegal migration. The Spanish government estimated that the 1991 regularisation failed to attract about 200,000 illegals, whilst other estimates of Spain's illegal migrant population in the early-mid 1990s go as high as 300,000 or more (see Cornelius 1994: 335). This would lead us to suggest a total migrant population of 650,000-700,000, equivalent to about 1.7 per cent of the Spanish total.

Spanish attitudes toward migrants

Prior to the recent immigration flows from less developed countries, Spanish society had not really formed an opinion on immigration issues. Spanish people still saw their country as one of emigration: their only contacts with foreigners had been through their own experiences as emigrants in North-West Europe, or meeting tourists visiting Spain. Hence the widespread view of foreigners was that of wealthy people, and the Spaniards considered themselves as non-racist compared to their counterparts in Europe (Diez Nicolás 1992: 35).

The last decade has significantly changed this situation. In the face of an erroneously-perceived 'avalanche' of migrants, public opinion has expressed some feelings of opposition and even outright racism. The suddenness of Spain's transition to the status of an immigration society may be a relevant factor here, for the 'traditional' countries of immigration such as France, the United Kingdom or Germany had effectively more time to form a more measured (but often no less racist) reaction.

According to a recent report by the Centro de Investigaciones sobre la Realidad Social (CIRES 1994), Spaniards' interpersonal experiences of migrants are still low, even negligible. Only one in three Spaniards had ever had a conversation with a Latin American, and only one in ten with an African. The same CIRES survey found that, on the whole, the Spanish population's attitudes to 'Third World' migrants were ambiguous, apprehensive, and variable according to the continent of origin (for English summaries of the CIRES and other Spanish surveys on migrants see Cornelius 1994: 358-62; Misiti et al. 1995: 179-80). Just over half of the people surveyed thought that there were too many foreigners living in Spain; only one third perceived immigration as a 'good' phenomenon. However, when different groups were discussed, significant variations emerged: Latin Americans more accepted, North Africans and Black Africans more rejected. Survey respondents considered that integration would be problematic for the Africans but relatively easy for Latin Americans, due basically to linguistic and cultural factors (Aguilera et al. 1993). However, it is also clear from these survey results (and indeed from the questions asked) that the conception of integration held in Spain is an assimilationist model of requiring migrants to adopt new modes of behaviour in strict concordance with those of the host population. Thus, when ethnic groups hold on to their own customs one finds assertions amongst the Spanish such as 'the Arabs do not want to be integrated into

Spanish society', or 'gypsies are not Spanish' etc. This dual assumption of the unwillingness of migrants to integrate and of their alleged need (as viewed by the Spanish) to completely assimilate is a dangerous ploy which can be used by racist movements as a pretext for their own tolerance and prejudice.

Opinions on the relationship between immigration and unemployment and delinquency are rather divided: 54 per cent of the respondents in the CIRES (1994) study felt that immigrants did not affect unemployment, and 60 per cent felt that delinquency was not increased by the greater migrant presence; on the other hand 46 per cent and 40 per cent, respectively, felt that immigrants had pushed up unemployment and crime. However, these assessments, like other opinions regarding migrants, are strongly conditioned by the age and educational level of the respondents. For instance, whereas 26 per cent of the total respondents believed there were 'too many foreigners living in Spain', most of these negative views were concentrated in the over-45 age group and in groups with low levels of formal education. By contrast, younger people and persons with good educational levels have much more positive attitudes towards migrants.

On the whole, most of the sociological research carried out so far on Spanish attitudes towards migrants shows that levels of 'discrimination' and 'rejection' are still low by comparison to those recorded in other European countries: this is confirmed by the periodic Eurobarometer surveys on xenophobia which show that Spain is the least racist EU nation (Misiti et al. 1995: 179). The Spanish survey data presented by CIRES (1994) do show, however, that there is a significant and worrying level of apprehension and scorn towards illegal migrants without employment and stable housing, and towards Moroccans in particular.

Interpretation of the CIRES, Eurobarometer and other social surveys on migration also have to take into account the recent political and social history of Spain. Above all, one has to bear in mind that, in the post-Franco era, the open display or discussion of racist attitudes is not well accepted in democratic Spanish society, and hence people tend to hide their feelings on these matters. Accordingly, the surveys mentioned above probably do not unveil the real face of discrimination against migrants. The historical rejection and discrimination suffered by the gypsies shows how unstable and imperfect Spain's self-identification as a non-racist society is. We would conclude that not only is racism incipient in Spanish society, but also that it is a more ingrained latent force waiting potentially to explode.

Gypsies apart, the main target for negative stereotypes is undoubtedly the Moroccan migrant. Moroccan immigration is perceived as the least desirable and the most problematic, challenging and 'threatening', both for Spanish society in general, and for the authorities. There are three main factors which help to explain the widespread social rejection of this group. First, Moroccans are now the largest foreign nationality in Spain. Second, they have one of the highest levels of illegality, related to their strong participation in the underground economy. And third, Moroccans are usually described by Spaniards as the most 'different' group in terms of culture, religion, language and race. They suffer rejection as a consequence of historically-grounded prejudices against *'los moros'*, who are today associated both with Islamic fundamentalism and with negative stereotypes of dishonesty, untrustworthiness and criminality. These barriers mean that Moroccans, more than any other group, face a real struggle to integrate and accommodate themselves within Spanish society (Bodega et al. 1995; Cazorla 1995; Pumares 1993a; Solé 1995).

Evolution of Spanish policy towards non-EU migrants

The relatively low salience of immigration issues amongst the Spanish population, the lack (so far) of widespread or systematic racial tensions and the absence of any extreme-right party campaigning on anti-immigration policies, are all correlated with politicians' low-profile stance on migration policy. As Cornelius (1994: 335) points out, the reticence of the political class to get deeply involved in debate about immigration reflects both their lack of confidence in dealing with such a 'new' issue and the country's ambivalence about the immigration question. Many Spaniards, and their politicians, still do not know what kind of immigration policy they really want. The regularisations discussed above were merely an attempt to recognise a *de facto* situation, namely the structural presence of large numbers of clandestine migrant workers. The amnesties could hardly be regarded as policies, although each was set within a wider legal and political context.

The legal framework

Until 1985 there was no legal framework regulating the rights and responsibilities of the foreign population in Spain; hence migrants and foreign settlers were under no obligation to regularise their legal situation. However, from the mid-1980s onwards, this situation changed as a result of three factors: growing immigration flows from 'Third World' countries, the alarmist reactions of some sectors of Spanish society, and pressure from European Community member states in the context of Spain's imminent accession and the creation of a 'common European space'.

In 1985 the so-called 'Foreigners' Law' was passed which unified hitherto dispersed regulations and had the following main objects.

- to regulate the entry and residency procedures of foreigners in Spain;

- to protect the national job market by taking action against clandestine employment;

- to guarantee acceptable working conditions for foreigners, as well as assist them to integrate, avoiding illegality and marginalisation;

- to harmonise Spanish immigration legislation with the rest of the EC, working within the EC unification process.

The *ley extranjería* was widely considered as controversial, restrictive and discriminatory against non-EU migrants. Its twin thrust was to tighten Spanish border controls against 'unwanted' immigration and to strengthen the powers of the police to deal with illegal migrants already in the country. However, the bureaucratic structures necessary for the law's proper implementation have been slow to develop and the complex Spanish legal system posed further obstacles. For instance, non-EU migrants had to provide the authorities with a contract from an employer, proof of earnings and a passport from their country of origin before being granted an official work permit (by the Ministry of Labour) and a temporary residence permit (from the Ministry of Interior). These complicated administrative hurdles, which can take years to overcome, have kept large numbers of migrants in an illegal state, working in the informal economy, even after the regularisations. Indeed not only has the flow of illegal migrants continued, but many 'legal' migrants have been forced into a clandestine position because of the necessity to re-apply for work and residence permits every time they change jobs; if they become unemployed they lose their resident's status and must leave the country.

In response to EU pressure, the main effort has been put into controlling clandestine entry. In 1991 visa requirements were imposed on arrivals from North African countries, and these have been selectively extended to certain Latin American countries such as Peru and the Dominican Republic, thought to be sources of significant flows of economic migrants. Maritime controls have been stepped up along the Andalusian coast and an agreement has been struck with Morocco that it should seek to control departures from its own shores (Misiti et al. 1995: 181). Within Spain the *'ley corcuera'* has given police the powers to stop suspected illegal migrants on the street and demand documents. Moroccans and black Africans were the main targets for the use (and abuse) of this legal tool, but expulsions have been relatively few. Unlike in Greece, there have been no mass round-ups and deportations: such highly visible, repressive actions would not be tolerated by most sections of modern Spanish society still sensitive about the Franco legacy (Cornelius 1994: 346). Under the 1985 law, employers are liable to fines (but not more serious punishment) for hiring illegal workers, but prosecutions are on a small scale and are usually limited to those in violation of other regulations such as health and safety law.

Little or no progress has been made on integration and other social measures. Schooling for all migrant children is now guaranteed, as are health care and unemployment payments for those who have paid social security contributions. Plans to set up migrant housing schemes, however, have yet to get off the ground (Misiti et al. 1995: 182).

The main lesson to be drawn from this short legislative experience is that the government cannot aim at devising an effective policy on immigration without resolving certain problems and contradictions. First, there is the basic problem of the failure to decide internally what kind of migration policy Spain needs: thus far the measures put in place have largely been driven by external (EU) pressures. Second, an immigration policy is difficult to achieve without simultaneously formulating a proper integration policy - and the means to accomplish it. To that extent, the Spanish government's approach to immigration proves to be ineffective, since it is basically centred around the need to control inflows using border patrols and police powers. This seems to have the perverse effect of increasing clandestinity without actually halting the flows. Finally the absence of a real drive to implement employer sanctions reflects the government's reluctance to confront the informal economy, the source of so much productive activity and employment in Spain.

Social consequences

To a certain extent, Spain's migration policy - or lack of it - has conditioned the social framework within which the social integration/exclusion of migrants is developing. As Martín Serrano (1993) points out, the legislators have unconsciously generated an administrative situation that in practice promotes marginalisation and the incipient formation of migrant ghettos. As noted at the beginning of the previous subsection, one of the key objectives of the Foreigners' Law was 'to guarantee acceptable working conditions for foreigners, as well as to assist them to integrate, avoiding illegality and marginalisation'. This objective has manifestly not been attained. Instead, by tightening controls at the Spanish borders in order to try to rebuff inflows, and by endowing police with special powers to approach and detain suspected illegal migrants anywhere in Spain, the authorities have indirectly fostered a growing clandestine migration and a significant stock of illegal migrants.

However, despite the lack of a properly-defined and comprehensive policy of social integration, the migrant communities in Spain are not completely excluded from all areas of society or all social benefits. The government has not blocked access to state schools or health care facilities for illegal migrants and their children. All migrant children are encouraged to attend state schools and free emergency and in-patient care is available to all migrants of whatever status. However, out-patient treatment is granted only to those with a residence permit, whilst the children of illegal migrants do not qualify for public scholarships or vocational training, nor can they receive any certification for their school years in Spain (Cornelius 1994: 356-7).

Faced by criticisms for being more interested in stemming migrant inflows than in providing social assistance to migrants already in Spain, in 1994 the socialist government of Felipe González passed a blueprint for the social integration of migrants, the *Plan para la Integración Social de los Immigrantes*. It is as yet too early to assess the impact of this 'active' policy, but we can confirm that in practice migrants are still suffering from restrictive and exclusionary measures which manifest themselves in many spheres of migrants' everyday lives such as education, employment, housing, social benefits, social integration and harassment.

The driving-force behind the Plan came from several quarters of Spanish liberal society, plus pressure from the trade unions, NGOs and migrant organisations, all of which were concerned to awaken Spanish society and the authorities to the harsh life conditions of the migrants. The new plan has set out as one of its main goals the allocation of leading integrating roles to civil society in general and to NGOs and other associations in particular. The work of the two main trade unions *(Unión General de Trabajadores* and the *Comisiones Obreras)* in the field of immigration has not been easy since it has been characterised by a compromise between protecting the jobs of union members and denouncing the working conditions of the migrants. However, the trade unions have not only focused on labour aspects but also on structural, personal and family considerations of the migrant condition.

NGOs have recently acquired a more prominent role in Spanish society and have been especially active in providing a variety of social and support services to migrants, including illegals. Funded both by the government and religious bodies and supported also by voluntary donations and work, NGOs such as Caritas, Cruz Roja and SOS Racismo offer services such as childcare for working mothers, soup kitchens, emergency accommodation, language teaching and legal advice for migrants irrespective of legal status. They are particularly important in big cities like Madrid and Barcelona and in southern Spain near the points of arrival (Aragón Bombín 1991). Also, not to be overlooked are the various migrant associations which play an essential role in acting as a bridge between migrants and the host society and in defending the interests of the former. The most important of these organisations correspond to the various national groups: ATIME for the Moroccans, ARI for Peruvians, Voluntariado de Madres Dominicanas for Dominican women and so on.

Whilst integration is relatively unproblematic for migrants from Europe and Latin America, African groups, and especially the Moroccans, suffer from multiple social exclusion. This is clearly seen in their patterns of housing. There is no doubt that a great deal of anti-migrant discrimination is exercised by landlords who claim to be concerned about alleged criminal activities, notably drugs trafficking (Cornelius 1994: 357). In Madrid there are many squatter-style settlements of shacks and informally-built housing on tracts of land which were formerly vacant: most of these shanty districts are occupied by Moroccans (Pumares 1993b). Barcelona has virtually none of these types of spontaneous settlements; here the trend has been for migrants to concentrate in the low-rent apartment blocks which formerly housed the earlier waves of poor internal migrants. It is to Barcelona and Catalonia that we now turn our attention, after a brief section on the Moroccan background.

The Moroccan context

The 'new' migration flows from Morocco to Spain do not represent the first contact between the two countries. On the contrary, a whole range of prior relationships have shaped both the flows themselves and how perceptions of Moroccan migration are constructed. For the sake of brevity, just three key processes are mentioned here. First, there is the historical and psychological legacy of seven centuries of Islamic dominance in the Iberian peninsula, which ended with the expulsion of the Muslim (and Jewish) populations and their migratory exodus to North Africa. Ever since the *reconquista* in the 15th century, when the Christians regained control over the south of Spain, the Moorish 'enemy' has been present in the Spanish collective memory. Although there is no real challenge to Spanish national security nowadays, the belief persists amongst public opinion that the 'threat' still emanates from the south (Martín-Muñoz 1994). This syndrome of the 'Moslem menace' tends to be reinforced by the activities of Islamic fundamentalists and by the generally ethnocentric and alarmist stance of the mass media towards this fundamentalism and towards illegal migration. Undoubtedly, the deeply-rooted negative image of Islam produces a backlash for the Moroccan migrants who want to live part of their future in Spain and who want to achieve a measure of integration with Spanish society.

The second significant historical fact with far-reaching outcomes for the migratory process has been Spanish colonialism in north-western Africa. This started in 1912 with the establishment of two protectorates - French and Spanish - over Moroccan territory. Two distinct areas were administered by Spain: the northern part, which included the Rif and Yebala regions; and the southern desert territory known as Spanish Sahara. The Spanish presence was maintained until 1956 in the north and until 1975 in Spanish Sahara. The main area of interest for our study of Moroccan migration to Spain is the north, inhabited mainly by rural Berbers. Migrants of rural Berber origin account for the largest ethnic element of the Moroccans in Catalonia, 40 per cent of whom come from the Rif, and particularly from the provinces of Nador and Larache (Roque 1994).

The third key historical moment concerns the role of Moroccans in the Francoist uprising which started in northern Morocco in 1936 and culminated in the Spanish Civil War. Some 75,000 Moroccans joined the Francoist faction, for two main reasons. On the one hand the nationalist faction was seen as a supporter and protector of Islamic traditions compared to the 'antireligious' republicans. On the other hand, persistent drought and famine in northern Morocco in those years meant that joining the Francoist army was seen as a way out of an extremely precarious economic situation by many Moroccan peasants. It is also important to point out that this support given to Franco's army reinforced even more the negative stereotypes of Moroccans in Catalonia, a region that during the Civil War was an important bastion of republicanism.

We now move from political history to demography. Since the establishment of Morocco as an independent country the population has grown from 10m in 1956 to 26m in 1994. Average annual population growth was 2.2 per cent between 1980 and 1993; it will be 1.9 per cent during 1994-2000. Although sheer demographic momentum constitutes a powerful 'push factor' for emigration, it is important to appreciate that demographic indicators are changing rapidly. The total fertility rate (TFR) - the average number of children produced by a woman over the reproductive life-cycle - fell from 6.7 in 1960 to 3.6 in 1993: a decline which has not been fully grasped by Western scholars who still seem obsessed with the 'explosive' growth of the population of Morocco and the rest of North Africa (Courbage 1994). Key factors explaining the drop in fertility are the rapid urbanisation of Morocco (urban birth-rates are significantly lower than rural), rising levels of female education leading to delayed marriage and new norms on family size, and the introduction of family planning programmes since the 1970s (Arango 1989).

The Moroccan economy has failed to keep pace with recent demographic growth and this situation seems likely to continue for some time. Despite recent urbanisation, the rural component of the economy remains dominant: 40 per cent of the active population are engaged in farming. Other structural problems such as declining prices for phosphates (Morocco's main primary industrial resource), deep recession in the 1980s and a heavy external debt burden provide the economic context for high levels of unemployment and hence pressures to emigrate. In 1992 the official unemployment rate was 16 per cent, but 30 per cent for young people aged 15-25. However, unofficial estimates suggest that youth unemployment could be as high as 70 per cent (Mir 1995: 58).

Colonial economic history dictates that the Moroccan economy is closely integrated into that of the EU but in an unequal partnership (Khader 1992: 223). France and Spain are the main trading partners. In 1994 two-thirds of Moroccan trade was with the EU, but with a deficit of 45 per cent on these

70 Into the Margins

transactions for Morocco. Tourism and emigrant remittances help to compensate for the large deficit on visible trade.

Moroccan emigration to Europe has evolved in two main phases. The first, covering the 1960s and early 1970s, was shaped by the crisis in Moroccan traditional agriculture and the strong demand for labour in post-war industrial Europe. The main destinations were France, Belgium, the Netherlands and West Germany. In this respect Morocco played a similar role to that of Spain, also a massive labour exporter at that time. The second period, the last 20 years, is shaped by continuing crises in the Moroccan economy together with the strong migration control measures taken by the traditional immigration countries of North-West Europe. The latter policies forced many migrants to look for 'alternative' destinations. Increasing numbers of Moroccan migrants ended up in southern Europe, notably Italy and Spain, either because these were the traditional staging-posts for migrants heading north, or because increasingly prosperous southern Europe was seen as a straightforward alternative to direct entry to northern Europe (King and Konjhodzic 1995: 49).

By the early 1990s, according to figures produced by the Bank al-Maghrib, there were more than 1.7 million Moroccans living abroad, equivalent to 7 per cent of the Moroccan population. Of these, 1.4 m were in Europe, with most of the rest in other Arab states. The chief European groupings were in France (720,000), the Netherlands (190,000), Belgium (170,000), Italy (130,000), Spain (90,000) and Germany (80,000).

Moroccan migrants in Catalonia

Earlier on it was pointed out that Catalonia, especially Barcelona, represented one of the major poles of attraction for Spain's 'new migrants', and that Moroccans were the most important migrant group, both in Spain and in Catalonia. In this section of the chapter we first examine the demographic and economic structure of Catalonia as a context for recent immigration, and then describe the arrival of Moroccans in Catalonia.

Catalonia: economic and demographic aspects

Migration has played a fundamental role in Catalan development, even before the arrival of Moroccans and other recent migrants. During the period 1950-75 Catalonia's population grew by 75 per cent, from 3.2 to 5.6 million. An immigration of 1.4 m people from elsewhere in Spain, mainly from the south, was the main contributing factor, together with a steady rate of natural increase of the Catalan population, boosted by the higher fertilities of the in-migrants from the south of Spain. By the late 1970s, 38 per cent of the Catalan population had a birthplace outside the region.

By contrast, the period since 1975 has been characterised by Catalonia's demographic stagnation. Internal migration more or less ceased, indeed many migrants returned home, and the region's birth rate collapsed from a TFR of 2.5 in 1975 to 1.3 in 1986, leading to a sharp ageing of the population. As internal in-migration faded away, the way was left open for migrants from abroad.

This demographic 'window of opportunity' for new immigration flows was reinforced by powerful economic developments operating in Catalonia in the 1980s and early 1990s. On the one hand these involved the more-or-less standard processes of post-Fordist economic restructuring: a sectoral shift from heavy manufacturing industry to high-tech production and services, an organisational change from mass production to more flexible and small-scale outputs, and a switch from rigid to flexible labour management (Blotevogel and King 1996). On the other hand were economic developments that were more specific to Catalonia - a reindustrialisation process financed by significant flows of foreign direct investment (in the late 1980s Catalonia attracted more than a quarter of the FDI entering Spain), a strong tertiarisation based on tourism and trade, the strategic geographical position of Catalonia in the context of Spain's EU membership and integration, and then, the *coup de grâce*, Barcelona's hosting of the 1992 Olympic Games. Finally, for both Catalonia and Spain, there was the gathering strength of the informal economy, reckoned to employ a quarter of the population and to account for a similar proportion of national and regional GDP. Casual labour operating within the informal employment market came to be particularly concentrated in agriculture, the service sector, small industry and construction: all sectors important in the Catalan economy and precisely those niches where Moroccan migrants are found.

Arrival and employment of Moroccan migrants

The first Moroccan communities in Catalonia resulted from the 'shutting off of the Pyrenees' in the mid-1970s; up to that time Catalonia was essentially a region of transit for Moroccans en route north. Barcelona contained the overwhelming majority of these initial migrants, most of whom were young males engaged in the construction and industrial sectors. The lack of any migration policy or controls by the authorities left these early Moroccan migrants in an irregular position, but this was hardly a practical problem since there were no obstacles to prevent them staying and settling down. (Subsequently they were able to regularise their positions if they wished). For about a decade, the Moroccan migrants consolidated their presence and spread also to other towns and provinces of the region, notably Girona and Tarragona. Some women and children arrived. The final phase, since 1986, is characterised by the legal framework (but delayed implementation) of the Foreigner's Law of 1985. As noted earlier, the introduction of this restrictive law has not weakened the flow of Moroccan and other migrants into Catalonia. Moroccan migrants have continued both to establish firmer bases for community development in Barcelona and to diffuse their presence throughout the Catalan region, especially to those areas where urban jobs, tourist employment and agricultural work are available. Moroccans are the biggest migrant group in all four Catalan provinces (Barcelona, Girona, Lleida and Tarragona); nevertheless Barcelona still accounts for 68 per cent of all Moroccans officially registered in Catalonia, and for over a quarter of Moroccans in Spain (López García 1993; IOE 1994). In Catalonia Moroccans accounted for over half of all legally present foreigners (27,150 out of *ca.* 50,000) at the end of 1992.

The age structure of the Moroccan population in Catalonia reflects a predominance of the economically active. Only 8 per cent are over 50 and only 0.6 per cent over 65. The modal groups are 30-49 years (43%) and 16-29 (36%). Nevertheless there are variations within Catalonia, and the situation itself is changing. Barcelona has a larger than average share of both elderly and infant Moroccans, reflecting its longer-established Moroccan community. By the same token the sex divide (79% males in Catalonia as a whole) is somewhat more equal in the Catalan capital (IOE 1994). The proportion of females in the Moroccan migrant population is tending to increase, along with the number of children, either born in Morocco or Spain. Generally, it can be observed that the family size amongst Moroccans in Catalonia is lower than in Morocco (Tapinos 1993: 35). However, not all Moroccan migrant women are 'merely' the wives of male migrants: there is a significant independent flow of single and divorced women, both students and workers, who are leaving their country in the quest for better work and study opportunities and a new life.

This group challenges the widely-held stereotype of submissive Moroccan women.

Regarding employment, Moroccans in Catalonia exhibit the very high activity rates typical of economic migrants: an average of 90 per cent overall, rising to 96 per cent in Lérida (Lleida) province (IOE 1994). In contrast to the indigenous Catalan population who are strongly concentrated in the tertiary sector (54%) and industry (33%), Moroccan migrants work mainly in construction (36%), services (30%), agriculture (20%) and industry (13%); it should be stressed once again that these data refer only to recorded migrants and exclude undocumented Moroccans. It is also important to bear in mind that, in the vast majority of cases, these jobs are at the very bottom of the labour hierarchy. There is a tiny minority - 2 per cent - of professionals, technicians and managers, whilst 4.6 per cent have an official license as shopkeepers or traders.

The most stably settled of the Moroccan migrants are found working as public employees (eg: street-cleaners), petty traders and as more-or-less permanent employees in small industrial workshops or on those farms where there is a demand for non-seasonal labour. The majority of these groups are legal migrants. The rest of the Moroccan working population, including many illegals, are found in those sectors of the economy where there is a need for a casual workforce, for instance in the construction trade, seasonal farm labour and the tourist industry. Some Moroccan women are found in domestic service. The precariousness of these kinds of work hinders the integration of migrant workers, prevents family reunion and tends to block access to proper housing.

To sum up, the employment pattern of Moroccan migrants in Catalonia follows that of migrants in other southern European countries, where employment tends to be round the edge of the formal labour market or in parallel informal markets where there is no union protection or collective bargaining (Iosifides and King 1996). Hence the migrants, especially those with no legal footing, are exposed to all kinds of exploitation and abuse by their employers. This situation does nothing except reinforce the already poor living conditions and social exclusion of the Moroccans, as we shall see in the next section.

Social integration and exclusion of Moroccan migrants in Catalonia

In this final main part of the chapter, we attempt to link the two themes of immigration and integration, drawing on our specific knowledge of Moroccans in Catalonia. In earlier sections we have seen how the 'new immigration' represents a considerable challenge for Spanish society which is still in the stage of being taken by surprise by the speed of the development of immigration. Hence the country's rather uncertain search for suitable policies, which must rely in turn on appropriate models of social integration on the one hand, and migration control (we would prefer the term 'management') on the other. The success of the process of integration is essential in order to create a more stable, fair and tolerant society in which human rights are respected and where the receiving society is enriched by the contact with other cultures. By contrast, the failure of social integration would configure a society based on permanent social conflict and high levels of marginalisation and exclusion.

Models of integration

This is not the place for an extended discussion on the integration of migrants in host societies. Instead, we will first offer a brief working definition of social integration, then outline three potential models of integration, and finally examine the Spanish-Catalan experience.

Integration can be defined as a process through which the indigenous population and a minority group settled in the same place gradually intermingle and move towards equality on the socio-economic, cultural and political levels. This conception differs from the notion of assimilation which implies the cultural, social and political subordination of one group by another, such that the minority group is deprived of its original identity.

According to Castles (1995) there are three main models of integration, which respond to the basic ways in which a receiving country can react to immigration. The first is the *assimilationist* model, in which, as noted above, the cornerstone of policy is the process by which migrants are expected to give up their distinctive linguistic, religious and other socio-cultural characteristics and become indistinguishable from the majority population. The active role of the state becomes essential in this transition, notably through insistence on the use of the dominant language. The assimilationist model has been applied at various times in the past by several countries, including France, the USA,

Canada and Australia. Generally, however, it has been abandoned over time and replaced by other policies of integration.

The second model is the *pluralist* model, characterised by the acceptance of migrants as ethnic communities that remain clearly distinguishable from the majority population with regard to culture, language, social behaviour and ethnic associations, even across several generations. This model implies that migrants are given equal rights to the indigenous population in all spheres of society, but without giving up their diversity and origins except where conformity to majority norms is unavoidable (for instance with regard to polygamy or repression of women). This model has many variants and has mainly been applied in recent years in the USA, Canada, Australia and Sweden.

The third model, that of *differential exclusion,* is the one that would seem to be closest to the one adopted in Spain and in Catalonia, as we shall see presently. This approach is characterised by a situation in which migrants are incorporated into certain areas of society, such as the labour market, but denied access to others, such as welfare systems, citizenship and political participation. Exclusion may be effected by legal mechanisms - refusal of naturalisation and sharp distinctions between the rights of citizens and non-citizens - or through informal practices such as racism and discrimination. In this model migrants become ethnic minorities who generally become marginalised by their ethnic 'difference' and immigrant status. Since such ethnic minorities usually become disadvantaged socio-economically, a powerful link between class and ethnic background is implied.

The differential exclusion model responds to the belief that the admission of migrants is only a temporary phenomenon, such as the recruitment of foreign workers to meet cyclical or seasonal upswings in labour demand. Permanent settlement is seen as a threat for the receiving country. This threat is commonly 'explained' by the social costs of long-term settlement, such as emands on social services and the danger of the emergence of an 'underclass'. Other reasons deployed are the challenges to national culture and identity, and political arguments such as the effects on political institutions and foreign relations.

Governments following this model adopt a dual strategy. On the one hand, they keep migrants in a temporary state by means of restrictions on residence rights and prevention of family reunion. On the other hand, they tolerate or even tacitly encourage illegal labour immigration. As Castles (1995) points out, such dual policies are clearly being used by southern European countries such as Spain.

Dilemmas of social integration in Catalonia

The question of immigration into Catalonia is more complicated, since the Catalan government has a stronger commitment to the integration of migrants than does the national government. For instance, the *jus solis* (i.e. the principle that the Catalan-born children of migrants, including other Spaniards, are considered as Catalans) is embodied in the political discourse of the *Generalitat de Catalunya* - the regional government of Catalonia. However, Spanish law, tied to the concept of *jus sanguinis*, does not recognise the children of foreigners, and since the application of this principle is the exclusive competence of the central government in Madrid, Catalonia is left without any power to apply the *jus solis* to the children of foreigners. The Catalan government can, however, still decide how to integrate its region's migrants. In this respect there is still a long way to go despite the 1993 enactment of the *Plan Interdepartamental de Inmigración* by the regional parliament. Among the various departments of the Generalitat, only that for education has a clear policy in favour of integration for migrants, with universal schooling rights guaranteed irrespective of the legal status of the children.

The Catalan language represents one of the main instruments of social integration (in contrast with Basque nationalism which is based on consanguineity). This explains why Catalonia never really had a problem integrating migrants from other Spanish regions, insofar as these internal migrants were able to assume the different elements of Catalan culture. Thus the Catalan model of integration as regards migrants from the rest of Spain is one of assimilation. However, the new migrant flows from Morocco and elsewhere have put into question the applicability of the traditional assimilation model, since these migrants obviously differ markedly from the previous ones in terms of language, culture, race and religion.

As regards social services to migrants, the Generalitat has contracted-out their provision to NGOs and supported their task by means of public subsidies. Whilst this tactic might be thought to be in tune with the general trend towards privatisation of public services in Europe, it also indicates the lack of a well-articulated policy to cope with migrants' practical needs. Meanwhile, the NGOs continue to increase and diversify their areas of action, reinforcing their active role as mediators between the indigenous society and the migrants.

Pathways to social integration depend on many factors: the 'objective' cultural distance between migrants and the host society (insofar as this can be measured); the barriers of prejudice and negative ethnic stereotyping; legal status; and the socio-economic conditions of different migrants, particularly with regard to access to work and housing. Moroccans are the group in Catalonia which faces the greatest problems of integration: in addition to legal obstacles there are also powerful social barriers. Perhaps surprisingly, access to housing for Moroccans is more problematic than access to work. Bearing in mind the nature of the Catalan labour market, most Moroccans tend to work in the informal economy, where work is characterised by precariousness, exploitation, low status and low pay. Stable jobs are hard to find, and hence one of the pathways to a more complete social integration is blocked off. Housing represents another route/barrier to integration which is difficult to traverse, partly because (more so than work) accommodation is highly spatially defined and therefore leads to a situation of ghettoisation. In the case of Moroccans in Barcelona, the main housing lies in the zones of low-rent, dilapidated tenement blocks previously occupied by internal migrants from the south of Spain in the 1950s, 1960s and 1970s. These hurriedly-built blocks were originally constructed without proper planning permission and hence are poorly equipped and poorly connected to the rest of the urban network. The Moroccans' high levels of residential segregation and overcrowding make social integration more difficult: progress out of these areas of urban degradation is hampered by the unwillingness of landlords and residents' associations elsewhere in the city to rent or sell to Moroccans.

Anti-Moroccan racism in the housing market and in other forms of informal social discourse still stops short of having an overt political expression in Catalonia and in Spain. The attitudes towards migration expressed by far-right parties such as *Frente Nacional* (which is highly sympathetic to Jean Marie Le Pen's *Front National* in France) and *Solidaridad Espanola*, mainly reflect a sense of nostalgia for Franco's dictatorship rather than a well-articulated feeling of racism against migrants. Nevertheless, during the last decade, big cities such as Barcelona have witnessed the emergence of neo-nazi groups who have mainly targeted their hostile and violent activities against migrants. The murder of a female migrant from the Dominican Republic by a neo-nazi skinhead in Madrid in 1992 was amongst the first of a number of tragic incidents which are beginning to shatter the myth of Spain as a non-racist society.

Finally, the treatment of Moroccans and other migrants and minorities in the Catalan and Spanish media has a determining role in generating and reinforcing negative perceptions and stereotypes. Considering the fact noted earlier that most Spaniards have almost no personal interaction with migrants, the media is the source of most of their 'information' about migrants. Portrayal of migrants in the Spanish mass media exhibits partiality, deception and unremittingly negative stereotypes. This misinformation is mainly due to the emphasis placed on 'bad news' regarding migrants. Moreover the real facts are often replaced by inaccuracies and false assertions. As illustrations we can note that implicit links repeatedly established by the media between rising unemployment in Spain and the increasing numbers of unskilled illegal migrants, and the frequent and sensationalist reporting of cases of migrants involved in crime, especially street crime and drugs trafficking. Thus the average Spaniard is persuaded to perceive a strong causal link between immigration, unemployment and delinquency. The Moroccans are nearly always the main target, and their marginality is constantly highlighted by repeated references to their clandestine jobs and their role in the underground economy. Hence when the social exclusion of Moroccans is discussed, the debate must involve not only the standard material and welfare parameters of this exclusion - housing, work, social services, spatial segregation etc. - but also include their right to a public image which is fair and accurate.

Conclusion: the global setting

This chapter has examined the new immigration into Spain, paying particular attention to Moroccans in Catalonia. Our analysis would be incomplete if it was not considered, finally, within the broader context of the globalisation of international migration. This is necessary not only because migration has become subject to global-scale forces, but also because contemporary migration is part and parcel of global social change and development (Castles and Miller 1993; King 1995).

The push and pull factors used earlier to 'explain' Moroccan migration to Spain focused on straightforward economic and demographic indicators: from Morocco the 'pushes' derived from high (but now decelerating) demographic growth combined with chronic unemployment and poverty; from Spain the 'pulls' involved increasing prosperity in the post-Franco, EU era, ease of entry and a recasting of Spain's traditional gateway function into a new destination role. The macro-structural contexts of these pushes and pulls now need to be drawn out.

Since the early 1980s Morocco has been undertaking a strict programme of economic adjustment directed by the World Bank and International Monetary Fund. This harsh economic policy has resulted in sharp cutbacks in social spending which have been exacerbated, for some groups, the already severe situation of poverty and inequality and hence the pressures for emigration. In this context it is important to point out that the European countries which are the backers (either directly or indirectly) of the World Bank/IMF structural adjustment programme have yet to accept any share of responsibility for the social consequences of adjustment, including emigration. This is particularly relevant to France and Spain, colonisers of Morocco until 1956.

On the other hand, the past twenty or so years have witnessed the evolution of the Fordist economic model towards a neoliberal model throughout Western Europe, with a profound effect on labour markets. Amongst the outcomes of this transition have been a more sharply patterned labour market segmentation, the proliferation of temporary jobs and an increase in the strength and dynamism of the underground economy. These pressures have been particularly marked in Spain and southern Europe; indeed they are a key part of the specific south European sub-model of capitalist development (Hadjimichalis 1987; Mingione 1995). Migrant workers from the developing world have been integral to the recent further development of this sub-model, although their full role is only now coming to be appreciated and analysed (Iosifides and King 1996). Part of this analysis is the use of the concept of labour market segmentation to resolve the paradox of buoyant migration with high unemployment in Spain (22% in 1996).

Important though these global economic restructuring processes are in shaping international migration at the present time, it should never be forgotten that migration remains at base a social process (Jackson 1986). The so-called 'stock effect' is a key factor in this regard since previous migrants exert a powerful influence over on-going migration flows. It is important to note in this regard that the Moroccan community started to settle in Catalonia in the mid-1970s. The social context of arrival is reinforced by 'spillover effects' back to the regions of origin - information flows and remittances are the key mechanisms here.

Finally we have seen how, despite some good intentions, Moroccans remain on the whole a marginal and excluded group in Catalonia. Their lack of integration reflects Spain's (and Europe's) unwillingness to incorporate new generations of 'third-country' migrants as fully-participating members of society, and the ideology that their presence will be temporary. Previous experience of European migration suggests that this view is likely to be a myth. On the other hand, trans-Mediterranean migration has less of the syndrome of migration being a 'single great journey' (as with transatlantic migrations of an earlier era) and involves more flexible patterns of to-and-fro movement with sojourns rather than lifetime migrations. The crucial question here is to know to what extent this temporality is a real reflection of migrants' own preferences for their migration behaviour, and to what extent it is constrained by the immigration regimes which have been put in place (or allowed to evolve) by the new immigration countries such as Spain.

References

Aguilera, M., González, M. and Rodríguez, V. (1993) 'Actitudes de la población española ante los immigrantes extranjeros', *Estudios Geográficos*, 54: 145-54.

Aragón Bombín, R. (1991) 'Hacia una política activa de immigración', *Revista de Economía y Sociología del Trabajo*, 11: 97-108.

Arango, J. (1989) 'Disparidades demográficas y potencial migratorio en el Mediterráneo', in M. Roque (ed.) *Human Movements in the Western Mediterranean*. Barcelona: Institut Català d'Estudis Mediterranis.

Blotevogel, H.H. and King, R. (1996) 'European economic restructuring: demographic responses and feedbacks', *European Urban and Regional Studies*, 3: 133-59.

Bodega, I., Cebrian, A., Franchini, T., Lora-Tamayo, G. and Martín-Lou, A. (1995) 'Recent migration from Morocco to Spain', *International Migration Review*, 29: 800-19.

Castles, S. (1995) 'How nation-states respond to immigration and ethnic diversity', *New Community*, 21: 293-308.

Castles, S. and Miller, M.J. (1993) *The Age of Migration: International Population Movements in the Modern World*. London: Macmillan.

Cazorla, J. (1995) 'La immigración marroquí en España: datos, opiniones y previsiones', *Revista Internacional de Sociolgía*, 12: 117-44.

CIRES (1994) *Survey on Attitudes towards Immigrants*. Madrid: Centro de Investigaciones sobre la Realidad Social.

Cornelius, W.A. (1994) 'Spain: the uneasy transition from labour exporter to labour importer', in W.A. Cornelius, P.L. Martin and J.F. Hollifield (eds.) *Controlling Immigration: a Global Perspective*. Stanford, CA: Stanford University Press.

Courbage, Y. (1994) 'Demographic transition among the Maghreb peoples of North Africa and in the emigrant community abroad', in P. Ludlow (ed.) *Europe and the Mediterranean*. London: Brassey's.

Diez Nicolás, J. (1992) 'Actitud de los españoles hacia los immigrantes', *Cuenta y Razón del Pensamiento Actual*, Noviembre-Diciembre: 35-40.

Grigg, D.B. (1977) 'E.G. Ravenstein and the "laws of migration"', *Journal of Historical Geography*, 3: 41-54.

Hadjimichalis, C. (1987) *Uneven Development and Regionalism: State, Territory and Class in Southern Europe*. London: Croom Helm.

IOE (1994) *Presencia del Sur: Marroquies en Cataluña*. Barcelona: Institut Català d'Estudis Mediterranis.

Iosifides, T. and King, R. (1996) 'Recent immigration to Southern Europe: the socio-economic and labour market contexts', in G. Lazaridis (ed.) *Southern Europe in Transition*, special issue of the *Journal of Area Studies*, 9: 70-94.

Izquierdo, A. (1994) 'Consecuencias de la regulación de trabajadores extranjeros 1991-1992', *Papers*, 43: 125-31.

Jackson, J.A. (1986) *Migration*. London: Longman.

Khader, B. (1992) *Europa y el Gran Magreb*. Barcelona: Fundación Paulino Torres Domenech.

King, R. (1995) 'Migrations, globalization and place', in D. Massey and P. Jess (eds.) *A Place in the World? Places, Culture and Globalization*. Oxford: Oxford University Press.

King, R and Konjhodzic, I. (1995) *Labour, Employment and Migration in Southern Europe*. Brighton: University of Sussex, Research Papers in Geography, 19.

King, R. and Rybaczuk, K. (1993) 'Southern Europe and the international division of labour: from emigration to immigration', in R. King (ed.) *The New Geography of European Migrations*. London: Belhaven.

López García, B. (1993) *Immigración Magrebi in España: el Retorno de los Moriscos*. Madrid: Mapfre.

Martín-Muñoz, G. (1994) 'El Islam en España hoy', in L. Martín Rojo, C. Gómez-Esteban, F. Arranz Lozano and A. Gabilondo Pujol (eds.) *Hablar y Dejar Hablar: sobre Racismo y Xenophobia*. Madrid: Ediciones de la Universidad Autónoma de Madrid.

Martín Serrano, M. (1993) 'Los efectos de la política immigratoria', *Política y Sociedad*, 12: 37-43.

Mingione, E. (1995) 'Labour market segmentation and informal work in Southern Europe', *European Urban and Regional Studies*, 2: 121-43.

Mir, P. (1995) 'Las economías del Magreb', *Papers*, 46: 57-75.

Misiti, M., Muscarà, C., Pumares, P., Rodríguez, V. and White, P. (1995) 'Future migration into Southern Europe', in R. Hall and P. White (eds.) *Europe's Population: Towards the Next Century*. London: UCL Press.

Pumares, P. (1993a) 'Problemática de la inmigración marroquí en España', *Política y Sociedad,* 12: 139-47.
Pumares, P. (1993b) 'L'immigration moroccaine dans la Communauté Autonome de Madrid', *Revue Européenne des Migrations Internationles,* 9: 9-27.
Roque, M. (1994) 'Percepciones controvertidas: migración marroquí en Catalunya', *Papers,* 43:79-87.
Solé, C. (1995) 'Racial discrimination against foreigners in Spain', *New Community,* 21: 95-101.
SOPEMI (1990) *Annual Report 1989.* Paris: OECD.
SOPEMI (1995) *Trends in International Migration: Annual Report 1994.* Paris: OECD.
Tapinos, G. (1993) *Immigración y Integración en Europa.* Barcelona: Fundación Paulino Torres.
UNDP (1996) *Human Development Report 1996.* New York: Oxford University Press.

5 British Expatriates' Experience of Health and Social Services on the Costa del Sol

Charles Betty and Michael Cahill

Introduction

Retirement migration is an important feature of the migration patterns to be found in Spain. Northern Europeans now form a substantial population in some coastal parts of Spain with the majority being older people - it has been estimated that about 80 per cent of the over 65 population in these coastal areas are Europeans (Misti et al 1995:161). They form a significant bloc of the migrant population in the country, being outnumbered only by Latin Americans and North Africans. Until recently there has been little research into north/south European migration and we lack firm data on the nature of migrants; such evidence as we have comes from casual observation, impressionistic newspapers reports and personal contacts (Warnes 1991; Champion & King 1993; Harbert 1993). Retirement migration in Spain is now being studied in greater depth and the research reported here is a contribution to the emerging policy debate. It is based upon Charles Betty's 70 face to face interviews and 152 self-completion survey questionnaires in Benalmádena on the Costa del Sol.[1]

In this chapter we will define the situation of migration for the British migrants on the Costa del Sol. The perceived necessity of establishing friendship and social network patterns is also examined through the vehicle of membership of British social clubs. This membership could, however, result in an inward looking philosophy, which might exclude members from inclusion in

84 *Into the Margins*

local Spanish society and activities, and emphasise the differences rather than the similarities between the two communities.

Health status is extremely important for older British migrants as they age, hence an examination is made of hospital and domiciliary aftercare. The Spanish state, whilst it has made dramatic advances in the two decades since the death of Franco, is still some way behind those of Northern Europe in the provision of social care services. We explore the implications of this for retired older British migrants, particularly through the issues of informal care and residential and nursing home provision.

Also, in later life the ability to speak sufficient Spanish is an important skill for British expatriates; here we consider the extent to which language is still a barrier between the two communities.

As the European Union moves towards greater integration at the policy level the position of the northern European migrants raises interesting questions as to the extent to which the notion of a common European citizenship is a workable notion. The findings reported here suggest that while the Spanish government is committed to a policy of integration of its migrant populations this is problematic. First, we look at the British migrants on the Costa del Sol, and then specifically in Benalmádena.

The British on the Costa del Sol

The major movement of British and other northern European migrants began in the 1960s and continued through the 1980s. A recent estimate is that there are at least a million and a half European migrants in the Spanish coastal areas and in the Canary Islands (Balao Parra 1994). All such figures need to be treated with extreme caution because there are many reasons why migrants might not wish to be included in the census returns or other local surveys. Nonetheless, there are now substantial populations of northern Europeans in the coastal areas, principally British, Dutch, Swedish, German and Norwegian. These have recently been joined by a growing number of people from the former USSR. The British Consul estimated in 1995 that there are approximately 50,000 British migrants residing in the area from Almeria to Cadiz and of these at least 20,000 migrated to the Costa del Sol in the 1980s (British Consul 1994). There is no legal necessity for British residents to register with the Consul. In 1996, approximately 35,000 British subjects were registered, and this figure includes people who may have left the country or died without informing the Consul, thus the registered figures bear little relationship to the actual figures of British migrants resident on the Costa del Sol.

Reports by Help the Aged estimate that there are between 200 and 300 thousand UK citizens living in Spain (Mullan 1992: 2). So in practice little is known about the actual numbers of British people who live on the Coast, or indeed other areas of Spain. As there are no checks at the frontiers, and local censuses can be unreliable, because many British residents avoid completing the forms, little is known officially about the British community or the number of individuals who decide to reside in Spain. What is clear is that we need to create a set of categories which permit analysis of differing patterns of visiting and settlement, including perceptions and values about the host country, and the country of origin. Migrants who reside for most of the year on the Costa del Sol are called residential tourists by the Andalucian Tourist Board and the National Federation of Town Planners (Mellado 1996: 6).

The British older community under study in Benalmádena generally refer to themselves as expatriates. But as a person who took part in the recorded interviews said, 'What does it matter what we are called? We are foreigners residing in a country, which we love, but I suppose the authorities would like a term, which would accurately describe us'. Before we attempt to categorise the British older population on the Costa del Sol the study area requires description.

The Municipality of Benalmádena

Benalmádena, adjacent to Torremolinos on the Costa del Sol, has a population of 25,000 - which doubles in the summer months and consists of three distinct but interlocked districts. Benalmádena Pueblo consists mainly of Spanish nationals living in a typical Spanish mountain 'pueblo blanco'; with 'urbanisaciónes' - residential developments - for foreigners consisting of villas and small apartment blocks. Arroyo de Miel is largely populated by Spaniards, and is considered the heart of the municipality. Benalmádena Costa is an area of hotels, large apartment blocks with many British residents, and developments devoted mainly to tourism. Many of the respondents in the Benalmádena study have previously spent holidays in the area, before buying property, or spending long periods of time holidaying after retirement.

Tourists, residential tourists, or residents?

There is a need to define the terms resident and tourist, and to examine in what ways there are discernible differences and similarities. Tourists - those who travel for pleasure - go in their millions to the Spanish Costas each year for the sunshine, relaxed way of life, the beaches and because the packaged holiday is cheap (Barke, Turner, Newton, 1996). As Urry has defined it, modern tourism is denoted by movement to and from destinations, and the places 'gazed upon' are not for purposes connected with work rather they are sites for pleasure. The tourist is the modern consumer on holiday, seeking pleasure in a different locale and escaping from the routine of everyday life (Urry 1990: 7). It can be argued that tourists appear to be quite different from the resident who lives for most, or all of the year, in Spain.

To the extent that migrants travel regularly to the UK, some for as many as four or five months a year, then it would seem that the term 'residential tourist' has some validity. These people will usually maintain two homes; one in the UK and one in Spain. Although they may have selected Southern Spain as their retirement destination because they first came into contact with the area as a tourist, they are now committed to living a major part of the year in Spain. Those who sell their property in the UK and move to Spain permanently are probably best compared to the thousands of older people who have swelled the population figures for the coastline from Worthing to Eastbourne, the 'Costa geriatrica' of Sussex (Karn 1977). Although it can be argued that the older migrants' lifestyles are fundamentally different from that of the tourist it is true to say that some residents and long stayers engage in some similar activities. However, an examination of the content of the activities reveals that excursions and trips made by some older people feature religious festivals and local village fiestas remote from their place of residence. In this respect they resemble the cultural tourists who travel in search of the 'real Spain,' and avoid the Costas.

Many older British migrants have taken with them a range of daily UK leisure and pastime activities to Spain. Their life pattern is very little different from that previously enjoyed in the UK, except that the temperate climate permits an outdoor life, and a sharing of joint household and living tasks Clearly, older people who have sold their homes in the UK and migrated to Southern Europe could hardly be considered to be tourists if the length of their residence was the criterion. Migrants to Spain are not registered in any systematic way by that country, and there are no clear distinctions between holiday makers, temporary residents, and permanent residents (Warnes 1994). In order to discuss the expatriate community some categorisation is required and the following section briefly examines different categories of residents.

Analysis of British expatriates

It is possible to categorise British expatriates in the following way:-

a) Registered residents
These are people who live more or less permanently on the Costa del Sol. They are registered at the local town hall through the national or local census, or for the purpose of voting in European or local elections. They hold a resident's permit, which indicates that they are legally registered and conform to certain financial and health requirements. Their health needs are catered for by the Spanish National Health Service. They may or may not still have a residence in the UK. In 1995 1,236 British people were registered in Benalmádena according to the local authority.

b) Non-registered residents
These are British migrants who are not registered at the local Town Hall, and do not hold a resident's permit to live in Spain. They have bought property and commonly spend a major portion of the year in residence. Most of them do not have a home in the UK, and their health requirements are met by private medical insurance, or in some cases by actually registering at the local Health Centre, provided they have notified the Overseas Branch of the Department of Social Security in the UK. These people have various reasons for not registering with the local authorities. Clearly a powerful motive is the fact that registration would often ensure liability for Spanish income tax. Recorded interviews, and observation in the social clubs reveal that many older migrants in Benalmádena are terrified of having their personal details put on computers. They are frightened of local government bureaucracy, and believe that registering would be counter - productive. There are some cases of elderly people not registering because they fall below the financial limit required for registration. These people migrated in the 1960s and 1970s when the Spanish cost of living was significantly below that for the UK and their personal pension would buy them more. Now this group are in their late seventies and eighties, and are feeling the impact of ageing, illness, disability, death of a

spouse and growing isolation where close family are over 1000 miles away. Pensions and personal savings were eroded by the subsequent weakness of sterling against the Spanish peseta. Since the advent of democracy in Spain in the late 1970s the Spanish population has become more affluent, prices have increased, and taxation takes a bigger slice of income, resulting in a lower standard of living for pensioners on a fixed income. An applicant for a resident's permit in the Province of Malaga is required to have a daily income of 5,000 pesetas (£25). So for a week, a total of £175 is needed to qualify for residencia. Clearly £175 a week is more than the single British National Retirement Pension, and this fact precludes a number of elderly people from being able to obtain a permit.

Another powerful incentive not to register with the local Town Hall derives from the fact that many unregistered residents invest their savings in local Spanish banks, and receive higher interest than that obtained in the UK., without the deduction of income tax at 25 per cent which is paid by registered residents. A pensioner commented, 'Where I keep my money, and what I do with it has nothing to do with the authorities!'

c) Long stayers
They are owners of flats, villas or dwellings in a purpose built complex, which are used as a second home for itinerant visits, or for long stays of between three and six months, usually during the winter. Their health requirements are covered by either form E111 and /or private medical insurance. Form E111 the 'certificate of entitlement to benefits in kind during a stay in a member state' enables EU citizens to receive emergency medical treatment whilst on holiday in a EU country other than their own. There are no statistics, which indicate how many long stayers are resident on the Costa del Sol.

d) The renters
These are people who rent villas and flats for periods of three to six months. They retain a permanent home in the UK, and spend the winter in Spain. They use private medical care or form E 111. Some of these people rent for several months before deciding whether they wish to reside permanently on the Costa del Sol. The renting period gives them the opportunity to see whether their perception of living in Spain matches or surpasses that previously held. Other older people prefer to rent so as to avoid paying local taxes, rates, and community charges which have to be paid by owners whether resident or not. So it would appear from the above that there is a difference between the

lifestyles of the tourist who holidays for a few weeks a year with those who spend long periods of time on the Costa del Sol.

Age is a significant factor in understanding the migrant community on the Costa del Sol. There are considerable differences with the lifestyles of the younger one or two week tourist 'hell bent' on returning to the UK sporting deep suntans, and feeling relaxed and ready for the work place. For the most part, these tourists do not involve themselves in the cultural life of the area and only occasionally venture out of their holiday homes on organised trips. They will frequent British bars, mix and talk to British people some of whom may be registered residents, long stayers, non-registered residents or renters. Apart from a common language and interest in British activities such as politics, and sport, their point of contact will be transient. Evidence from interviews reveals that many older migrants have a well-organised lifestyle which differs considerably in content and detail from the younger tourist. Their reasons for living for most of the year in Spain are many and varied.

Recorded interviews with residents and long stayers (including renters) demonstrate that older British migrants have a well-organised lifestyle, which differs considerably in content and detail from tourists. The interviews reveal that many older migrants have developed a rich and fulfilling life for themselves since migrating. Outdoor activities are pursued with vigour and interest especially during the winter months because of the beneficial climate. Club members are given opportunities to travel to various parts of a Spain, particularly to areas of cultural interest such as Madrid, Galicia, Toledo, Granada and Cordoba. A long stayer commented: 'Since spending the winter in Spain I have had the opportunity to visit lots of places of cultural interest, which I could not do before I retired and when I was a tourist'. The interviews also show that many migrants believe that their lifespan has been extended, because of the relaxed way of life in Spain, and the excellent health facilities especially at primary care level. Jane, an 82 year old widow said,

> I am positive that my health has improved since living in Spain. Before I used to be breathless when I walked, but now I can walk much further, and I have the support of a good Spanish doctor.

An interesting revelation from the interviews is the sharing of household and shopping tasks by men and women, which differed from the accepted practice before retirement. As a 73 year old permanent male resident remarked:

> When I was working I couldn't, or didn't share the household tasks, or accompany my wife to the shops. Now I feel it is right to help in the house; to share the shopping and indeed, I now do most of the cooking. This is a complete change for me, and I am enjoying it.

The analysis shows that some interviewees have benefited from membership of local social clubs, so why do people join these clubs; and what are the positive and negative aspects of belonging to an exclusive club?

Membership of social clubs

Many of the migrants interviewed in this study are members of clubs which were originally founded to cater for the social needs of older British expatriates. Practically all their members are retired and are either residents or long stayers. There are four social clubs for British migrants in Benalmádena with a combined membership of over 1,500 people. The clubs provide an opportunity to develop social networks which are an important prerequisite of successful adaptation to a strange environment. Membership of a club can be a substitute for family support which geographical distance precludes. One respondent said of the decision to join a club:

> It was the best thing I have done since migrating to Spain. The clubs have given me access to many, many more friends. I do not feel so lonely now I know that I have people I can call upon in times of need. I look forward to the trips, especially the long ones because I can get to know my friends even better.

Occasionally the clubs organise trips of a week's duration to other parts of Spain which enable people to make lasting friendships which could be of considerable benefit when help of various kinds is required. A special feature is the amount of information members are given about financial matters, Spanish law and taxes, and talks by experts on various aspects of Spanish life and culture. The clubs are an integral part of many older migrants' daily lives. Indeed, some migrants are members of several clubs which provide opportunities for the building of friendship patterns. This is especially important for widowed people. A 75 year old widow said:

The clubs are marvellous. You make lots of friends; more than you would at home. This is one of the biggest bonuses of living out here. If you are lonely it is of your own volition. You must go out and join a voluntary organisation like the Royal British Legion which I did. They are the mainstay of my life out here.

These clubs - and similar organisations for other nationalities on the Costa del Sol (Nordic, German, Dutch, Asian, South and North American) whilst welcoming Spanish members, in fact have few, if any. The problems of adequate language communication and differing cultures result in social clubs which are practically 100 per cent British. Even if some older Spaniards might wish to join foreigners' clubs, there is very little likelihood that they would speak sufficient English to enable them to enjoy the range of cultural and British traditional activities which are usually organised for members. Indeed, some of the clubs celebrate traditional British customs such as Saints' days, Guy Fawke's nights, dinner dances playing British music, talks by officials from the British Consul, and seminars on pension rights. In fact the events which attract British members could be counter-productive and further distance them from the host nation.

It can be argued that the elderly expatriates protect their identity, and isolate themselves from the Spanish community by forming exclusive clubs, which whilst not forbidding Spanish members do not encourage them to join when the only medium of communication is English. So it can be seen that the formation of the clubs clearly fill a need for friendship and support, but at the same time they provide a form of self imposed exclusion from participation in the country where they have decided to spend their later years.

One of the major topics which is revealed in the interviews, and is keenly debated in the social clubs is the issue of personal health. As the migrants age they become more concerned about the maintenance of adequate health standards, and worries about the future, especially if they are widowed. However, the general opinion about the Spanish Health Service is that it compares very favourably with the British system, which is seen as under funded with too many patients and long waiting lists for operations.

Spanish hospitals and after care

Many elderly expatriates in Benalmádena condemn what they see as the erosion of the National Health Service in Britain. The length of time it takes to see a specialist or consultant, or to reach the top of a hospital waiting list is contrasted with the facilities available in the Málaga province; namely the opportunity to see a medical specialist or consultant within a matter of days. It is also felt that there is a lack of pressure on hospital beds in the province particularly in the Marbella area because a new hospital has recently been opened. This hospital, to which Benalmádena patients have partial access, has some of the mostly modern medical technology available (Hooper 1995:253). Nearly half of the interviewees had been in hospital since living in Spain and reported that they had had excellent medical treatment. Yet all remarked that the nursing care was far from satisfactory and compared unfavourably with similar care in the UK. As one observed:

> I was treated extremely well in hospital. My only criticism is the lack of nursing care as we understand it in the UK. The nurses in Spain seem to only check temperatures, and give injections. My personal washing requirements were carried out by my wife.

It is expected that families help with washing, feeding etc. So what happens if an elderly person enters a Spanish hospital who has no family?

In this study seven out of every ten people who had received state hospital care in the Málaga province reported on the paucity of after care when leaving hospital. One man said: 'There is no after care at all. The service in hospital is excellent but as for after care – none'. Similarly, an eighty year old widow remarked: 'There is a lack of after care. Generally it is the family who look after you in Spain.. If you are on your own, you are on your own! That is what is missing - after care'. A former British nurse, now a retired migrant added:

> I used to visit a disabled woman and help nurse her. On a number of occasions she had infections, and I found that the doctor would not call. In the end she went back to the UK where she could get the necessary care. I doubt very much whether she would have survived much longer had she remained in Spain.

So what help can be obtained from the social services and voluntary organisations? All registered inhabitants resident in Benalmádena, whether native or expatriate, are entitled to access to all facilities for aftercare and domiciliary help provided by the local municipality which has the responsibility for social services. Lavishly illustrated booklets outlining what appears to be a comprehensive aftercare and home care service are available. In reality, little of what is published is available. A national health system was not formally created until 1987, although it built on measures introduced since 1942 (Rodriguez 1992: 19). Much of the responsibility of organising a national health service was given to the seventeen autonomous regions with delegated powers to the municipalities. It covers 99 per cent of the population. There is a wide gap, however, between the provisions of the 1986 General Health Law and its full implementation. The development of the health service has been uneven with slightly different priorities, and financial resources (Tudor Hart 1990: 225, Elola Somoza 1996).

The local Health Centre in Benalmádena was built in 1992, and has a large staff including fourteen doctors, eight nurses and one social worker. Membership of the local health centre gives full medical care to older migrants. The only discrimination they receive is self imposed, that is to say, their inability to speak Spanish. This problem has been reduced somewhat by the creation of a volunteer interpreter service at the health centre, filled largely by British migrants, which assist those patients who cannot speak Spanish.

In a number of cases hospital doctors have recommended social work support, but in Benalmádena this is difficult to obtain. There are only three social workers for a population of over 25,000 people, and only one of them speaks English. The current economic position of the municipality of Benalmádena has meant a cut in the provision of domiciliary help. A number of people interviewed contrasted the position unfavourably with that in the UK where, although local authority home care services have diminished in recent years, none the less, there are still a variety of domiciliary services provided by local authorities and voluntary organisations. In Benalmádena the local Health Service will provide the services of a nurse for house calls, but only one speaks English, so in practice there is no community nurse support. Most older Spaniards can rely on close family support and a network of extended family help whereas the families of most British older migrants are in the UK. But what happens to older migrants who reside far from their roots, when they become ill, and unable to look after themselves?

Residential and nursing home provision

The Benalmádena older migrants were asked about the future as they aged and become frail. Most of them said that they would prefer to remain in Spain, rather than return to family or friends in the UK. An 80 year old widow said: 'I will remain in Spain if I become very ill. I do not wish to return to the UK, and be a burden on my family. They have their own lives to lead'.

Care in state and private residential homes is very limited in Andalucia, in Benalmádena and the neighbouring town of Torremolinos. There are only five homes prepared to take foreigners. In practice very few are admitted because of language difficulties. 'How could I enter a home which is for Spaniards? I can't speak Spanish, so how would I communicate? It is not an option for me', commented a widower aged 88 years. This lack of suitable accommodation has led to the realisation by some entrepreneurs - both British and Spanish - that there is a market for suitable homes to attract older expatriates. Unfortunately these premises are not subject to regular inspection by the local authorities as would be the case in the UK. There is little likelihood that the Spanish State will be able to provide more suitable accommodation and the private sector has financial constraints which could mean that they have insufficient resources to enter the market. The choice for the very ill and infirm older British migrant is either to stay in Spain, and hope that some help may become available from neighbours and voluntary organisations, or to enter Spanish accommodation with the subsequent absence of English speaking staff, or to return to the UK. To be able to return to the UK depends on personal financial assets. There is some evidence that a growing number of older people who are living on fixed incomes are in dire financial straits and unable to return to the UK (Mullan 1992: 4).

A 76 year old woman living on a small state pension with diminishing assets remarked: 'What is to happen to me when my money runs out? I haven't sufficient money to be able to buy a house or flat in the UK. I don't know who to turn to.'

What happens to these people? The British consular services can only help in extreme cases if there is a guarantee that the expense of repatriation can be recovered. Some of the voluntary organisations, such as the Royal British Legion, have well developed welfare services for ex armed forces personnel and their dependants. They can arrange return journeys to the UK and into suitable accommodation, provided funds are personally available. But the other Benal-mádena clubs do not provide this service. Therefore, there is a need to find ways of informal caring, possibly by the migrant community itself.

Informal care

Spain has made vast strides towards the implementation of a general welfare state since the death of Franco in 1975 and can now be considered to be an intermediate welfare state (Mangen 1996). There are fundamental differences between the British system of public financing of the National Health Service and the pluralist approach to welfare provision in Spain. Although during the last few decades the influence of the Catholic Church care provision has declined in importance, it nevertheless has a decisive part to play in supplementing state provision, particularly in the field of hospital and residential nursing home care.

In Spain the family is a basic point of reference in the social structure. Spanish families still maintain their ties with the extended family (Rossell & Rimbau 1989). The family holds a central position in Catholic social policy in Spain, and this has been an important factor in the development of family policy (Valiente 1996). This tradition emphasises philanthropic solutions to welfare provision by institutions such as the Catholic church, the family and private charity along with state organisations (Coote 1989). Through its religious orders and organisations, such as Caritas, the church provides a significant amount of social welfare. Indeed, until the end of Francoism, all social work and social work training was provided by the Church.

The supply of domiciliary and day care is generally inadequate and dependence on care provided by women in the family system is high. The vast majority of carers are women who give caring and nurturing functions relatively high priority (Jamieson 1990). Women, since Franco died, have had more independence and better employment prospects and it might be expected that their commitment to a caring role within the family will wane.

'The First Plan of Equal Opportunities for Women' (1988-1990) included measures which provided legislation prohibiting discrimination for reasons of sex. The Second Plan (1993-5) contains additional measures which aim to improve women's position in culture, education, health and employment. Extra resources and services directed at women have been provided by the central State, the Autonomous Communities and local government. This has accelerated the process of change in Spanish society, and provided more opportunities for career advancement by women. The proportion of working women at the present time is 34.3 per cent. This is an increase on 26.8 per cent in 1981, and reflects a trend which is likely to have a profound effect on informal care (Ministerio del Portavoz de Gobierno 1993: 327).

This trend in the number of women wanting and accepting paid employment could mean that there may be a different attitude to the caring of elderly relatives as a full time job. This has clear implications for residential and nursing home care provided by state and voluntary bodies. The key age group are those aged between 45 and 69 who might be expected to take on the care of an ageing relative. There has been a reduction of 62 per cent in this age group relative to the number of older people in Spain. Furthermore, in this age group there has been a sharp increase in the number of women in the work force. They came to maturity during the Franco years when there was official discouragement for those women who wished to engage in work outside the home. In contrast, in the 1980s the government encouraged women to participate in the paid labour force. Inevitably this will mean a reduction in this pool of informal female carers (Cousins 1995; Threlfall 1996: 137-41).

A survey of older people in the European Community in 1992, asked whether families were less willing to care for older people than in the past. Around two thirds of older people thought that this was the case. However, in Spain 80% of older people agreed with the statement and 58 per cent of older British people agreed with it (Eurobarometer Survey 1993 cited in Means and Smith (1994)). This was higher than the overall per cent of those in agreement in the EU. Residential and domiciliary care for older people in Spain is scarce and one of the lowest percentages for the European Union countries (Hugman 1994: 125-7). How does this pattern of provision affect the elderly migrant? In Benalmádena, the social worker based at the Health Centre reports that she has assisted very few older foreigners. The majority of those helped are desperately anxious not to have to return to Britain, and seek help or advice on those terms. The social worker occasionally visits foreigners in their own homes accompanied by an interpreter. However, people who live near Spanish families often obtain assistance from local Spaniards if help is needed. The social worker said that it was very difficult indeed for those housebound foreigners living in high rise blocks of flats, and without help from Spanish people, especially when migrants did not speak sufficient Spanish to be able to verbalise their needs.

Language and identity

The inability or desire to speak sufficient Spanish to negotiate the local and regional bureaucracy is often cited as a major deterrent to the assimilation of British retirees in the local Spanish community (Champion & King 1993; Mullan 1992). Their lack of interest in all but the most superficial elements of local culture are seen as elements of the inward looking philosophy of British residents. These observations are confirmed by the Benalmádena recorded interviews, and discussions with club members. 'What is the point of learning Spanish? Most of the people in the shops and restaurants speak English, so there is no need to learn the language' commented a 68 year old long stayer. And a 77 year old man remarked, 'I attend local fiestas, and watch processions, even though I do not always understand the significance of them'.

The vast majority of British residents read only British newspapers, listen to English speaking community radio stations, and watch satellite television. Very few older Britons watch Spanish television, or read Spanish newspapers, except for the weather forecast! Indeed it can be argued that since the arrival of British satellite television several years ago, the British community has been even more inward looking and surrounded by the English language, so that even those people who regularly watch Spanish television, now have no reason for doing so. It is as if the advent of global communication has allowed extra barriers to be erected against the infiltration of the Spanish language thereby further excluding British migrants from integrating with, and understanding, the local Spanish community. One of the most interesting episodes to witness is the eagerness of the British population to obtain the two free English newspapers. This fact demonstrates again that Britons are eager to keep up to date with British news, events, and local club activities and the global media enable them to do so. The 'problem' of the lack of Spanish language skills is not seen as such by many migrants, for their decision to move to this part of Spain was prompted in part by the fact that there were large numbers of native English speakers resident there and a great many Spaniards spoke and understood English. It is difficult to see how a community composed largely of older people will ever be in a position where large numbers will be fluent Spanish speakers, participating fully in the local community. The notion of ethnic exclusion from the Spaniards may be less applicable if there was a move towards a more European concept of citizenship, with the provision of voting rights, social security, third age education and health issues.

The European Union is in fact very important to Spain and Spanish membership has been seen as a crucial factor in the modernisation of the country. It is unsurprising then that the response from the Spanish government to the health and social service needs of the northern European migrant population has been to see it as a European Union problem. The Northern European migrants are viewed as 'European Citizens'. It might be argued, however, that the position of the older British migrants on the Costa del Sol illustrates the limitations of such concepts as 'European citizenship' (Martiniello 1995). Although enjoying the right of freedom of movement and residence and soon to be able to vote, the British migrant community does not display a great interest in the political life of the areas where they live. Indeed, as we have noted, it is the case that some Britons resent the fact that they are liable to taxation. The British community derives much of its identify from the link with the UK. This is not only attributable to the fact that they are older people, for the same insularity characterises many younger British migrants on the Costa del Sol. Social integration would have more chance of success as a project if the British migrant community were domiciled in Spain permanently but, as we have shown, the proximity by air travel to the UK makes this unlikely.

The Spanish response to the older European citizen

The government introduced a Gerontological Plan in 1992 which outlined a series of measures the central state planned in association with the autonomous communities. However, the Plan did not mention the situation of the foreign residents among the elderly population. This has now changed and in the 1995 Gerontological *'trienio'* - three year plan - there was a separate section on 'European citizens' under the heading of 'social integration'. To this end the *trienio* proposes that there should be regular meetings between the European organisations in Spain and the autonomous communities (Ministry of Social Affairs 1995). It also sees a role for cultural exchanges between the northern European communities and the host Spanish community.

Clearly the Spanish government, with some justification, wants to see the problems of the older northern Europeans as a policy area for the European Union. In her report for the Social Affairs ministry Pilar Balao recommends that a European network is established which would work out proposals for agreements between the member states. The areas regarded as a priority are: social security, housing, domiciliary help, cultural activities, leisure pursuits, the role of the helping professions, voluntary organisations and language

(Balao Parra 1994). The income problems of those who are not eligible for assistance from ex-service persons' organisations such as the Royal British Legion, demand some further consideration from the UK and Spanish governments. The representatives of migrant organisations argue that attendance allowance and disability benefits should be payable in Spain. Some greater attention to these problems can be expected as more of the migrants become eligible to vote in Spanish local and central government elections. At the municipal elections in Spain in May 1995 only the residents of Norway, Sweden, Denmark and Holland were able to vote. The *'Ciudadanos Europeos'* (European Citizens) organisation has links with the governing Partido Popular and is gaining in influence. At the local political level the Partido Popular is making definite moves to attract the support of the Northern European migrants in anticipation of their being granted voting rights in 1999.

All are agreed that one of the most useful services that could be provided is information offices for foreign residents. Some of the municipalities which contain high numbers of foreign residents - notably Alfaz de Pi, near Alicante and Mijas, Benalmádena and Fuengirola in Andalucia - have already opened these 'Foreigners Bureaux' which deal with issues such as tax, purchase and sale of property, residence permits, driving licences.

Conclusion

There can be no doubting the vitality and strength of the British migrant organisations which cater for the needs of the older population. They provide an impressive range of voluntary social service functions for their members. The ex-service persons' organisations such as the Royal British Legion, which has six branches on the Costa del Sol, and SSAFA (Soldiers Sailors And Air Force Association) are also able to provide direct financial assistance as well as access to nursing and rehabilitative care. More intractable and difficult to assist with is the social isolation and neglect encountered by those who are not members of these organisations or known to members. The bereavement of a spouse, the onset of Alzheimers Disease or chronic, long term illness or disability can prove to be emotionally and financially crippling for those who are socially isolated and thousands of miles from family, even if any survive. Many preventative measures can be taken to warn intending migrants of the darker side of life on the Costa del Sol. A much greater stress on the acquisition of language is clearly necessary yet - quite correctly - migrants point out that in areas like the Costa del Sol, unlike vast areas of the rest of Spain - it is difficult to practise one's Spanish. Alcohol provides solace for many isolated people and again there is a role for greater stress on the dangers of alcohol abuse in a country where wine is so cheap. These and many other ideas to warn people of some of the pitfalls of later life in Spain are being implemented by organisations such as Age Concern in the UK, working in conjunction with migrant organisations. Yet the UK migrant population on the Costa del Sol will soon have many more members in the 75 plus age range when chronic illness and disability become more prevalent. The extent of state or voluntary sector residential or nursing home care is minimal, as we have seen, and cannot be expected to grow dramatically in the next few years.

Some clues as to the future direction that voluntary welfare provision could take among the migrant population on the Costa del Sol is provided by the self activity of British migrants on the Costa Blanca. It too has a large British community with many of the problems found on the Costa del Sol (Lishman, et al 1993). Volunteers - mainly British pensioners - provide community services in medical and other kinds of emergency. There are eight branches along the length of the Alicante coastline and in the province of Valencia. The volunteers visit sick people in home or in hospital, providing all night care if necessary, liase with medical and social services, provide basic nursing and in addition assistance with transport, shopping and interpreting. Another example of mutual assistance which tries to compensate for the inadequacies of the Spanish welfare system is the overseas branch of Age Concern England on the island of Majorca. This provides for the welfare and social needs of British older people on the island. Again it is the non-joiners, the unclubbable, who can be most in need but are outside these networks.

It can be expected that these initiatives will grow in the next few years as the British migrant population sees more of its members enter the over 75 age group who make greater use of health and social services. Such a development is in line with the pervasive emphasis in Spain on the important role of non-state forms of social welfare where several big voluntary organisations and numerous smaller ones dominate much social service provision. As we have noted the extent of state or voluntary sector residential or nursing home care is minimal and cannot be expected to grow dramatically in the next few years. The Spanish state will in the twenty first century have to attend to the problems of ageing Spanish population more of whom will require residential care because of the decline in family size and the greatly increased involvement of women in the labour market (Council of Europe 1996). The future developments in the provision of residential care may be expected to be led primarily by voluntary provision. In that sense the vigour of the British migrant voluntary organisations could lead them to assuming a more overt role in home care and residential provision working alongside the municipalities. They would be supplying for the British migrant populations a complementary service to that supplied by organisations such as Caritas, the Red Cross and other Spanish voluntary organisations.

The Benalmádena study partly concentrates on members of exclusively British social clubs and has exposed a major problem which the migrant community must address, that of social exclusion. Other ethnic migrant groups on the Costa del Sol also face the same dilemma of exclusion from the host community. The ethos, structure and organised activities of the clubs prevent Spanish people from being actively involved in them. Clearly, as has been stated, the need to speak Spanish is vital in counteracting social exclusion. But it would be widely optimistic to suggest that older migrants will become proficient in Spanish.

The study shows that a few people do make valiant attempts to become fluent in the language, but they rarely advance beyond the elementary stage. So it is unlikely that there will be sufficient relevant verbal communication between the ethnic groups. This might mean that the present social exclusion of older migrants will continue. But what can be done to ameliorate the situation? The solution may rest within the migrant community. Extra efforts could be made by social clubs to discover alternative ways of communicating and integrating with Spanish people. The migrant clubs might perhaps forge links with local schools and colleges, where English is taught. There is often an affinity between young and old which could be beneficial for both groups. As many young Spaniards speak English, they may be able to articulate the problems and concerns which face older Britons, and thus become the 'voice' of cooperation with the municipal bureaucracy and other Spanish organisations. The migrant social clubs have a good deal to offer the local community. The task is to harness the strengths and experience of migrants to the welcoming attitudes of the Spanish community. This would result in improved mutual understanding and would be an important step towards social integration of the migrant community.

References

Balao, Parra, P. (1994) Ciudadanos Europeos Mayores: Residentes en Espana

Apporoximacion a la situation actual. Ministerio de Asuntos Sociales, Madrid.

Barke, M., Turner, J. & Newton, M.T. (1996) *Tourism in Spain - Critical Issues*, Cab International Publishers.

British Consul Málaga, (1994) *Personal Communication with Charles Betty*, December

Champion, A.G.& King, R. (1993) 'New Forms of European Migration'. *Geographical Viewpoint* 21, 45-56.

Coote, N. (1989) 'Catholic Social Teaching' *Social Policy and Administration*, 23, 2, 150-60.

Council of Europe (1996) *Recent demographic development in Europe*, Strasbourg.

Cousins, C. (1995) 'Women and Social Policy in Spain: the development of a gendered welfare regime'. *Journal of European Social Policy* 5 (3) 175-197.

Elola Somoza, J. (1996) 'Spain: The case for Politicising the Health Debate.' *Contemporary European Affairs* 134-135.

Harbert, W. (1993) *British Elderly People in Spain*. Help the Aged, London.

Hooper, J. (1995) *The New Spaniards*, Penguin, London.

Hugman, R. (1994) *Ageing and the Care of older People in Europe*, Macmillan, London.

Jamieson, A. (1990) 'Informal care in Europe', in Jamieson, A. & Illsey, R. (eds.) *Contrasting European Policies for the Care of Older People*, Avebury.

Karn, V. (1977) *Retiring to the Seaside*. Routledge, London.

Lishman, G., Morrall, L,, Wilkins, N., Singer, S., Harbert, W. & Mullan, C. (1993) *Older British People Resident in Spain*. Age Concern: London.

Mangen, S. (1996) 'The "Europeanisation" of Spanish Social Policy' *Social Policy and Administration*, 30, 4, December: 305-323.

Martiniello, M. 'European citizenship, European identity and migrants: towards the post-national state?'; in Miles, R. and Thranhardt, D. (eds.) (1995), *Migration and European Integration: The Dynamics of Inclusion and Exclusion*, Pinter Publishers: London.

Means, R. and Smith, R. (1994) *Community Care - Policy and Practice*, Macmillan.

Mellado, V. (1996) 'Government Study of Resident Foreigners' *Sur in English* Malaga 29 November 1996.

Ministry of Social Affairs, (1995) *Plan Gerontológico Política Integral para las personas mayores Trienio 1995-1997* Madrid.

Ministerio del Portavoz del Gobierno (1993) *Spain*. Madrid.

Misiti, M., Pumares, C., Rodriguez, V. and White, P. (1995) 'Future migration into Southern Europe'. in Hall, R. and White, P. (eds.) *Europe's population Towards the next Century*. London: UCL Press. pp.161-187.

Mullan, C. (1992) *A Report on the Problems of the Elderly British expatriate Community in Spain*, Help the Aged: London.

Rodriguez, J.A. (1992) 'Struggle and Revolt in the Spanish Health Policy Process: the Changing role of the Medical Profession' *International Journal of Health*

Services 22, 1, 19-24.

Rossell, T. & Rimbau, C. (1989) 'Spain - Social Services in the post Franco Democracy' in Munday, B. (ed.) *The Crisis in Welfare*, Harvester Wheatsheaf.

Threlfall, M. (1996) 'Feminist Politics and Social change in Spain' Chapter 3 In Threlfall, M. (ed.) *Mapping the Womens' Movement*. Verso, London.

Tudor Hart, J. (1990) 'Primary Medical care in Spain', *British Journal of General Practice*. 255-258.

Urry, J. (1990) *The Tourist Gaze: leisure and travel in contemporary societies*, Sage, London.

Valiente, C. (1996) 'The rejection of authoritarian policy legacies: Family Policy in Spain (1975-1995)' *South European Society and Politics*, 1, 1 (summer).

Warnes, A.M. (1991) 'Migration to and Seasonal residence in Spain of Northern European People'. *European Journal of Gerontology*:53-60.

Warnes, A.M. (1994) 'Permanent and Seasonal Migration: the Prospects for Europe'. *Netherlands Geographical Studies*, 1, 73, Department of Geography, University of Utrecht.

Note

[1] The case studies and interviews were selected randomly at the local Health Centre. A semi-structured questionnaire was used, utilising questions raised at focus group discussions. Interviews were tape recorded and then usually transcribed to highlight topics and problems.

6 The Helots of the New Millennium: Ethnic-Greek Albanians and 'Other' Albanians in Greece

Gabriella Lazaridis

1. Introduction

Since the 1980s, Greece has been faced with two new challenges: first, unplanned, unorganised and uncontrolled influxes of large numbers of economic migrants, political refugees and asylum seekers (Lazaridis 1996; Lazaridis and Romaniszyn 1998); second, a sharp increase in recorded crime[1] (Karydis 1996). The combination of the two phenomena at a time of economic and social crisis has made the ethnicisation of crime or the criminalisation of migration very appealing.

Media interest has centred on and is particularly, but not solely, preoccupied with one group of migrants, the Albanians (Lazaridis and Wickens 1999), as these constitute the largest group of undocumented migrants in Greece.[2] The tactic employed by the mass media of connecting Albanian migration with criminality and its characterisation as 'imported criminality' provokes a feeling of growing insecurity in Greek society. This has led to xenophobic and racist reactions against the dangerous 'others', disregarding any historical, cultural, political and individual differences amongst migrants coming to Greece from Albania. Thus, dichotomic categories like criminal/non-criminal, dangerous/non-dangerous, good/bad, are often used by the mass media to characterise migrants from Albania.

This growing feeling of insecurity in Greek society coupled with pressures from outside (e.g.: Schengen partners aiming to create what has come to be known as 'Fortress Europe') invite for strict controls at the borders, aiming at partly recuperating the lost control over the uncontrolled influx of third-country migrants from the borders and thus preventing the alleged threat these flows pose on the security and stability of the country. Such securitisation of migration can be found in many intergovernmental agreements concerning immigration control like the Schengen, Dublin agreements, TREVI and the Ad Hoc Group on immigration (see paper by Kostakopoulou is this volume for details). The effectiveness of these is arguably limited as far as the South European member states are concerned, since their extended sea and mountainous borders are difficult to control; in other words, the effectiveness of restrictive measures in controlling illegal flows of migrants through the country's porous borders has been limited (Lazaridis 1996). Moreover, the absence of a common European migration policy and the desire of the Southern member states to improve their ability to compete in world markets, has allowed them to appreciate cheap unregulated labour and exhibit some tolerance towards the hundred of thousands of undocumented migrants the majority of whom work in the underground economy. At the same time, however, the political rhetoric is used for internal and external consumption with regard to immigration control. Thus the inability of Greece to control its borders functions as a mechanism facilitating the expansion of the underground economy and the survival of many small family-owned businesses. This is despite the introduction of law 1975/1991 which, among other things, stipulated that entry in the country without appropriate documents and work without a permit are criminal offences for which the offender faces up to five years imprisonment (for details see Lazaridis 1996).

Employers benefit primarily in three ways from the use of undocumented migrant labour: the inherent flexibility of labour which is hired only when there is work to be done; low employment costs, that is low wages, no social security costs, tolerance of poor working conditions and long working hours; and low capital costs since there is little incentive in investing on labour-saving capital equipment (see Lazaridis and Romaniszyn 1998; Lazaridis and Wickens 1999). Despite the ILO (International Labour Organisation) convention which prohibits wage differences and several bilateral treaties which set minimum wages, wages of foreign unskilled workers (even those who work legally) can be up to 50 per cent below those of Greeks (Diktakis 1993:26). It is not surprising therefore, to see that many Greek employers (particularly in the primary and service sectors) are increasingly recruiting casual labour from the Albanian migrant population. This tolerance is compromised however, by laws (e.g.: article 4 of law 1995/1991) enacting the procedure of deportation of undocumented migrants, which has resulted in raids aiming at 'sweeping the streets' clean from Albanians.[3]

This chapter looks at the character of Albanian migration into Greece. It desires to take a distance from the logic of Albanian migrants as comprising a homogeneous entity, as well as the trap of dichotomic approaches. The aim is to analyse the processes through which the stigmatisation and social exclusion of 'other' Albanians as opposed to ethnic-Greek-Albanians, are conducted in Greek society; it also looks at differences, however subtle these may be, in the treatment these groups receive, taking into consideration their different historical, political and cultural identities. I will argue that the 'other' Albanians are treated as people of a lesser human worth, and hence that it would be appropriate to characterise them as the 'helots of the new millennium'.

2. Background context

After almost forty years of self-imposed isolation from the Western world and a policy of collectivisation implemented by Hoxha, in 1990 Albania decided to unlock its gates to the rest of the Western world.[4] Hundreds of thousands of Albanians flew into Greece and Italy. The Albanians who come to Greece are not a homogeneous group. Some are of Albanian origin; these cannot be defined as refugees since their own country did not persecute them.[5] Others belong to the Greek-Orthodox minority, which has lived for centuries in the Southern part of Albania, called by the Greeks 'Northern Epirus'.

The situation prevailing in Albania during Hoxha's regime can partly explain the mass exodus during the early 1990s of penniless Albanians into Greece and Italy. After World War II, in 1946, Albania proclaimed itself a people's republic. With the assistance of Tito, Hoxha established communism in Albania. In the late-1950s, he condemned de-Stalinisation and later strengthened Albania's links with China. Through systematic propaganda Hoxha campaigned against 'bourgeois attitudes', embraced with great enthusiasm Mao-Tse-Tung's 'cultural revolution' and sent intellectuals into the countryside to get closer to the people and teach them Marxist-Leninist doctrines. During Hoxha, Albania became the first self-proclaimed atheist state in the world (Hamilton 1992) and as a result revoked the charters under which the Muslim, Roman Catholic and Orthodox communities operated. Albanians could not leave the country, the mail and media were censored, and any type of anti-socialist propaganda was punished with at least ten years imprisonment accompanied with hard labour (Hall 1994). At the same time state propaganda was trying to persuade Albanians that they had the highest standard of living in Europe (Hall 1994).

During the time when Hoxha was in power, various attempts were made to establish a Greek-Albanian relationship. In January 1970, Greece signed a trade agreement with Albania; six years later, the two countries re-established diplomatic relations and a year later a direct airline connection between Athens and Tirana was established. In 1985, a few months before Hoxha's death, the Greek government opened its borders permitting small numbers of the Greek minority living in Albania to visit relatives in Greece (The Economist, 23 April 1988). In 1987 Greece renounced its territorial claims on Northern Epirus (ibid). The then government received a lot of criticism however, for not securing guarantees for the Greek minority's human rights. In 1990, Alia lifted the ban on religion, issued foreign passports and thousands of Albanians started to emigrate. In early July 1990, 4,500 Albanians arrived in Italy (Antonopoulos 1995) and another 5,000 to 6,000 took refugee in various foreign embassies in Tirana (CE 1991). Following that, thousands left the country and crossed Greece's borders. At the same time, Alia's democratisation process was under way; the effects on the economy were dramatic: a 13 per cent fall in national income, 10 per cent unemployment, 200 per cent inflation, a 50 per cent drop in agricultural and industrial production (CE 1991). Poverty and unemployment, as well as political, religious and ethnic conflict, led to an increase in numbers of emigrants from Albania to neighbouring countries. In 1992, the number of Albanian migrants in Greece reached 250,000 (Ta Nea, 12 Dec. 1992), despite an agreement reached the previous year between Greece and Albania for the latter to stop the flow.[6] The relative ease of entry into the country through the numerous islands and the 15,000kms of Greek coast or via the 1,181 kilometres of land, and the need for seasonal labour especially in the primary sector, in construction and in tourism, have also acted as pull factors encouraging Albanian migration into Greece. As a response to rising hostile public opinion and external pressures from the Schengen partners, the Greek government began mass expulsions of Albanians and at the same time sent military detachments and armed police forces along the Greek-Albanian borders. In 1997 however, Greece and Albania signed an agreement which guarantees Albanians the right to work on a seasonal basis in Greece and despite previous reservations, now Albanians are included in government's recent efforts towards regularisation of undocumented migrants (see Lazaridis and Poyago-Theotoky 1997 for details).

The tension between Albania and Greece dates back to 1939, when Greece occupied 'Northern Epirus'. In this part of Albania there is a relatively large Greek-Orthodox minority. The size of this minority is estimated by the Albanian authorities to be around 59,000 whereas the Greek government places this number at 260,000. 'Most Greek sources explain this disparity in terms of the "statistical genocide" committed by the Albanian governments in order to weaken the Greek minority and violate its human rights' (Droukas 1998). Today, this Greek minority, irrespective of its size, allegedly suffers maltreatment by the Albanians. During the Hoxha years, there was the abolition of religion, a discouragement of the use of Greek language by this minority and the abolition of Greek names. A large proportion of those who emigrated to Greece are members of this minority.

Greece has viewed 'Northern Epirus' as territory which should be included within Greece's frontiers. Today, a Greek minority lives in Albania. 'The violation ... of the ethnic-Greek-population's human rights has since the early 1990s served to undermine both Greece's and Albania's efforts at peaceful regional cooperation' (Lazaridis and Romaniszyn 1998:21). In their efforts to escape the status of minority members in a totalitarian regime the ethnic-Greek-Albanians migrated to Greece. In Greece they found out that, despite their Greek origin, they too were discriminated against and experienced social, economic and spatial exclusion, along with the rest of Albanians (see Lazaridis and Psimmenos 1999), this time within the 'motherland'. As the overwhelming majority of them did not possess the necessary documents which would permit them to stay legally in Greece, their status has been defined as 'illegal' by the Greek government and police alongside the status of non-ethnic-Greeks or as I call them here, 'other' Albanians. When they emigrated to Greece they became a 'minority' in the motherland, suffering discrimination and exclusion similar to that experienced by non-ethnic-Greek Albanians.

Based on ethnographic data, this chapter discusses some preliminary findings concerning the experiences of Albanians in Athens. In particular, it focuses on the experiences of Albanian migrant workers, who enter into the country illegally and find themselves in the fringes of the labour market. Both ethnic-Greek Albanians and 'other' Albanians come to Greece seeking better prospects than they can find at home. Unlike ethnic-Greek-Albanians the majority of the 'other' Albanians are 'sojourners', that is temporary migrants, with an intention of someday returning home.

The comparative analysis focuses on the experiences of these two minority groups and particularly on their experiences in Greece. Fieldwork over several years (1994-1998) has shown that both types of migrant worker constitute a 'replacement labour force', filling the undesirable, low paid menial jobs in the primary and tertiary sectors which have recently been deserted by Greeks (see Lazaridis 1996). It is argued that although both these social groups are found in low-paid occupations, the ethnic-Greek-Albanian is treated more favourably by the hosts than members of other ethnic minority groups, such as the 'other' Albanians. The latter not only experience exploitation and discrimination in employment but are treated as scapegoats in various 'games' played in the political arena. For example, as shown below, although both groups are likely to be stopped and searched by the police for petty crimes, such as theft, due to pre-conceived perceptions of them as criminals, the 'ethnic-Greek-Albanians' are less likely to be victims of prejudiced actions of law enforcement agencies. The paper argues that the 'other' Albanians are trapped in a condition of inferiority, immobility and 'ultra-exploitation'. It shows the contradiction between economic inclusion on the one hand, albeit in the informal economy, and different degrees of social exclusion on the other, that these two ethnic minority groups experience.

In the following sections, the two cases of Albanians are discussed; these show that the two categories of 'ethnic-Greek-Albanian' and 'other-Albanian' partly explain the differential treatment of these strangers by the host community; the former are marginalised, that is living at the edge of society whilst the latter are excluded, that is have been shut off completely from the kinds of social relationships which 'ethnic-Greek-Albanians' have. The Greeks behave as if they have no obligations to them. Social exclusion affects them in multiple ways, not only in income, but also matters of health, access to education, access to services, housing etc. So social relationships are a primary source of disadvantage. Integration is difficult. As a group defined by their 'deviant' behaviour, they are subject to considerable prejudice and to active discrimination.

3.   Methodology

The chapter is based on ethnographic data collected during field work in the spring and summer months of 1994-1998 in Athens. Semi-structured in-depth interviews were carried out with 38 migrants from Albania and various Greek key informants allowing them to express their perceptions of Albanians. The majority of the Albanian respondents were between 24 and 46 years of age and had arrived in Greece sometime between winter 1990 and spring 1995. Although I am relying on a relatively small number of informants, I have tried to embrace heterogeneity of experiences and accounts.

Because many Albanians, in particular those working clandestinely, were reluctant to participate, the 'snow-balling' technique was employed for obtaining access to the respondents and for selecting people for interview. What are being reported here are the interviewees' versions of 'reality': their views, their subjective accounts and interpretations of events. The aim of this chapter is to 'tell it like it is' from the point of view of the respondents and to try and achieve an understanding of the way these 'strangers' perceive and interpret their experiences.

4. Subjective experiences in the host country

Ethnographic evidence gathered over the period 1994-1998 reveals that both ethnic-Greek and 'other' Albanians in Greece work in the secondary labour market performing poorly paid jobs, experiencing poor working conditions, little or no job security and opportunity for promotion and seldom come across offers on-the-job training. They come to Greece as a 'replacement labour force' (Peach 1968), to take jobs which are no longer attractive to local people, such as cleaning in hotels, washing up in tavernas, bar work and construction work (both household construction and public works). Their employment is informal, undeclared and concealed from the state authorities by employers and is characterised by high rates of turnover (on average 6-7 times a month). As argued elsewhere (Lazaridis and Romaniszyn 1998) their illegal status renders them helpless against exploitation. They form an 'undocumented underclass' (ibid) being hired illegally to perform often unhealthy, heavy menial jobs and paid lower than subsistence levels, receiving as low as six US dollars per day for eight or more hours of work. They are therefore part of what Cohen (1994) called an 'underprivileged "helot" class'. As Gregoris, a 42-year-old ethnic-Greek Albanian from Gjirocaster said:

> I came to Greece in 1993, for the children. Life in Albania is dangerous. I set off full of dreams and hopes for a better life ... I was soon to be disappointed ... I have to work hard to simply survive ... I take any job I find. I have worked in the construction industry, I have washed dishes in tavernas, and I

was employed as a decorator in houses. I work for lower wages and for longer hours than the Greeks ... I do not intend to go back, I will stay (interview, summer 1996).

Moreover, as stated elsewhere (Lazaridis and Wickens 1999) there is job segregation by sex, in that most women are confined in certain types of work, such as domestic work, washing up and cleaning[7] (see Lazaridis 1995), whereas men, regardless of educational background, take up agricultural work in rural areas and are employed in the construction industry (both household construction and public works via subcontractors) and other macho low-paid low status jobs, which require physical strength and little skill. Both men and women have stated that they face hostility from Greek employers. As a 34 years old woman from Gjirokaster said,

In the one of the houses that I worked, the woman I worked for was always watching me. She watched the way I cleaned, the way I washed the dishes, the way I swept the floor. She did not trust me. She was treating me as if I was worthless. At least this is how I felt.

Another woman said:

I was expected to clean the house, look after the kids, cater for parties and ... gradually the boss's husband made it clear that he was expecting sexual favours from me (interview, summer 1997).

There is therefore diversity in employers' demands. The women's illegal status and the vulnerability derived from this, means that the employer can step outside the web of rules and obligations and conventions which govern domestic work and make sexual advances and yet evade all social and financial obligations that go along with sexual relations commercial or non-commercial. Such situations literally coerce an Albanian woman, a person with no power to escape, no ability to exercise rights or claims, into a slave-like relationship. Their illegal status dissolves their entitlement to protection and respect accorded to non-illegal women. They have no civil rights, and therefore they become the property of any man; theoretically, she can leave, but the risk in doing so is great in terms of her economic survival in a hostile world. So, many choose to transfer rights of commands over their body in exchange for a false security.

Regardless of their educational background, all Albanians, even those who used to be employed back home as doctors or teachers are pushed into low status, poorly paid occupations with very few opportunities for advancement, because of their poverty-stricken situation. As a 28-year-old woman, Maria, who was a qualified doctor in Albania said:

> I am working as domestic looking after an elderly relative of my boss. They know that I have qualifications but they treat me like a slave. I am working for long hours and receive only insults. I have no choice. I am illegal, I am not insured. I receive 1,000 drachmas per hour and I work more than 12 hours a day. I only go out on Sundays (interview, summer 1995).

Whether these educated Albanians will gradually move into higher paid, higher status occupations in Greece, remains to be seen.

The legal and labour market situation of the ethnic-Greek-Albanian and the 'other' Albanian does not differ much as long as both are illegal; at some point through the migration process, however, the ethnic-Greek-Albanians can manage to call upon their Greek ancestral ties, and therefore gradually obtain the right to stay and work in Greece. As most have crossed the borders illegally without documents, it often takes a long time to be able to satisfy the authorities of their 'Greekness'. At the same time, 'other' Albanians, bearing in mind the privileges enjoyed by ethnic-Greek-Albanians, make a conscious attempts to learn and speak the Greek language and not only to learn something about the way of life and customs of the Greek people, but to adopt them. This conscious attempt made towards confirmation of self-identity as Greek includes Greek-Orthodox baptism and change of first names into Greek names. As Maria, said:

> I was treated like a slave, working for a family with four children, until I met a really good woman who baptised me. She helped me to find another job. I now feel safer (interview, summer 1995).

So in an attempt to lessen the cultural racism directed towards them, instead of wanting to assert their difference, they try to conceal it. This is an attempt to adopt 'Greekness' in order to assimilate, or to achieve, if possible, the production of bonds, sentiments and solidarities relating to collective origin and belonging (Anthias 1998a: 513). Thus the ethnic heterogeneity between those of Greek origin and 'other' Albanians becomes blurred. So one often hears them say: 'I am of Greek-Albanian origin', 'I am an ethnic-Greek Albanian', 'I am a Greek who has lived in Albania for years', but almost never one hears them say: 'I am an Albanian', 'I am an Albanian living in Greece'.

In other words, they seem to be building and discarding self-definitions, depending on the degree of need for self-presentation as 'Greek', for 'belonging'. The latter, i.e.: 'Greekness', relates to their life chances in Greece; it is able to reproduce advantages and privileges, the forms and degrees of which may depend upon gender, class differences, different levels of education, religious values and so on, which may interplay with those of 'Greekness' to produce hierarchical outcomes for the individuals (see also Anthias 1998a: 520).

The concentration ethnic-Greek-Albanians and 'other' Albanians in the secondary labour market points to the consistent disadvantages suffered by the people interviewed. The migrants I interviewed find themselves employed casually, intermittently and/or for limited periods of time. More importantly when work is scare, they are likely to be unemployed. As a result, they are likely to move through various types of ephemeral labour, including temporary employment, casual work with no tenure; they often experience periodic spells of unemployment (Spicker 1993: 84). Although this approach explains some of the problems experienced by these two minority groups in employment, it is limited in its explanatory power for the differential treatment of these groups. It fails for instance to account for the racist ideology which leads to the relatively higher degree of marginalisation and social exclusion experienced primarily by the 'other' Albanian migrants. In what follows the differential treatment of these two minority groups by the hosts will be discussed.

5. Differential treatment of ethnic-Greek-Albanians and 'other' Albanians[8]

Both ethnic-Greek and 'other' Albanians are strangers to the host culture, in the sense that they have not 'belonged to it from the beginning' and that they import 'qualities into it that do not and cannot stem from the group itself'. In coming to temporarily stay in the host country, they bring with them some 'qualities of the stranger' that is their value systems that are different from that of the host community. As Cohen (1972: 166) has observed 'not even modern man is completely ready to immerse himself wholly in an alien environment ... For man is still basically moulded by his native culture and bound through habit to its patterns of behaviour' (ibid.).

The concept of the 'stranger' can be usefully applied to the phenomenon of migration. In Park's work the migrant is conceived of as a 'marginal man' who lives in two worlds, in both of which he is more or less a stranger (Levine

1979: 23). Park suggests that many migrants by migrating give up old values but do not acquire the norms of the host community. While Park's interpretation of Simmel's (1950) stranger explains the marginality experienced by many minority groups in Greece it does not provide an adequate explanation for the different treatment of the ethnic-Greek-Albanian and the 'other' Albanian migrant.

As mentioned in the previous section, unlike the 'other' Albanians, ethnic-Greek-Albanians as long as they are able to 'prove' their 'Greekness', they are not seen by the Greeks as undesirable intruders and hence they are generally welcomed and rarely treated with hostility; 'auti ine diki mas, Vorioepirotes; I alli ine xeni, Alvani' (these are one of us, Greeks from Northern Epirus; the others are foreigners, Albanians' or 'afti ine Vorioepirotes, then ine xeni san tous Alvanous' (these are Greeks from Northern Epirus, they are not foreigners like the Albanians) one often hears Greeks saying. Evidence from fieldwork shows that Greeks are negative towards the 'other' Albanian workers, perceiving them as 'cunning', 'primitive' and above all 'untrustworthy' (see Lazaridis and Romaniszyn 1998). 'All Albanians are thieves', 'Albanians are responsible for increasing crime rates in our cities' 'Albanians are murderers; they can murder someone for 100 drachmas', 'Did you hear of that murder? It must be Albanians, what else? Who else would kill so brutally an old couple for 5,000 drachmas?' are common expressions in the Greek vocabulary and everyday conversation. These stereotypes enjoy wide currency and stigmatise the majority of the 'other' Albanians, which, in turn, justifies their 'ultra-exploitation' in the labour market. 'Other' Albanians are generally seen as a 'problem' and are most likely to experience hostility. For example, in September 1998, a man entered a ground floor flat in Athens and held as a hostage a young woman – he was holding a grenade that eventually exploded. When the incident reached the evening news bulletin, an immediate assumption was made that the intruder was an Albanian. It was said: 'The intruder is most probably an Albanian'. It was not until later that he was identified to be a Romanian living in Greece since he was a young kid. When I asked an Albanian how he felt about this, he replied:

> How did they know he was an Albanian? Whenever a foreigner does something bad, he has to be an Albanian. It is very difficult to deal with this kind of prejudice against us. People here see us with hostility. They avoid us, they are frightened of us, they are angry with us (interview, September 1998).

This antipathy towards them is reflected in government policy in the early 1990s to limit their numbers by 'exporting' them - the so-called operation 'skoupa' or 'sweeping operations'. The decision by the Greek authorities is primarily based on what I have called 'Albanophobia' - fear that Greece will be swamped by a massive influx of Albanian migrants and fear that the societal cohesion of the country will be threatened by these 'foreign criminals' or 'foreign thieves' as they are often labelled by various Greek newspapers (Lazaridis and Wickens 1999). Thus, while Greece is benefiting from these 'peripheral' workers, widespread fear and insecurity, stimulated by media reports of criminal activities such as thefts, armed robberies by 'other' Albanians is partly responsible for the government's decision in the early 1990s to send many Albanians home by force (ibid.).

In contrast, as mentioned above, ethnic-Greek-Albanians are, 'one of us' and hence, they are welcomed and treated more favourably. These workers adapt rapidly and see themselves as part of the Greek 'ethnos'. Their belief that they have always shared with the Greeks of the motherland a historic territory, Northern Epirus, common historical memories, common cultural traditions, the survival of which they had often to fight for, leads them to believe that they 'must' be granted equal rights and duties with the host population. Their inability however to speak fluent Greek and often to produce valid documents proving their 'Greekness' creates boundaries which distinguishes and/or differentiates them from the national Greek community. The host society is prepared to accept and welcome them as long as they prove that they are part of the in-group. Since, however, because of lack of appropriate documents or other evidence in support of their 'Greekness', their Greek identity is 'imagined', its reality lies in the host community's perception of the validity of a common belonging, its willingness to accept them on an equal footing as *'authochthones'*, namely those born within the national territory (Clogg 1992: 48). Their 'Greekness' is put into question until they provide proof of their Greek-ethnic origin. This is important in drawing the line between Greeks and the 'others', and in providing the ethnic-Greek-Albanians with a right to Greek social and political citizenship.

In contrast the 'other' Albanians interviewed remain distinct from the wider society and foster their own cultural features and life-style. Hence the host society is treating the Albanian as 'inferior', 'ignorant', 'backward', the 'not belonging' Such stereotypes coincided with Alia's amnesty to a couple of hundred political prisoners in 1991. Newspapers published articles about the release of these prisoners who could commit crimes once they entered the country. During the same period (early 1990s) there was a 40 per cent increase in the number of crimes committed in Greece (Karydis 1996: 92). This increase in criminality in Greece together with allegations that 60 per cent of all crimes committed by foreigners are committed by Albanians (newspaper 'Kathimerini' Dec. 1996), have, as argued elsewhere (Lazaridis and Wickens 1999), led to a moral panic and contributed to the 'construction of the Albanian as 'dangerous', 'criminal' and to false conclusions that 'every Albanian is a criminal'. Crimes committed by Albanians found their place in newspapers front pages thus playing a leading role in the construction of the image of Albanian criminal and in triggering public prejudice against them (Drouka 1996). One could read in the main newspapers headline like the following: 'Illegal migration reaches explosive dimensions in Greece' (Apogevmatini, 15 September 1991); 'Albanians and Bulgarians have taken criminality to its peak' (Kathimerini, 1 November 1991); 'Albanians ... a crime per day' (Apogevmatini, 5 January 1992); 'Albanian Mafia went Ballistic' (Niki, 7 September 1992).

This 'xenophobia' or 'Albanophobia' on the part of the mass media and lack of acceptance by the Greeks that Greece is a multi-ethnic state in which ethnic and cultural diversity exists, provide at least part of the explanation for the differential treatment of these 'strangers' in this host community.

The responses of most Albanians, show that they feel themselves to be 'the victims of discrimination'. They often experience open hostility and abuse. The work 'Albanian' acts as a label that causes many Greeks to perceive them in a negative way and to treat them accordingly. For instance, as mentioned elsewhere, evidence shows that many Albanians are stopped and searched by the police and even arrested for petty crimes, such as thefts (Lazaridis and Wickens 1999). As an Albanian migrant said:

> It is not possible to be an Albanian in Greece and not have had any encounter with the police. A few months after I arrived in Greece I was arrested for not possessing the appropriate documents; I was expelled from Greece; the conditions in those coaches were humiliating. The filth was unbearable. I stayed a couple of months in Albania, I bribed soldiers on the border near Kakavia – the tariff can be anything up to 400,000 drachmas per person – to let me and my wife cross the borders without visas. I have a permanent fear ... In many cases employers turn their employees to the police so that they evade paying them their daily wage (interview, September 1997).

Another person said:

> If the police realise that you are an Albanian, they immediately stop you and search you and sometimes they take you to the station for no reason (interview, September 1997).

To quote Karydis (1992:100) 'On the level of law-enforcement an increasingly extensive policy action took place in the form of raids in order to clear off the streets and the country from Albanians'.

Trapped in conditions of inferiority and occupational immobility, they feel powerless to make any representation of grievance, against harsh and racist police treatment. Discrimination in employment and political attack inspired by Greek Nationalists, ensure that these peripheral workers occupy an inferior position in the host community. Moreover, the use of the word 'Albanian' adds another level of meaning to their disadvantaged position. For instance, the expression 'I am not your Albanian' that is, 'I am not your slave', is often used by the Greeks to refuse a job which is seen as menial and underpaid (Lazaridis 1996).

Clearly, what has been emerging in Greece over the last few years is an 'underclass' consisting largely of these recent illegal immigrant workers (Lazaridis and Romaniszyn 1998). These workers are denied the basic legal and social rights of the rest of the labour force and are confined to low paid, insecure work. Discrimination in employment, racist police practice and political attacks inspired by Greek nationalism ensure that these illegal migrant workers occupy an 'inferior position' in this host community.

6. Concluding remarks

In this chapter I have looked at ways in which processes by which the migrant population from Albania is constructed as 'deviant and dangerous'. I have also looked at ways in which aspects of exclusion and inclusion of ethnic-Greek-Albanians and 'other' Albanians spans a number of important sites of differentiation depending on how the categories ethnic-Greek-Albanian and 'other' Albanian are constructed and presented. I have looked at strategies employed by the 'other' Albanians to blur the ethnic or cultural differences between them and the Greeks. So one cannot treat the migrant population from Albanian as unitary and static. It seems that ethnic and cultural identities here are rather fluid and dynamic; and there can be strategies employed by some groups to remove their culture-visibility believing perhaps that in this way they blur boundaries of ethnic identity and/or origin, thus establishing bonds of commonality with the Greeks and by doing so exclusions, disadvantages and multiple forms of discrimination they may encountered as 'undesirable others' will potentially disappear.

Greece has recently been transformed from an emigration to an immigration society with a plethora of other cultures living within its territorial boundaries. These changes have been challenging notions of citizenship based on acquisition of Greek nationality and a call for 'a recognition of citizenship as properly involving rights to pursue diverse cultures and ways of life ... this ... requires a great deal of dialogue ... as well as a serious concern with redressing economic and social inequalities ... There needs to be a refocusing of the terms of reference of policies and politics towards issues of greater inclusion (not assimilation or integration) and democratisation as a strategy on the one hand, and a focus on campaigns at the local level on the other' (Anthias 1998: 17).

References

Anthias, F. (1998a) 'The Limits of Ethnic "Diversity"', in *Patterns of Prejudice*, Vol. 32, No.4, pp.5-19.

Anthias, F. (1998b) 'Rethinking Social Divisions: some Notes towards a Theoretical Framework', in *The Sociological Review*, Vol. 46, No.3, pp.505-535.

Antonopoulos, E.A. (1995) *Albanian and Greek-Albanian relations 1912-1994*, Athens: Okeanida (in Greek)

CE (Council of Europe) (1991) 'Report on the situation of Albania', Document 6496, Geneva, 13 September.

Clogg, R. (1992) *A Concise History of Modern Greece*, Cambridge: Cambridge University Press.

Cohen, E. (1972) 'Towards a sociology of international tourism'. in *Social Research* Vol. 39, pp.164-182.

Cohen, R. (1994) *Frontiers of Identity: the British and Others*, London: Longman.

Diktakis, A. (1993) *Greek immigration policy in the European context: third world immigrants and repatriated Pontians*, M.Sc. Thesis, School of Social Sciences, University of Bath, UK.

Drouka, E. (1996) 'The problem of illegal migration in Greece: the Albanian case', MPhil Thesis, Criminology, University of Cambridge, UK.

Drouka, E. (1998) 'Albanians in the Greek informal economy', in *Journal of Ethnic and Migration Studies,*, Vol. 24, No.2, pp.347-365.

Hall, D. (1994) *Albania and the Albanians*, London: Pinter.

Hamilton, B. (1992) *Albania: Who cares? The exclusive inside story*, Grantham: Autumn House.

Karydis, V. (1992) 'The fear of crime in Athens and the construction of the 'dangerous Albanian' stereotype', in *Chroniques*, Vol. 5, pp.97-193.

Karydis, V. (1996) *Criminal activity of migrants in Greece* (I englimatikotita ton metanaston stin Ellada), Athens: Papazisis.

Lazaridis, G. (1995) 'Immigrant women in Greece: the case of domestic labourers from Albania and the Philippines' in European Forum for Leftist Women (ed) *Nationalism, Racism, Gender*, Salonika: Paratiritis.

Lazaridis, G. (1996) 'Immigration to Greece: a critical evaluation of Greek policy' in *New Community*, (renamed Journal of Ethnic and Migration Studies) Vol. 22, No.2, pp.335-348.

Lazaridis, G. and Poyago-Theotoky, J. (1997) 'Illegal migration: issues of regularisation' paper presented at the ISS/FES international conference 'Central and Eastern Europe: new migration space', Pultusk, Poland 11-13 December.

Lazaridis. G. and Romaniszyn, C. (1998) 'Albanian and Polish Undocumented workers in Greece: a comparative analysis' in *Journal of European Social Policy*, Vol.8, No.1, pp.5-22.

Lazaridis, G. and Psimmenos, I. (1999) 'Migrant Flows from Albania to Greece: Economic, Social and Spatial Exclusion' in R. King, G. Lazaridis and C. Tsardanidis (eds.) *Eldorado or Fortress? Migration in Southern Europe*, Basingstoke: Macmillan.

Lazaridis, G. and Wickens, E. (1999) 'Us and the Others: ethnic minorities in Greece', in *Annals of Tourism Research*, Vol.26, No.3. (in Press).

Levine, D.N. (1979) 'Simmel at a distance: on the history and systematics of the sociology of the stranger' in Shack, W.A. and Skinner, E.P. (eds.) *Strangers in African Societies*, Berkeley: University of California Press, pp.84-106.

Peach, C. (1968) *West Indian Migration in Britain*, Oxford: Oxford University Press.

Simmel, G. (1950) 'The stranger' in Wolff, K.H, (ed) *The sociology of George Simmel*, New York: Free Press.

Salt, J. (1997) 'Reconceptualising migration and migration space', paper presented at the ISS/FES international conference 'Central and Eastern Europe: new migration space', Pultusk, Poland 11-13 December.

Spicker, P. (1993) *Poverty and social security: concepts and principles*, London: Routledge.

Notes

[1] During the early 1990s, the total number of arrests of foreigners increased from 9,631 in 1990, to 211,742 in 1995 (Drouka 1998:335). This imported crime coincides with the period when large numbers of Albanian migrants started coming into Greece. Their visibility and illegality lead in media presentation of the Albanian as criminal. The absence of victimisation surveys and of reliable data contributes to the process of creation of the Albanian as criminal.

2   For example, in 1994 the Ministry of Public Order estimated the number of undocumented migrants in Greece to be around 350,000, half of whom were migrants from Albania.
3   Between 1991 and 1995 the Greek government deported approximately one million illegal Albanian migrants (Drouka 1998:353).
4   This is not the first time that Albanians emigrated. For example, during the 16th and 17th centuries, many Albanians were forced to migrate due to hunger and oppression by the Ottomans who since 1931 took a large part of Albania under their control (Hall 1994).
5   1951 UN Convention on refugees; 1967 Protocol.
6   As argued elsewhere (see Lazaridis and Wickens 1999) 'approximately half of the illegal migrants [in Greece] are Albanians. Nevertheless, illegal migration as a phenomenon can be said to be 'statistically invisible', in that documentation of its nature, rhythm and impact is incomplete. This is partly due to the 'hidden' aspects of many activities and transactions, partly due to the embryonic state of research in this area, partly due to double counting at the borders and partly due to incompatibility of sources, conceptual and definitional problems. As a result, it is not possible to gain more that an informed estimate of the numbers of illegal migrants, where they are moving to and from, who they are (Salt 1997). So the data available cannot be used to provide an accurate assessment of the migration realities of the 1990s'.
7   For a detailed account see Lazaridis 1995.
8   This section rests on ideas explored in another paper (Lazaridis and Wickens 1999).

7 The Presence of the Polish Undocumented in Greece in the Perspective of European Unification

Krystyna Romaniszyn

1. Introduction

Contemporary mass economic migrations have led to debates and controversies between, generally speaking, the defenders of the individual's human rights of free movement and settlement versus the defenders of the nation-state's rights and obligations to guard their national boundaries against masses of potential immigrants. On the one hand, from a liberal point of view, migration has been explained in respect of the exercise of human rights or as a factor working against poverty and political oppression (Dowty 1987; Richmond 1994; Zolberg 1989). On the other hand, from the point of view of conservative (often right-wing) political theorists, it has been seen as a threat to social cohesion, and even to the sovereignty of nation-states 'swarmed over' by bearers of different cultures (Stolcke 1995). And both sides believe that they have good reasons for defending their stand.

Western European democracies are characterised by the implementation of restrictive and exclusive immigration policies and the adjustment of the monitoring systems in order to protect their nation-states against immigration flows now coming also from Central and Eastern European countries. This, in fact, is a continuation - in a new, more radical, and explicit form - of policies adopted since the mid-1970s when the controls on immigration became ever more restrictiveafter an earlier period of being characterised by freedom of border entry. Such a switch in immigration policies occurred after a relatively long period of planned foreign labour recruitment during which labour migration was institutionalised by the implementation of the guest worker system. This lasted from the early post-war period until the mid 1970s. More restrictive immigration policies introduced by western states have also gone hand in hand with anti-immigrant political movements, actions and attitudes.

Measures to stop people from migrating in search of a better life or higher wages do not succeed fully. Heightened levels of illegal immigration, noticed in developed European countries, may be largely attributed to the restrictions put on legal migration. This is more so, because such restrictions clash with the interests of numerous employers in the high-income countries who benefit from the supply of cheap labour and, hence, risk hiring *'illegals'*. As Malcolm Cross argues the cycle of contradictions between a political and an economic logic lies at the heart of the current European debate on immigration (Cross 1996: 197). Also the rapid growth of the so-called *'world'* or *'global cities'*, in Europe and elsewhere, facilitate migrations, illegal ones included, by providing a social base for the reception and insertion of newcomers, as explained by the social capital and migrant networks theories (Fielding 1993; Portes and Borocz 1989; Salt 1989).

Other objective factors are noted by the world system perspective (Miller and Denmark 1993), such as intensification of communication and the development of relatively cheap transportation systems. They further facilitate the flow of information and, thus, of migrants. The increasing real (also perceived as such by potential migrants) international inequalities in living standards have the same effect. In addition, the collapse of Central and Eastern European regimes backed by the Soviet Union, and the democratisation processes which followed, have resulted in the release of a number of migrants who readily exercise their newly-obtained permission to travel abroad. Restrictions imposed by Western European democracies on entry, stay, and work permits - which are aimed at reducing the inflow of potential migrants - may be overcome by illegal or undocumented migration. Hence, despite the restrictions imposed, conventions signed, or debates held, numerous individuals try their luck at illegally undertaking jobs in the parallel economy of host Western and, recently, also Southern European countries (Cross 1993). The Polish undocumented in Greece provide but one such example of illegal labour migration from Eastern to Southern Europe. Although, Polish migrants, particularly the undocumented, suffer clear social disadvantages attendant on their status and social position (discussed later), this paper aims at investigating the phenomenon of their presence and work in Greece within the perspective of European unification, and the assumption that this involves the growth of mutual understanding and collaboration. The paper will argue that political inclusion must be necessary adjunct to social acceptance.

2. The context of individual experiences

After 1989, as a result of the democratisation process, Polish citizens acquired the right to leave their home country at any time they so decided. The old problems with obtaining a passport ceased to exist. The new problem which has appeared derives from the growing difficulties in getting a paying job in the former labour-exporting countries of Western Europe. Westward trips undertaken by most Poles in the previous decades were aimed precisely at earning money due to the strikingly different levels of income between their home and the Western Europe countries, such as Germany and Austria. The economic recession from which the latter have suffered from, and the restrictive immigration policies they have adopted, have drastically reduced work opportunities in these countries. When opportunities arose in Southern Europe, a new stream of economic migrants from Poland headed to Greece and other countries of this region, namely Italy and Spain. The lack of valid data makes it impossible to establish the exact number of the Polish undocumented in the specified countries, and only estimates have been available. According to Italian estimates, Polish illegal labour migrants comprise some 80 per cent of the Poles who live in the country (Cieœliñska 1995: 36); in 1990 there were as many as 16,966 Poles legally settled in Italy (Rosoli 1993: 284). As for Spain, the Polish consulate in Madrid estimates that in 1996 some 8,000-20,000 Polish undocumented were staying in this country (Nalewajko 1997: 3). In Greece the existing estimates differ greatly; some claim that in 1993 there were approximately 100,000 Polish undocumented workers (Petrinoti 1993), while others stated that there were 30,000 of them in the same year (Panoi 1993: 8). Greece became a labour-importing country after 1980, and most economic immigrants, originating from a number of countries, are illegal, like the Poles (Lianos, Sarris and Katseli 1996: 449).

This section is based on the findings of my three-month fieldwork carried out in Greece in Autumn 1993. Basically it was conducted in Athens. Short, additional trips were made to the island of Santorini and Crete, and the Peloponnese where small groups of the Polish undocumented dwelled. To identify the undocumented, the research involved a multifaceted technique of focused interviewing (Minichiello, Aroni, Timewell and Alexander 1991: 89);

observation of the undocumented in the places where they concentrate and where various services are offered to them, such as the 'Polish' church, the 'Polish' disco and tavern, the 'Polish' travel and dentist offices, the 'Polish' shop, etc.; and the examination of the Catholic parochial documents. Focused interviews were conducted with 22 informants; these were Polish undocumented workers who had stayed and worked in Greece for at least a year, and who were selected by the referral method.

According to the research, the only economic sector in which Polish economic migrants can find jobs in Greece is the informal one, or in other terms, the Greek parallel economy. Generally speaking, there are two economic niches in which the Polish undocumented can get jobs; these are: domestic service for women and building construction for men. Jobs available in agriculture seem less popular especially among the more 'permanent illegals' some of whom stay in Greece for a few years. Similarly, jobs in the tourist industry are basically undertaken by seasonal illegal workers. On the whole the Poles, like other foreign illegal workers, take up labour intensive jobs in enterprises that operate outside the direct control of fiscal authorities. Their inflow into Greece consists of two categories, seasonal and permanent workers. This characterises all illegal immigration into Greece (Lianos, Sarris and Katseli 1996). The Poles who come only for a short-term job tend to disperse all over the country; permanent illegal migrants tend to be concentrated in Athens.

During their stay and employment, both categories of Polish migrant workers come into contact, in one way or another, with Greek institutions as well as individuals. These contacts will determine the migrants' knowledge of, and attitude towards, Greek society and culture. Of course, the influence is stronger and more formative in the case of 'permanent' migrants. They come into longer lasting contact with the host society and its culture, and may acquire some of its elements.

First of all, this is noticeable in the sphere of language. Polish workers will try to learn some Greek and acquire some conversational skill, especially in the area of their job duties and everyday life situations such as shopping, eating, etc. It is worth noting that some informants who have stayed and worked in Greece for a few years pronounce even Polish words with a Greek accent. Whether this is done on purpose - to show how familiar they are with this foreign language - or not, this fact reveals that they try and are successful to some extent in learning it. Another sphere in which some influence of the elements of the host society culture on Polish labourers is particularly visible is body language, e.g., the language of gestures and mimicry. Some of these gestures, unknown and never practised in Poland in contrast with Greece, are imitated, consciously or not, by the Poles living in this country.

A deliberate interest in Greek culture is manifested by those of the Polish undocumented who go sightseeing, visit historic sites or museums. In this context, an interesting habit of those who get married in Athens should be mentioned. Almost as a rule they include in their celebration a visit to the Acropolis, documented on a video cassette they order and pay for.[1] Taking pictures of each other posed against the background of the historic monument - which are to be sent back home and shown to friends and relatives - seems to be yet another practice of some Polish workers in Greece.

Another example of becoming familiar with and/or acquiring particular elements of Greek culture is provided by baptism documents gathered in the Athenian church of Christ the King. Altogether there were as many as 826 Polish children baptised there from 1986 until October 1993.[2] In numerous cases, the Greek-born children of the Polish undocumented were given Greek names such as Nikos for boys,[3] and Olympia and Eleni for girls. Other names such as Aphrodite and Dimitri were also frequent, and there was even one Socrates. Of course, among the baptised children some were given typically Polish names, and a number of them English, or Polish ones combined with Greek. This is possibly intended to serve as a help for the child who is to live outside Poland. The documents also show that, in some cases, a child had been named after his/her Greek godparent. Asked for the motivation behind the decision to name her Greek-born son, Nikos (written down in this form in the baptismal certificate) one woman explained: 'Let him have a souvenir from Greece'. Among other things, such practices may indicate the desire to manifest publicly a positive attitude towards Greeks, important in the situation of being undocumented, but it may also reveal a truly positive attitude towards Greece.

Generally, for all who have stayed in Greece and who have had friends or relatives there, Greece is not an 'abstract' country, located somewhere and known only from history and geography lessons. It is a country to which personal experiences and memories are attached, and which is a part of a **personal biography**. This very fact undoubtedly takes down barriers of ignorance and indifference, but whether and to what extent it brings members of the two societies closer together depends on the kind of experiences they have come through.

One result of these frequent or regular contacts between the Polish undocumented and their Greek hosts is the process of stereotype creation. On the whole, popular stereotypes of Greek people are not found in Polish culture - and probably *vice versa* - before the contemporary mass economic migration from Poland to Greece. Thus, the current situation of culture contact is fertile ground for studying the process of creation of stereotypes. Material gathered in the course of fieldwork provides a starting point for relevant study, and allows one to assume that, as a side effect, stereotypes have emerged in the recent decade out of regular, broad contacts made and maintained on an unprecedented scale by numerous members of both societies, and from experiences they have acquired. It may be therefore claimed that the process of stereotyping has already begun. Informants frequently expressed - seemingly an already common belief among the Polish undocumented - that 'Greeks are difficult to put up with' which they nevertheless manage to do. On the other hand, all interviewed - who were young people, aged between twenty and thirty, with technical and vocational training, originating from small towns - were sensitive to the image of themselves in the host society. They voluntarily brought this subject into our conversation claiming that the opinion of Polish migrants held by Greeks is positive and that, 'We have a good presence here' which they were visibly proud of. This refers to the problem of representing the home country and its culture in the host society. Immigrants see themselves as bearers of their home culture, and are often perceived as such. In this sense, any migration involves the migration of cultures (Zamojski 1995: 27). Indeed, by their work, behaviour, and appearance Polish migrants articulate their home culture and represent their home land to host society members.

At this point it is worth including an episode significant in the matter discussed regarding the self-esteem of the Polish undocumented. On one Greek island where they have stayed and worked in larger numbers, a group of initiates commissioned a Greek artist and paid for a painted copy of the icon of the Black Madonna of Czêstochowa - both a religious and national symbol for Polish Catholics. The copied icon was ceremonially placed in the local Roman Catholic Church on November 11, 1993 - on Polish Independence Day. Sermons and speeches, in both Greek and Polish, were made in front of a large audience of Poles and a handful of local Greek Catholics. Explaining the incentives for the idea one person said 'We will not settle here but, nevertheless, we want to leave behind our mark in the place we have lived'.

Of course, the whole event might well serve the immediate interest of the undocumented. The formal co-operation between them and Greek citizens (the painter, church officials, and local Catholics) built upon this event was meant to legitimise, to some extent, their prolonged presence on the island. The initiative also brought together the Poles and their Greek host, making room for the establishment of closer contacts between them.

The same end was served by yet another episode which took place in Athens in March 1993 where the Polish undocumented workers organised a concert, lottery, and trade fair in order to collect funds to purchase medical supplies for the Polish child of an illegal worker. Among the participants were Greek friends and/or employers, some of whom donated considerable sums.[4] This event, again, may be viewed as a contact-building one and as a manifestation of social solidarity, and one may say, against legal barriers. In contact-building, however, more important than unique events are everyday affairs which result in the creation of mutual, and in many cases, friendly links between Poles and their Greek employers or landlords who rent them flats, and invite them, as clients, to their pubs, clubs, or restaurants. Such contacts serve as a powerful factor in linking members of society, and people involved may be viewed as *contact-builders* between two societies (Simila 1995).

In the light of these arguments based on fieldwork findings it may be assumed that the Polish undocumented workers do not face social rejection in Greece. In this respect their situation differs noticeably from that experienced by another population of clandestine workers, namely, the Albanians. The commonly held belief associates the latter with criminal activities (Lazaridis and Wickens 1995). According to research carried out in Northern Greece on the impact of illegal immigration on local communities, Greeks are tolerant towards immigrants without being particularly friendly or hostile (Lianos, Sarris and Katseli 1996: 465). It should not be overlooked, however, that this attitude may well change. The authors have already noticed that there seems to be a *general* sense of dissatisfaction as far as the presence of illegal migrants in the country is concerned (ibid: 465).

Presently, through successful personal contacts with the host society, through the expression of interest in that society's culture, the knowledge acquired about it, and the assimilation of its elements, Poles - despite their 'undocumented status' - may help to forge a link between the two societies, as migration networks theory implies (Salt 1989). Economic migration within Europe, therefore, might facilitate the unification process by intensifying contacts and thus linking societies. However, this might be effective in facilitating unification, provided that the objective legal, economic, and political factors are in place and respective governments have decided for unification. In other words, **political inclusion** of clandestine workers, by which I mean legalisation of their recruitment, should follow any **social acceptance** already experienced by the Poles in Greece if unification is to be fully achieved.

3. The context of Greek immigration policy and its determinants

The presence of the clandestine workers in Greece, among them Polish ones, apparently violates legal acts implemented in the country aimed at regulating immigration. The official stand of the Greek authorities as reflected in immigration legislation is firm and oriented toward minimising immigration. The new Law of 1991 basically addresses the problem of illegal labour immigration. It stipulates expulsion of illegal immigrants and severe penalties on Greek citizens for employment of undocumented workers and on those who facilitate their entry. As a critic stated, the document mainly reflects a preoccupation with **public order** without mentioning ways of legalisation or integration of immigrants into Greek society (Tapinos 1994: 10). In other words, it does not address the problem of political and social inclusion of immigrants who already stay and work in the country. The law is also viewed as ineffective as the dynamics of immigration flows are far from being curbed. To a large extent this results from the fact that the law acts against the Greek tradition of openness to travellers and traders (Lazaridis 1995: 8). Aristotle observed, in his *Politics,* that laws which are not rooted in tradition and customs are ineffective. Of no less importance is the fact that such laws operate against the vital interests of those citizens who make profit out of the employment of the foreign undocumented workers.

The situation is complex. On the one hand, there is still demand for cheap labour, basically provided by foreign workers. On the other hand, the ruling principle with regard to work permits holds that 'any citizen of a non-EC country entering Greece with the intention of working as an employee must have obtained prior approval, which is granted by the Ministry of Foreign Affairs, providing the job cannot be done by a Greek or EU member-country citizen' (Gulbenkian and Badoux 1993: 75). In practice, this means that *legal* mass labour migration from outside the EU into Greece is impossible.

Seemingly, general rules and conditions for admitting foreign workers do not regulate real labour immigration. This results in the build-up of a huge bulk of illegal immigrants which, in 1993, amounted to some 300,000 persons

(Petrinioti 1993: 18) or according to another source in 1992 numbered almost 280,000 persons (Lianos, Sarris and Katseli 1996: 452). This is an obvious outcome of the situation of high demand for cheap labour accompanied by legal principles which prohibit foreign labour recruitment. In fact, the presence of the undocumented in Greece is not so much due to the imperfect monitoring system at the border crossing; it results from the fact that their presence brings profit to the private sector of the Greek economy. Foreign illegal workers add to the development of the Greek parallel economy which accounts for some 30 per cent of the Greek GDP (Pavlopoulos 1987). Furthermore, in spite of increasing unemployment there is a large number of unskilled jobs not filled by Greek workers whose job aspirations and wages expectations have also increased (Lazaridis 1996: 339). To a certain extent the matching of supply and demand of labour operates through illegal foreign labour recruitment since illegal migrants act as a substitute for Greek workers, particularly in the unskilled labour market. Therefore, the mechanisms of the labour market can prevail over legal and institutional restrictions implemented to curb illegal immigration, especially if the restrictions are alien to local traditions.

The situation described is further complicated by Greek membership in the European Union. The present stance of the EU towards labour immigration is generally unfavourable, and the presence of a huge bulk of illegal economic migrants in Greece is inconsistent with the Union immigration policy. All these cause Greece to manoeuvre, more or less deliberately, between the *Scylla* of losing the profit provided by illegal labour migration, and *Charybdis* of losing its credibility among the EU countries. It may be one reason for the lack of an explicit, labour-importing immigration policy on the one hand, and toleration of the undocumented workers on the other. The other, no less important reason, is that the country has learned a lesson provided by former labour-importing Western European countries which, at present, face the consequences of their former policy. It thus seems that Greece, while accepting the present advantages of the situation, tries to avoid its future costs and consequences. In contrast to Italy and Spain, no attempt was made in Greece to change the status of illegal immigrants by legalisation regulations, and there are numerous documented cases of illegal immigrants having been deported or expelled from the country.

It may be said that those who pay the highest price are the illegal migrants themselves, being underpaid, excluded from any security and pension systems, and existing on the margins of the host society. Even those 'illegals' who come for short-term, taking advantage of the high level of informality in Greek economy in their search for better wages, do suffer being deprived of welfare provisions in Greece.

There are some advantages and disadvantages of undocumented worker 'status' which need to be explained. The apparent advantage of being undocumented is tax avoidance and being more competitive on the labour market. In numerous cases, the cheaper undocumented worker will be able to find a job more easily than the indigenous worker. This is the reason why some Greek trade unionists propose a legalisation of Polish migrants' stay and labour. They hope that as legal foreign workers (and thus not as cheap as they are now) the Poles would be less competitive vis-a-vis the domestic labour force - one piece of research has shown that adjusted wages for illegal immigrants can be 60 per cent lower than the corresponding Greek wage (Lianos et al., 1996: 465). The advantage of tax avoidance and being more competitive is balanced by certain disadvantages, namely: lack of social insurance and benefits (however, as a rule construction firm owners do pay health insurance for their Polish undocumented workers), exclusion from pension systems, and above all the ever-present danger of expulsion. It is also true that as clandestine migrants they may fall prey to exploitative Greek employers. There are a number of ways in which the latter may cheat their 'illegal' employees, such as: lowering of pre-arranged rates of work, paying by post-dated cheque, not paying at all. In such cases, however, all clandestine workers, may be able to claim their rights as victims despite their 'undocumented status'. This is due to the fact that Greece has signed several conventions which provide for immigrants' protection; also according to the Greek Constitution of 1975 every person who lives in Greece is entitled to full protection. This, unfortunately, is not implemented.

As the above shows, the actual situation of the Polish undocumented is quite complex; being technically illegal these migrants are tolerated by the state, although at an arguably exploitative level. They are also deprived of welfare state returns. However, what many of them actually look for is legalisation of their stay in the country, not so much as permanent settlers and recipients of welfare protection, but as legal migrant workers not subject to expulsion. The Polish government has also been interested in a bilateral agreement which would formulate principles of legal recruitment of Polish workers wishing to take up jobs in Greece. Prospects for such an agreement are, however, neither immediate nor encouraging. For the time being, the only bilateral agreements aimed at setting up rules and regulating legal employment of Polish citizens have been signed with the following countries: Germany

(1990), Belgium (1990), France (1990, 1992), Switzerland (1993), Ukraine (1994), and Lithuania (1994). They guarantee legal access to the labour market for Polish citizens, specify the character of employment and the category of employee, the maximum legal duration of employment, and, in some cases, the annual quotas accepted. The legal solution adopted in these countries provides legal status for seasonal, and other, jobs, and, in the case of the seasonal worker system, it gives initiative to the employer. It might well be followed by Greece arriving at an effective means of legalisation, at minimum social cost, to cover the present illegal employment - the more so as the existing law allows for short-term work permits for foreign workers. It stipulates that work permits may be granted for a specific time period and a specific job, in a specific area, and with a specific employer (Gulbenkian and Badoux 1993: 76). Implementing this would solve the present problem of the huge bulk of the undocumented foreign workers, among them the Poles. For the time being, however, the Polish undocumented, who on the level of individual experiences and interests may be viewed as contact builders between the two societies, may be perceived as law violators.

4. The context of European unification

Economic migration from Poland to Greece takes place at a time when the process of the unification of Western and Southern European countries is being finalised. The restriction on migration, implemented by the European Union, may interfere with the process. Indeed, present policies towards intensified economic migrations within and into Europe may be viewed as a challenge to the ongoing unification process. It is ironic that integration of one part of Europe also means, and leads to *protection against* the inflow of potential economic and other migrants from the other part of the continent and elsewhere.

The unification process is being carried out on two platforms, economic and political, aiming both at gradual integration of national economies, and at construction of a 'Europe of citizens' free from physical borders. This began in the 1950s and was initiated by France, Germany, the Benelux countries, and Italy. In its first stage it was prepared by the Treaty of Rome in 1965. The next stage was the Single European Act, signed by the EU member states in 1986, which set up the principles and time schedule for further political and economic integration (Gulbenkian and Badoux 1993: 3). Another, parallel step forward towards unification was taken the year before (1985) in Schengen where an agreement was signed by the Benelux countries, France, and Germany, later joined by Spain, Portugal, Italy, and Greece. This entrusted the signatory states with the task of establishing an area within which physical borders would be eliminated.[5] The Schengen Agreement of 1990 decisively finalised the long process of creating a 'Europe of citizens' where freedom of movement for persons, services, and capital has been secured (Lary 1993: 4).

This includes only a part of Europe; meanwhile, there have appeared new candidates to this 'Europe of citizens' - the countries freed from the Soviet 'commonwealth' and their citizens anxious to match their living standards with that available in the EU. The dramatic changes in 1989 and soon after, followed by democratisation taking place in the Central and Eastern European countries, situated the ongoing process set out in the 1950s into an entirely different setting. In other words, in the course of the successful Western Europe unification, a rather unexpected event occurred which changed 'the European scene' dramatically, creating a new context for the finalisation of the unification process. European countries of the EU have faced, and feared, the inflow of the released, impoverished masses from Central and Eastern Europe. Under such circumstances unification could easily slip into a 'Fortress Europe' building process, as a response to the threat of any mass immigrations not only those coming from the Central and Eastern European countries. The gradual elimination of inner borders between the EU member countries is accompanied by growing reinforcement and protection of the external borders, and by implementation of ever more restrictive immigration policies. In the situation where, for the time being, a vast part of Europe does not take part in the process, this may be viewed as the creation of a 'Western Europe Fortress'.

Talks are being held by some of the Central and Eastern European states and the EU on the possibilities, conditions, and timetable for the former to join the European Union. At the same time many individuals from these states, without waiting for state-level agreements, set out in search of better pay and/or living standards. The spontaneous and unwelcome, clandestine economic migration from the former Eastern bloc countries further compels the EU to introduce tougher measures against all kinds and nationalities of undocumented migrants, and thus to strengthen the already built 'fortress'. The other possible responses, which may be more effective, would be: working out system(s) based on bilateral agreements of legal, short-term employment of presently clandestine migrants; countering xenophobic attitudes towards economic migrants often seen as rivals and hence unwelcome (Jaakkola

1995);[6] and creating alternatives for economic migration, such as economic co-operation or free trade regions.[7] It may be that the time has come either for realisation of the plea and plans for a 'new international division of labour' put forward by labour-importing countries upon the closure of their borders in the mid-1970s, and/or for short-term legal employment of the undocumented from Central and Eastern European countries. For the time being, however, EU policy discourages further immigration from the South and the East. The measures implemented by the European Union to deal with East-West and South-West economic migrations are aimed at curbing or, at least reducing them. In the long run, the strategy might not be effective since it does not address the 'root' or fundamental causes of economic migrations, at present identified with the push factors of unwanted migration (Amersfoort 1996).

5. Conclusions

The economic migration of the Polish undocumented to Greece follows the rational model of East-West migration, rather than the Doomsday one - to use Robin Cohen's notions (Cohen 1991). The Polish illegals come to work in Greece because they find wages there attractive, and because there is demand for cheap labour. This migration continues because, for the time being, it is mutually beneficial. However, the rhetoric of exclusion may develop in Greece as it has elsewhere in Western Europe. Polish undocumented workers do not seek out welfare state returns in Greece but search for wages, saving for future investment and consumption back in Poland. This does not imply, however, that these migrants are entirely satisfied with their present 'undocumented status' in Greece. As mentioned previously illegal jobs have certain advantages perceived by those concerned, but at the same time the principal disadvantage of their present situation is perceived as being illegal migrants. The existing Greek law allows for short-term work permits for foreign workers, hence, at a minimum social cost, these migrants may be granted stay and work permits for a specific time period and on stipulated conditions. This certainly would strengthen social acceptance already experienced by the Poles in Greece. Now, they may be justifiably portrayed, concurrently, as contact builders, as Greek immigration law violators, and as a nuisance in the ongoing unification process.

References

Amersfoort van, H. (1996) 'Migration: the Limits of Governmental Control', *New Community* 22(2): 243-257.

Cieœlińska, B. (1995) 'The Poles in Italy - Images of the New Emigration', *Przegl'd Polonijny*, 3: 35-46.

Cohen, R. (1991) 'East-West and European migration in a global context', *New Community* 18(1):9-26.

Cross, M. (1996) 'Editorial', *New Community* 22(2): 197-200.

Cross, M. (1993) 'Migration, Employment and Social Change in the New Europe', in: R. King (ed.) *The New Geography of European Migrations*, Belhaven Press: London.

Dowty, A. (1987) *Closed Borders: The Contemporary Assault on Freedom of Movement*, Yale University Press: New Haven.

Fielding, A. (1993) 'Migrations, Institutions and Politics: the Evolution of European Migration Policies', in: R. King (ed.) *Mass Migration in Europe*, Belhaven Press: London.

Gulbenkian, P. and Badoux, T. (eds.) (1993) *Immigration Law and Business in Europe*, Chancery Law Publishing: London.

Jaakkola, M. (1995) 'Polarisation of Finns' Attitudes to Refugees and other Immigrants', a paper presented at the *ESA Conference*, Budapest.

Lary de, H. (1993) 'The Legal Basis and Practical Methods of Control of Migratory Movements in the Context of the EC after 1 January 1993', *OECD Madrid Conference*, material OECD/GD(93)19, OECD: Paris.

Lazaridis, G. (1996) 'Immigration into Greece: A Critical Evaluation of the Greek Immigration Policy', *New Community* 22(2): 335-348.

Lazaridis, G. and Wickens, E. (1995) 'Use the "other": Ethnic Minorities in the Greece', a paper presented at the *BSA Conference*, Leicester.

Lianos, T., Sarris, A. and Katseli, L. (1996) 'Illegal Immigration and Local Labour Markets: The Case of Northern Greece', *International Migration*, 34(3): 449-483.

Miller, M. and Denemark, R. (1993) *Migration and World Politics: A Critical Case for Theory and Policy*, Center for Migration Studies: New York.

Minichiello, V., Aroni, R., Timewell, E. and Alexander, L. (1991) *In-Depth Interviewing: Researching People*, Cheshire: Longman.

Nalewajko, M. (1997) 'New Polish Migration to Spain', in print in: *Migration and Society*, vol. 3, Polish Academy of Science: Warsaw.

Panoi, S. (1993) 'Immigration into Greece', *Kathimerini* 2 December.

Pavlopoulos, P. (1987), *Parallel Economy in Greece*, Athens.

Petrinioti, X. (1993) 'Immigration into Greece', *Odysseas*: Athens.

Portes, A. and Borocz, J. (1989) 'Contemporary Immigration: Theoretical Perspectives on its Determinants and Modes of Incorporation', *International Migration Review*, 23(3): 606-630.

Richmond, A. (1994) *Global Apartheid: Refugees, Racism, and the New World Order*, Oxford University Press: Toronto.

Romaniszyn, K. (1995) 'Economic Migration from Poland to Greece', a paper presented at the *ESA Conference*, Budapest.

Romaniszyn, K. (1996) 'The Invisible Community: Undocumented Polish Workers in Greece', *New Community*, 22(2): 321-333.

Rosoli, G. (1993) 'Italy: Emergent Immigration Policy', in: D. Kubat (ed.) *The Politics of Migration Policies. Settlement and Integration The First World into the 1990s*, Center for Migration Studies: New York.

Salt, J. (1989) 'A Comparative Overview of International Trends and Types, 1950-80', *International Migration Review* 23(3): 431-456.

Schutte, F, (1994) 'German Programmes for Training and Short-Term Employment Labourers from Central and Eastern European Countries', a paper presented at the *OECD Seminar*, Warsaw.

Simila, M. (1995) 'Minorities as Contact Builders between Nation States', a paper presented at the *ESA Conference*, Budapest.

Skotnicka-Illasiewicz, E. (ed.) (1992) *Dilemmas of European Identity*, Warsaw.

Stolcke, V. (1995) 'Talking Culture: New Boundaries, New Rhetorics of Exclusion in Europe', *Current Anthropology*, 36(1): 1-24.

Tapinos, G. (1994) 'Migration Policy of OECD Countries', a paper presented at the *OECD Seminar*, Warsaw.

Zamojski, J. (ed.) (1995) *Migracje i Spo³eczeństwo: Zbiór Studiów* (Migrations and Society: Collection of Studies), The Polish Academy of Science: Warsaw.

Zolberg, A. (1989) *Escape from Violence: Conflict and the Refugee Crisis in the Developing World*, Oxford University Press: New York.

Notes

[1] I learned about this practice from a person who makes these video films. Getting married in Athens became popular among the Polish undocumented from 1986 on. I elaborate on this phenomenon in a paper presented at the ESA Conference, Budapest, 1995.

[2] This number was estimated as of October 19, 1993 on which day I had access to these parochial documents gathered in the Roman Catholic Church in Athens to which Poles were given access.

[3] This is an interesting case for two reasons. Firstly, this name has its equivalent in the Polish language, *Miko³aj* which is apparently ignored by these parents. Secondly, they insist on registering into documents a diminutive version of the Greek name, i.e., the version they probably hear most often.

138 *Into the Margins*

4   A detailed report of the event was published by the Polish language weekly, '*Kurier Atenski*', issued in Athens by, and for the Polish undocumented. According to the report, the sum collected amounted to $2,200.
5   It followed the EC initiative of 1984, put forward at the Fontainebleau meeting and partly realised by the Franco-German agreement of Saarbrucken of 1985.
6   For example, a study on the attitude towards economic migration carried out in Finland shows that foreign workers, and even more so, economic migrants are less accepted categories of immigrants (see: M. Jaakkola 1995: 5). Addressing a similar problem, Skotnicka-Illasiewicz states that former, cold war period barriers have been replaced in Europe by barriers built on stereotypes and resentments resulting from unverified images of the world from 'outside the wall' (see: Skotnicka-Illasiewicz 1992: 20).
7   One such example from outside Europe is provided by the NAFTA agreement which, among other things, is intended to help the economic development of Mexico and thus to reduce its migration potential. An argument raised in favour of NAFTA - that it is 'better to have Mexican goods than Mexican undocumented' - applies to the present situation in Europe which is divided into affluent and poorer parts.

8 Racism and New Migration to Cyprus: The Racialisation of Migrant Workers

Nicos Trimikliniotis

Introduction: The context of new migration in Cyprus

This paper sets out to examine the processes of racialisation of temporary migrant or 'foreign'[1] labour in Cyprus, a country traditionally exporting migrants but recently transformed into one of hosting migrants. It considers policies and rights relating to migrant workers and examines discourses around migration found in the Greek Cypriot press and magazines. It also examines the role of employers and trade unions in the racialisation of migrant workers. It considers how conceptualisations of 'race' and racism, and their interrelation with class are useful in understanding and explaining the processes by which people are excluded, inferiorised and exploited.

Cyprus is the third largest island of the Mediterranean and is situated in the far eastern part of the sea, historically adjoining Europe, Asia and Africa. It became an independent Republic in 1960 following a turbulent history. In post colonial times, there was inter-communal strife and constant foreign intervention of one kind or another, until 1974 when a coup by the Greek junta and local para-fascists, the EOKA-B,[2] was followed by a Turkish invasion and the subsequent division of the island (Hitchens 1997; Attalides 1979). Turkey still occupies 34 per cent of the territory, whilst 200,000 Greek Cypriots remain refugees. The Turkish Cypriots inhabit the north of the island i.e. the occupied territories. Attempts to resolve the Cyprus problem have not been successful for over twenty years. Cypriot policy makers now hope that accession to the EU will be able to act as a catalyst in the effort to

140 *Into the Margins*

find a settlement (Kranidiotis 1993; Charalambous et al 1996; LSE and Hellenic Centre Conference 1996).

Cyprus has for years been a traditional exporter of migrants. As a former British Colony, many Cypriots migrated to the UK, as well as other destinations such as Australia, the United States, South Africa; in fact the number of Cypriots living abroad nears half the population of the island (Anthias 1992a). Cyprus has seen extensive economic development, from the time that the Greek junta coup and the Turkish invasion of 1974 left the society and economy devastated: an 18 per cent fall of the GNP between 1973 to 1975, a 30 per cent rise in unemployment, mass poverty and a loss of 37 per cent of the country's territory (PIO 1997b). Cyprus has been transformed into a society which acts as 'host' to immigrants, from different countries, who occupy a range of employment positions, from labourers, to professionals and entrepreneurs as well as retired persons.

Methodology

This paper examines Government policies and public discourses and debates and is not based on qualitative research. The sources it analyses are official statistics and publications, a range of other statistics such as those provided by trade unions and the media, and newspaper reports and articles. There is only limited literature available which includes some Planning Bureau Publications, the Reports by the Parliamentary Commissions on Human Rights and the Parliamentary Commissions on Employment and Social Insurance and some statistics provided in official publications of the Press and Information Office (PIO). Other than these and some trade union publications, the main source is newspapers and magazines. This paper draws mainly on press cuttings, which are content analysed and critically evaluated as well as statistical data. Some press cuttings have been collected by the researcher, whilst others are taken from archives of anything that has been published on the subject of migrant workers between 1995-97,[3] with emphasis given to the years 1996-97. From January 1996 to March 1997 there have been 189 articles/news reports that refer to migrant workers, racism or attitudes towards them[4] (See Appendix 1 for Political Orientation of the Cypriot Press). The Press is a valuable source to begin to research this area and provides insight into everyday discourse, at a popular level. The use of the press in analysing social and political events is long established (See for example Schlesinger and Elliot 1991a and 1991b).

Some statistical data on migrant workers is available but it is ridden with deficiencies. Numbers are disputed and contradictory and there may be a 'numbers game', whereby numbers are a key method of racialising groups, as shown later. Statistical information is incomplete, and statistics may be presented in different years, under different headings, refer to different time periods and adopt different definitions of the groups analysed.

The national problem and migration

Migrant workers arriving to Cyprus find a Cypriot population of about three quarters of a million. Prior to 1974 the population consisted of 78 per cent Greek Cypriots, 18 per cent Turkish Cypriots and smaller minorities (Maronites, Armenians, Latins and others) (PIO 1993). Today the actual size of the Turkish Cypriot population is disputed; Turkey, which occupies the northern part of the island, has been following a policy of colonisation and bringing in settlers. The population, currently residing in Cyprus is reported to be 735,900, of whom 623,000 are Greek Cypriots and 90,000 Turkish Cypriots (PIO 1997a).

The recent history of Cyprus has been marked by rapid economic development since 1974. The development of Cyprus has been structured by a number of 'external' factors such as the Turkish occupation of the north since 1974. This, by default, created the preconditions for rabid modernisation, in spite of the severe drop in the GDP during 1973-75 and the sharp rise in unemployment and mass poverty (PIO 1997a). Cheap labour was provided by the 200,000 Greek Cypriot refugees, who were forcibly expelled from the northern part and lived in refugee camps. This fact, together with a concerted effort by the government, political parties and trade unions, created the conditions for the kind and level of development that was subsequently experienced in Cyprus (Anthias and Ayres 1983; Christodoulou 1992; Panayiotopoulos 1995; 1996).[5]

It has been suggested that the level of growth led to a growth in the demand for labour, that exceeded the supply of labour from indigenous sources (Matsis and Charalambous 1993). The slow down in the growth of the economy in the 1990s in comparison to the late 1970s and 1980s,[6] together with the rise of inflation, was the basis for the abandoning of the restrictive labour policies practised up to 1990. In contrast with the restrictive policies, 1990 saw a radical change in government policy. For the first time migrant labour was allowed to enter on a much larger scale, to meet the labour shortage in those sectors of the economy that were no longer popular with Cypriots. Matsis and Charalambous explain the reversal of the policy on 'foreign' labour as a result of 'excessive demand pressures and the near full exploitation of the indigenous labour supply' (1993: 38). The same authors suggest that the policy to allow entry of migrant labour, is due to pressure from employers and the fear of inflation resulting from index linked wages. They suggest that 'the employment of foreign labour will eventually lead to a containment of wage increases' (1993: 42). Migrant workers primarily take up menial, low pay and low status jobs that Cypriots do not take; their occupational structure is similar to that of migrant labour in Europe in the 1950s and 1960s (Matsis and Charalambous 1993: 43).

Additionally there are international or global factors that have influenced the policy to open up the Cyprus labour market. These include regional changes, such as the collapse of Beirut as centre of the middle east, the collapse of the regimes of eastern Europe (with the resulting 'release' of investment in financial services) and the Gulf war. There has also been a world wide growth in tourism and migration flows. Global factors, in conjunction with the socio-economic orientation of the Cyprus Government are the main reasons for increasing migration to Cyprus. The whole history of Cyprus is affected by global and regional economic, political and social developments; thus the economic development of Cyprus is best understood in a global and regional perspective as shown by some writers (Christodoulou 1992; Wilson 1994).

Migrant workers: new migration trends to Cyprus

From the information given last October to trade unions and employers, for the first nine months of 1996 by the Ministry of Labour[7] the figures show 27,500 documented migrant workers: 10,500 workers are occupied in sectors that require 'approval' by the Ministry of Labour and 17,000 in sectors not requiring such reference.

The official figure of migrant workers, as a percentage of the active work force, was 2-2.5 per cent in 1990 and rose to 5.5 per cent by 1993 (Planning Bureau 1993). If we look at the trend of employment of migrant workers, with the exception of 1992-93 (Gulf war), we see a steady rise from the time the policy changed and allowed 'foreign' workers to be employed in 1990. There may be a distortion of the picture if one considers that some figures exclude

Greeks from the Greek Republic with the exception of 1994 (See Table 7). However, the total number of migrant workers varies in different estimates (See Table 7). The total figures also do not include undocumented workers, who are roughly estimated to be about 10,000. This figure is often quoted by newspapers, the Ministry and the trade unions and employers and is the figure given by the Report of the Employment and Social Insurance Parliamentary Commission (House of Representatives 1997a). Others estimate the total number of migrant workers to be about 45,000 (*I Alitheia* 18.1.97); and yet others estimate it at 36,000 (*I Simerini* 18.1.97). The official estimate is roughly around 35,000 (House of Representatives 1997a). If we take the mean as 40 thousand, then today we can estimate migrant workers as 13.3 per cent of the economically active population.[8]

An analysis of the data reveals some interesting facts about emerging trends (All Tables 1-7 are in the Appendix section). Firstly, from those workers that do not require reference or approval by the Ministry of Labour, the single largest occupational group are domestic helpers or maids (6200), followed by managers (3700), in off shore companies and then followed by 'artists' and 'dancers' (Table 4). Also there are about 3500 Greeks and 2000 migrants married to Cypriot women, referred to as 'foreigners' (αλλοδαποι) The latter category is an anomaly discussed later. About one third of all Greeks are occupied in the service sector and one fourth in managerial or qualified and technical work (Table 6).

The statistics providing ethnic/national and occupational breakdowns necessary, are somewhat dated (for the year 1994 see PEO 1996, Table 6) and do not account for undocumented workers. On the basis of the above statistics, apart from 3500 Greeks (Table 4), migrants come from four regions: from eastern Europe (about 6000), from south eastern Asia (4680), from the middle east (about 3000), and northern/central Europe/ USA (about 2500) (See Table 6).

The vast majority of Eastern Europeans are concentrated in production/industry, services, farming and 'artists/dancers'; jobs that are at the lower end of the market in terms of pay and status. With the exception of the Lebanese and to a lesser extent the Jordanians, who include a large proportion of managers/qualified and technicians (over 50% and just under 40% respectively), workers from the other two middle eastern countries, Syria and Egypt, are concentrated in production, services and farming. South eastern Asians are concentrated in services, farming and production. Two thirds of all

Sri Lankans and Filipinos are in services (mainly maids); whilst the rest are concentrated in farming and production.

The feminisation of entire sectors of the labour market is of particular significance. Domestic helpers/assistants consist entirely of Asian, and primarily Filipino women, reported as being over 6,000 (see Table 4) and attracting much media 'attention', as shown later, whilst cleaners are again mainly Asian women, from Sri Lanka and the Philippines (Table 4). Other sectors, such as building and construction, are male dominated (Syria, Egypt). There are both men and women in low paid jobs in production and services; however there are industries with sectors that consist entirely of men or entirely of women.[9] Even where there are both men and women in a particular sector, a sexual division of labour may be found, as well as wage differentials. In the hotel industry for example many employers may employ women in what they consider 'feminine' jobs (cleaners, room attendees etc.) and men in more 'male' jobs (such as bar work, waiters, kitchen etc.) though this is not always the case.

A sector made up entirely of women is the 'sex industry' and is found under the classifications of 'artists', 'dancers' and 'musicians', mainly working in 'clubs' and cabarets. The 'entrepreneurs' of this 'industry' (i.e. pimps) are mainly Cypriots. The number (1,100 Table 4) may be an underestimate as the 'sex industry' also includes other women who are officially 'tourists' and in other sectors and do not appear in the statistics. The regime governing female 'artists' (καλιτεχιδες) is strict, as they can only stay for 6 months and then they must stay abroad for 6 months with a right to be re-employed in Cyprus (*I Simerini* 2.3.97).

Prior to the collapse of the Eastern European regimes the 'artists and musicians' sector was dominated by Filipino and Thailand women; in 1994 the figures show 228 and 88 respectively (Table 6) but with the collapse of these regimes, the sector is now dominated by eastern Europeans: Romanians 482; Bulgarians 163; Russian 52[10] in 1994. (Table 6) The numbers vary significantly, as these women are constantly being moved around in a sector that operates at the fringes of the law. The sector attracts media attention from time to time, but not as much as 'domestic helpers'. Interestingly one newspaper report had the headline 'Cyprus comes first in the world in [female] domestic helpers and [female] artists' (*O Phileleftheros* 15.4.94). More recently there has been talk of areas in Limassol and Paphos being transformed into 'ghettos of legal and illegal workers' where 'prostitution and drug usage and crime are flourishing' (*O Phileleftheros* 4.10.96). However one has to be cautious of these linkages, as will be shown further on in this paper.

A closer examination of the various sectors employing migrant workers requires a consideration of the legal regime and rights enjoyed by these communities. The question of rights is intrinsically connected with citizenship laws and this will be next looked at.

Government policy, citizenship and the rights of migrant workers

The policies and practices governing migrant workers from the moment of entry, their work conditions and their legal and social rights, are set out in the agreement of the Government, the employers organisations (OEV and KEVE)[11] and trade unions (PEO, SEK, DEOK and some sectional unions),[12] known as the 'tri-partite system'. Prior to 1990, Government policy towards migration to Cyprus was restrictive, only allowing entrepreneurial positions and certain highly skilled managerial or technical posts to be filled by non-Cypriots. Work permits to 'foreigners' were granted only in exceptional circumstances and wherever there were no Cypriots with the relevant qualifications.

The policy change, allowing the entry of migrant workers, was seen as a necessary step in resolving the labour shortage. Migrant workers were to be granted the same employment terms and all other rights enjoyed by Cypriot workers, based on existing collective agreements and social security schemes. One relevant study, by the Planning Bureau, however refers to 'taking into account the element of temporality as well as other factors' (Planning Bureau 1989: 3). This allows flexibility in the interpretation of the policy, and may allow employers to evade the express condition that states that pay terms will be the same as with Cypriot employees (1989: 5). Furthermore the same study recognises that there are 'no efficient mechanisms to monitor this' (Planning Bureau 1989: 4). This problem is also recognised in the recent Report of the Parliamentary Commissions on Employment and Social Insurance (House of Representatives 1997a) and on Human Rights, (House of Representatives 1997b).[13] With the change of policy in 1990, the criteria for granting permits were extended and a procedure was outlined for employers to recruit staff from abroad, (Planning Bureau 1989). For administrative purposes, there are two categories of 'foreign' workers: those employed in sectors which require reference[14] (from the Ministry of Labour) and those employed in sectors that do not. The sectors are described in Tables 3 and 4.

A precondition for granting a permit is that the specific need by the employer cannot be covered by local workers. The period of stay was originally put at 2 years but was subsequently extended to 4 years (Matsis and Charalambous 1993:42-43). Different sectors have different criteria for stay periods. Musicians and singers in hotels can stay for 2 years, then they must stay abroad for another 3 months before being employed in Cyprus again; seasonal farming workers can only be employed for 3 months, providing they have obtained a reference from the Ministry of Labour.

There are two main ways that migration flows are regulated. One is the regulation of the types of jobs that may be taken by migrant workers. The Ministry of Labour grants permits to employers of such workers. This is based on 'controlling' employers, rather than the employees. The second is a direct control on migrant workers and this comes under the jurisdiction of the Immigration Department and the Police.[15] The presence of migrants in Cyprus is regulated by the **On Aliens and Migration Law** which, inter alia, empowers the authorities to deport migrants without the relevant documentation as 'illegal immigrants'. From the 1st of January 1997, this law was amended to become harsher against those who employ undocumented workers, providing up to 5 years imprisonment or Cy£5000 fine (or both). The court also has discretion to prohibit the employment of foreign workers by such an employer (PIO Press Release 30.12.96).

Originally, trade unions had their misgivings about the change of policy, fearing that employers would use migrant workers to undercut wages and unions bargaining power (See PEO 1995). However, they eventually agreed in the tri-partite meeting which set out the terms of employment and special conditions.[16]

The problems with government policies

It was agreed in the tripartite agreement that migrant workers would enjoy the same employment rights as Cypriots. However there were a number of problems with the way this was conceived. There is a lack of a proper legislative framework to deal with the possible problems, and a lot of the changes seem to have been rushed through on an ad hoc basis, to a great extent as a result of media and at times populist pressure. The Reports by the

Parliamentary Commissions on Employment and Social Insurance (House of Representatives 1997a) and the Parliamentary Commission on Human Rights (House of Representatives 1997b) recognise that legislation is anachronistic and must be reviewed.[17] The Report by the Employment and Social Insurance Commission has as a title precisely this issue: 'The problems that are created as a result of the absence of a relevant legal framework which must regulate their presence in our country'. The two reports put into perspective, from the point of view of the policy makers, a number of problems with government and other administrative policies on migrant workers and they indicate the need for debate on the subject and a concern about the rights of migrants.

There has been a tightening of regulation regarding 'agents',[18] which has been fuelled by press reports about 'agents', who allegedly profit, at the expense of the desperation of workers to emigrate. Networks of 'agents' make a 'profit' by getting massive 'fees' from migrants willing to pay to find a way out of the poverty and deprivation in their own countries. Until recently there was no legal protection against this (Protopapas 1996). The new 'draconian' laws[19] are flawed, however, because it is difficult for migrant workers to change employer and occupation. This may act as a disincentive on the part of migrant workers to report any employer malpractice and harsh conditions, as they may deported if the employer is found guilty of any such practice.

There is no mechanism for monitoring or enforcing the tri-partite agreement, noted as far back as 1989 by the Planning Bureau (1989). The institutional responsibility on monitoring whether the criteria and conditions of permit are met by employers lies with the Immigration Department, but in practice are carried out by the Ministry of Labour (House of Representatives 1997a). This raises questions of accountability and confusion.

The emphasis of the same Report (House of Representatives 1997a) however, in line with other public discourse, is dominated by the question of how to minimise the presence of migrant workers, and in particular undocumented workers.[20] In its conclusion the Report places emphasis again on the one hand, on combating 'illegal Immigration' and, on the other, it 'recognises the problems of inclusion in the Cypriot Society, as well as their needs such as practising their own customs, cultural, religions etc. that derive from their culture and their country of origin' (1997a: 11). It recommends that information is sought from abroad on the ways in which to deal with problems from European countries which have more experience in dealing with theses issues (1997a: 11-12).

Furthermore, there are problems to do with administration and law enforcement in Cyprus.[21] Part of this is due to inadequate staffing and training. The Report of the Parliamentary Commission on Employment and Social Insurance, (House of Representatives 1997a) notes the 'inadequacy of staffing' and that the 'control is not that which is expected'. The state bureaucracy, in general, is not very organised, but also its clientelist tendencies render it prone to arbitrary discretion in the enforcement of rules. Over and above this there seems to be an 'administrative laxity' by the administrators when it comes to enforcement of the agreement in controlling employment and protecting wages (Matsis and Charalambous 1993). Even the Interior Minister has admitted, before a Parliamentary Committee, that migrant workers are badly exploited and Cyprus is exposed to the international community as a result (*O Phileleftheros* 4.10.96). Matsis and Charalambous (1993: 46) note that Government policy is not conducive to the declared policy goals as set out in its strategic Development Plan for technological up-grading and controlling tourism development.

Moreover there have been reports, claiming reliable 'inside' sources, of allegations about immigration officers who have 'illegal give and takes with employers or are importing illegal aliens'. These have recently led to sweeping changes in the Immigration Department (*Haravyi* 7.2.97). Reports of the repression of clandestine migrant labour appear regularly in the press. During 1996 the Head of the Police revealed that there were 1500 'recent' deportations of undocumented workers and 150 employers who were before the courts in connection with this (*O Phileleftheros* 4.10.96), though we cannot deduce what period this covers. A press conference, given by the Interior Minister, recalled that there have been a total of 5,000 deportations, presumably referring to all deportations since 1990 (*O Phileleftheros* 7.2.97).

Citizenship rights

A comprehensive study of the rights and the position of migrant workers ought to involve an examination of the procedures of entry.[22] The laws regarding Citizenship, as set out by the 1960 Constitution[23] and the Citizenship Acts are extremely narrow in scope, not allowing citizenship, as a matter of right, to be extended on grounds other than those provided by blood or marriage. Women who are foreign nationals married to Cypriot men, after one year of marriage become 'denizens', not full citizens but second class citizens or 'semi-citizens', and may apply for citizenship. However, their children are entitled to citizenship.[24] Foreign men, on the other hand, who marry Cypriot women can only become citizens after five years of stay (*On Citizenship Law 1967* as amended in 1972 and 1983). There is a proposal by AKEL to amend the law to bring about equality between the sexes.[25] For non-Cypriot nationals working in Cyprus, a ten year stay period is required before they can *apply* for citizenship; even then it is not granted by right, but is a prerogative of the Council of Ministers. Dual citizenship is allowed in Cyprus but that is not much use when it comes to acquiring citizenship rights in the Republic.

Cypriot policy makers are very reluctant to grant citizenship to migrant workers, as they are seen as 'temporary' and part of 'a transitional phase'. The fact that the Cyprus problem remains unresolved and is considered to be a 'national priority' makes Greek Cypriot policy makers reluctant to alter the demography of 'the population' by granting citizenship rights to non-Cypriot origin people. The Turkish policy of settlement and colonisation of the occupied territories makes Greek Cypriots ultra cautious when it comes to altering citizenship laws.

None of the major political parties or political organisations is calling for the granting of citizenship rights to migrant workers.[26] Party opinions range from the 'pragmatic' viewpoint, which views migrant workers as a temporary and transient reality, to believing that they should never have been there in the first place. The Cyprus problem is a partial explanation for the attitudes of political parties. Two additional factors need to be considered; the role of the state and its policy on migrants and the question of racism, as an ideology, but also as a structure in Cyprus. With the exception of the two very recent Parliamentary Reports referred to above, there has been little serious effort by policy makers of the main political parties to enhance the rights of migrants. Indeed it was the policy, right from the start of the change of policy on granting permits, that 'foreign' labour would be a temporary phenomenon, (Planning Bureau 1989). Enhancing migrants' rights might be seen as encouraging them to stay longer.

The Parliamentary Commissions Reports refer to ways of enhancing the rights of migrant workers. In particular, the Report by the Human Rights Commission is very critical of the existence of racism and xenophobia in Cyprus. This calls for measures, including legal responses, to the question (1997b). However the Report by the Employment and Social Insurance Commission, whilst referring to the need to enhance migrant rights, also contains racial stereotypes and construes the presence of migrant workers as a problem. For example it refers to 'the negative aspects of employing

150 *Into the Margins*

foreigners' such as 'marriages of convenience to ensure presence', 'committing crimes', 'inadequate raising up of children', 'xenophobia and racism' (even racism seems to blamed on migrant workers themselves) and 'extra-marital affairs' (1997a: 7).

Debates and discourses on migration: media amplification

The role of the media in the racialisation of groups in society cannot be overstated, as it is by and large via the media that representations of collectivities are made and their role in the shaping of attitudes and opinion is crucial. The media, which involves different communication networks, has the power to shape attitudes, as the classic study by Stuart Hall and his colleagues (1978) on mugging and media amplification has shown. The Glasgow Media group has shown the existence of selective representation, and therefore distortion of news, through the ability to decide what 'news' is and what is not. Chomsky's 'manufacture of consent', (Peck 1988), as well as other works, has shown how US policy goals outweigh any consideration of objectivity and fairness in the flow of information, for example. If we accept these arguments then we need to consider the role of the media in Cyprus.

The following section involves a discourse analysis from the content of the 189 press reports and articles, which referred to migrant workers, between 1996 to March 1997.[27] This involved following through the headlines and content of the press during this period and looking at the way in which migrant workers are dealt with.

Replaying the 'numbers game' and racialisation through representation

Moore (1975), writing about Britain, spoke of a pernicious 'numbers game' whereby migrants were constructed and stigmatised as a 'problem'. Migrants thus become **the problem** in the minds of the media and in the eyes of the readers. The 'numbers game', though presented in the guise of ensuring 'good race relations', in fact accentuates racism. The preoccupation with figures constructs 'migrants as a problem', and includes 'discussions' on the 'optimal number', and how to control the numbers of 'these rampant people'. The term 'numbers game', as used here, illustrates how the debate around the number of migrants in Cyprus contributes to the racialisation of migrants as they are presented as a problem for society.

The 'numbers game' is being replayed in Cyprus today. Out of the 189 reports/ articles analysed only 18 did not refer or respond to the question that there are 'too many foreigners', either as undocumented immigrants or as documented workers.[28] The language of the headlines is indicative: 'We are swamped by foreigners' from the right wing daily newspaper *O Agon* (18.9.96).[29] The more liberal establishment and most popular daily *O Phileleftheros* follows the same approach: '50000 Foreign workers- when Cypriot are unemployed' (1.9.96); 'Flood by foreign workers' (20.10.96); 'Illegal immigrants are a plague' (26.10.96); '..in a dangerous zone' (20.12.96); '..a headache' (25.12.96); 'The illegal workers are invisible' (7.2.97) '.. incurable cancer' (4.3.97). The extreme Right-wing *I Machi* refers to illegal workers as 'a plague' (19.1.97). *Ergatiko Vima*, the newspaper of PEO, the Left wing trade union adopts a more cautious approach but has used an alarmist language: 'Foreigners, everywhere foreign workers' (8.9.93) (See Appendix I for Political Orientation of Press).

These are but a few headlines, as all papers seem to take a similar alarmist approach. Out of the 15 reports which were more 'sympathetic' to migrant workers articles/reports, 7 still considered that this number should be restricted (*O Phileleftheros* 1.10.96; 3.10.96; 14.10.96; 24.10.96; 31.12.96; 1.1.97; *Haravyi* 1.12.96). *Haravyi*, the newspaper of AKEL (Progressive Party of Working People) seems more cautious in using such headlines, due to the Left wing and working class/internationalist ideology it claims to promote, and takes up cases of super-exploitation or oppression, but the difference seems at times to be of style rather than substance (See *Haravyi* 4.20.96; 25.10.96; 1.12.96; 5.12.96; 1.3.97). Neolea, which is the youth supplement in Haravyi, and is the organ of the General Council of EDON (United Democratic Youth Organisation), is the most sympathetic newspaper to migrant workers.

It is paradoxical that many Cypriots are, and have been, subject to this same treatment abroad. Cypriots in fact, together with other ethnic minorities such as Hungarians suffer discrimination (Daniel 1968). More recent studies again reveal a pattern of discrimination and racism directed against Cypriots in Britain, albeit in an uneven and more subtle manner depending on the class and gender position of the people examined (Anthias 1992a). In the way that Italians do not seem to have learned from the experience of racism, faced by Italians who emigrated abroad, in their treatment of migrant communities to Italy (Vasta 1983), so Cypriots seem not to have learned from racism many Cypriots have experienced abroad.

In the Cyprus context the 'numbers game' is instrumental in orchestrating 'moral panics' in the classic way, via 'media amplification' (Hall et al 1978). 'Mugging' was coined and connected to black people in Britain as if there is somehow a 'natural' link. The rising numbers of 'illegal foreign workers' in Cyprus has been connected to the rise in crime rates, (see House of Representatives 1997a). The media is ignoring the pouring in of Russian investment and the rise in the drug trade. Hall et al (1978) pointed out that the construction of 'mugging' in the 1970s 'can only be understood in terms of the way society -more especially the ruling-class alliances, the state apparatuses and the media - responded to a deepening economic, political and social crisis'. In a similar way there is a scapegoating of migrants with regard to the rising crime rate in Cyprus. The connection between migrants and crime is a recurring theme in official Reports and the media. Sometimes pictures of arrested people appear next to reports on migrant workers (*O Phileleftheros* 4.2.97). They are blamed for a rise in crime, violence and drugs (see *O Phileleftheros* 24.4.96; 1.1.97; 6.2.97; *I Simerini*; *To Periodiko* 29.11.96), as well as for 'social problems' such as marriages of convenience (*O Phileleftheros* 21.1.97), divorce and illegitimate children (*O Phileleftheros* 6.2.97).

In Cyprus, the most common explanations for arguing against migration are either that Cyprus is 'too small' and it is justifiable to feel the need to 'protect' its 'national culture and heritage'; or more authoritatively, that it is a semi-occupied and threatened country and its national survival needs to be ensured by all means necessary (*O Phileleftheros* 20.11.97). The alleged 'protection of national culture and heritage' from 'alien cultures' of migrant workers, as claimed in Cyprus, is part of nationalist discourse as Balibar (1991) has shown. Hence a SEK leader (the Right wing trade union) called for the withdrawal of all working permits given to temporary migrant workers when their contracts expire, unless they were of Greek origin (*O Phileleftheros* 28.7.96). The dominant model is not one of 'assimilation' or 'integration' of these workers; it is a 'host-immigrant' model whereby the 13-15 per cent of temporary workers are considered a threat to the fabric of society as a whole.

Kitromilides' (1979) observation of what he branded as a 'dialectic of intolerance', partly as a historic legacy of colonialism and structured around the institutional framework of Cypriot political life, also finds expression in 'ethnic' intolerance today. This may also be an indictment of the lack of a strong 'public opinion' and debate in a 'small society', where education is more concerned with technical or professional qualifications, rather than the development of critical faculties. However, it cannot be assumed for certain that the outcome of any debate would necessarily lead to the concern with the rights of migrants, as the supposedly more 'open' debates in western Europe illustrate (see the debates on racism and anti-racism in France and Europe, Anthias and Yuval-Davis 1992; Solomos and Wrench 1993, Solomos and Back 1995; Lloyd 1994).

An unsavoury connection in some report is made between migrant workers and disease, crisis, and dirt. Headlines such as 'Foreign workers are a real cancer' (*I Simerini* 19.10.96) appear or reports may quote the Interior Minister remarks: 'Foreign workers are an unsalvageable cancer' (*O Philelephtheros* 4.3.97). There are references to the undocumented workers as 'a gangrene' (*I Alitheia* 4.3.97), as well as 'plague'; 'headache', as shown above. A favoured connection, since the rise in unemployment in Cyprus from 1.8 per cent in 1990 to over 3,0 per cent in 1996 (PEO 1996), is that of employment and the numbers of migrant workers: 'Working people victims of employment of foreigners - mass dismissals' (*I Simerini* 1.3.97); or 'Unacceptable: Hundreds of Cypriots dismissed as foreigners are employed' (*Haravyi* 1.3.97). Structural or other causes of unemployment are ignored. The scapegoating of migrant workers is in fact a regular feature in the media and this involves connecting them to all sorts of social evils, as *Neolea*, (4.10.96) in an article critical of the media coverage on the subject, pointed out.

The social Welfare Department, in reply to questions by journalists, had 'expressed concern' about some 'social problems resulting from the presence foreign workers' such as marriages of convenience. The spokesperson speaks of 'suffering of under-age children as a result' as well as 'affairs mainly by Cypriot men with female workers' many of which lead to 'the break up of marriages' (*Ergatiko Vima* 8.9.93). These were more or less repeated in the Parliamentary Commission Report (1997a). However, one has to look specifically at the racialisation of women workers, since the process is gendered.

Gendered and racialised labour market: the racialisation of domestic workers

The headline in the most popular but 'serious' newspaper is revealing: 'Instead of every house and a Castle, Every House and an Asian Woman' (O

Phileleftheros 14.2.97). This is paraphrasing the well known phrase by the veteran leader of EDEK,[30] who was for years advocating that 'every house [be] a castle' in the face of Turkish expansionism. The report was mocking the fact that many Cypriots today, to gain 'prestige' and status, have recruited Asian women as maids. Asian women have become the stereotype of domestic workers/servants and are seen as a 'necessity' for every household that can afford them. In fact the term 'Asian woman' (Ασιατισσα) is used in many instances interchangeably with Filipino woman (Φιλιππινζα) or Sri Lankan woman (Σριλανκεζα). A common phrase used in popular discourse is: 'What do you think I am? Your Asian/Filipino woman?'

The expression 'I work like a "black"' (μαυρος), with its racist connotation, was used before the wave of new migration, but has now reached wider application in popular discourse and found in casual talk among people. It is also used as a term of abuse against migrant workers. As one migrant worker himself vividly illustrated in the English speaking newspaper *Cyprus Weekly* (30.9-6.10.97): '... I cannot sit on my own balcony without getting verbal abuse from Cypriot people, who call me "mavro" or shout other bad words...'.[31]

Colour is only one of the signifiers of racism, not exclusive or necessarily the most important. It has been suggested that darker people are more **likely** to be the target of racism. Regarding Cyprus one may crudely suggest that people from different geographical areas are concentrated in different occupations, with 'whites' (northern/ central Europeans/ Americans) concentrated in more office type works, with a very large number as managers. 'Black' people (northern Africa/Arabs, and south east Asians, with the exception of Lebanese and Jordanians), on the other hand, are more likely to be concentrated in manual jobs. However this is a crude and at times misleading picture: there is an anomaly with east Europeans, who, depending on their class position of course, generally occupy jobs at the lower end of the market. This is also the case for the Lebanese and to a lesser extent Jordanian migrants. Therefore, we can argue that racism cannot be reduced to a phenotypic prejudice solely based on colour, without wanting in any way to underestimate the historical and systematic racism faced by black people. (Gilroy 1987; Miles 1989; Anthias and Yuval-Davis 1992: 132-140.)

As for the gender dimension, there is a clear division of labour based on racial background: eastern European (white) women are the first preference for the sex industry (prostitution and 'artists'/ 'dancers'), with some continuity with the stereotype of the 'exotic' Asian women in some clubs. Asian women are preferred for home care and 'caring jobs', perhaps linked to some stereotype notion of the 'black (or dark) maid'. The cultural basis for the position of the Asian maid was found in the category the 'kori' in traditional society, where the woman, daughter and wife, 'served' the man. This operated together with class, as lower class women were the cleaners and maids in the houses of the rich (αρχουτικα).

In one report (*O Phileleftheros* 14.2.97) the case of a Sri Lankan woman is presented, who worked from 7:00 am until 10:00 p.m. every day except Sunday, serving four related families on very low pay. The example illustrates how racism and class and oppression work together and how the position of these individual needs to be seen within particular locations: race, class and gender (Anthias and Yuval Davis 1992). When the representative of the trade union SEK (Right wing) was asked to comment on this, he spoke of how revealing this case is 'in denying three Cypriot cleaners of work'! (sic).

The antipathy of the Cypriot press towards domestic workers and xenophobia against them was demonstrated when a group of organised Filipino workers were condemned by the newspapers in big headlines for their 'Self-proclamation as a Community' (*O Phileleftheros* 28.9.97 and *I Simerini* 30.9.97). One reader, through the readers columns, regretted the attempts to 'legitimise' the presence of Filipinos and blamed Cypriot housewives for wanting 'foreign' maids, warning of the possibility of 'racial discrimination and trouble' (*O Phileleftheros* 6.10.97). The matter was exposed by *Neolea* (4.10.97), the only newspaper which has consistently defended the rights of migrant workers and has spoken out against racism.[32] In this paper the writer of the article spoke of the treatment of migrant workers as 'symptoms of a wider malaise and misleading attitude, a racism that underlies this attitude and is gradually being established in Cyprus'.[33] One must consider the connection between gender and 'race', and racism and sexism, if one is to understand the position of migrant women labour and the kind of racialisation they face. We are reminded that 'racialized and ethnic minority women are concentrated in the most arduous and poorly paid work' (Anthias and Yuval-Davis 1992: 117) and the experience in Cyprus clearly shows this, if one looks at domestic workers and the way the media portrays them.[34]

A crucial dimension in the racialisation of migrant workers is in their capacity as labour, in the labour market. This requires an examination of their employment position.

Migrant workers and employment

Employers and migrant workers

The labour shortage in Cyprus has been invoked by employers to put pressure for the import of 'foreign' labour but in spite of the original agreements there are reports of wage differentials between migrant workers and locals (*Ergatiko Vima* 27.9.95). Moreover the kind of occupations migrant workers are concentrated in are so low paid that no Cypriot would take them (Matsis and Charalambous 1993). There are disputes on the question of 'designated' job descriptions and contracts, as the employers induce migrant workers to do different types of work or tasks, over and above their contractual agreements. There is no significant trade union intervention; if there are no trade unions operating in the firm there is no intervention (*Ergatiko Vima* 27.9.95). Employers consider the presence of migrant workers as positive for the economy of the country, but primarily for putting a downward pressure on wages and keeping a check on inflation, something also reflected in the Report by the Parliamentary Commission (1997a).

Anastasiades, speaking from the employers' viewpoint, (*O Phileleftheros* 4-5.12.96) sees migrant workers as useful in making Cypriot products more competitive and he argues that the low wages paid to migrant workers will yield high wages for Cypriot workers (in the long term). The increase in profits and productivity, it is suggested, will lead to an increase in exports and taxes, a reduction in unemployment and crime, and eventually to increased wages for Cypriot workers (Anastasiades, *O Phileleftheros* 4-5.12.96). These claims are regularly repeated by representatives of the Employers Associations, who also point to the 'positive contribution' of migrant workers, especially in agriculture and industry (Pierides for OEB *I Simerini* 19.1.97; and for KEVE *O Phileleftheros* 4.2.97). Employers' representatives, however, always appear tough on undocumented workers calling on authorities to take the necessary measures for their removal (Loizides in *O Phileleftheros* 4.2.97).

The Cypriot labour movement and migrant workers

Traditionally the Cypriot labour movement had a strong internationalist approach, stressing the unity of all workers, including Turkish Cypriot workers, in the labour struggles. However, recent publications of AKEL (Progressive Party of Working People) do not even refer to migrant workers as being part of the 60.7 per cent of the economically active population who are estimated to be working class (AKEL 1996: 94).[35] This is at a time when AKEL, *Haravyi*, (the AKEL daily) PEO and other Left wing organisations regularly discuss and debate the issue and numbers of migrant workers.

Despite regular reports in the Cypriot press on the plight of migrant workers and reports of 'super-exploitation', 'sub-letting' and 'lending' them to friends and relatives for the weekends, little has been done by the Labour movement to organise migrant workers. Headlines include: 'Subletting of foreign workers' (O Phileleftheros 3.10.96); 'Vicious exploitation' (*Haravyi* 20.5.1994). *Haravyi* (20.5.1994) presents the case of a worker who was paid Cy£13.90[36] per week, rather than the agreed Cy £54.10 entitled; far too excessive hours of work, up to 36 hours continuous work. In another report it is reported that a severe beating of arrested migrants has reached the European Committee against Torture (*O Phileftheros* 19.2.97).

Trade unions, however, have failed, on the whole, to take action to support or demonstrate their solidarity to migrant workers. One must distinguish between the Left-wing and the Right-wing trade unions, as there are differences in emphasis and ideological leanings. PEO has be to considered in conjunction with AKEL and the broad Left. SEK (Confederation of Labour of Cyprus) is ideologically and organically tied to the Right-wing party DESY (Democratic Rally). Having said that, there is a consensus in their opposition to the presence of migrant workers. They agree that they are to blame for rising unemployment and they have taken common action against migrant workers in the hotel industry in Paphos (*Haravyi* 12.12.96; *O Phileleftheros* 13.12.96).

A SEK spokesman is quoted stating that 'they [migrant workers] are stealing our bread' (*O Phileleftheros* 2.12.97), which is an illustration of SEK's approach. SEK is also more vocal on how migrant workers 'contaminate our culture', and blame them for rising criminality and other 'social problems'. A SEK official,[37] in line with a number of other similar statements by his union, is alarmed by what he calls 'the danger' of creating 'a third minority', beyond the Turkish Cypriots and the illegal settlers brought by in Turkey. He refers to 'an Afro-Asian "minority" and other aliens with dangerous consequences for a country that faces a problem of invasion, occupation and alteration of its demographic character' (*O Phileleftheros* 28.7.96). The super-exploitation and human rights of migrant workers may be discussed as another justification for their deportation, as they are not well treated anyway (Interview with Assistant General Secretary of SEK, Demetris Kittenis, *Ergatiki Foni* 30.10.96).

In contrast the Left, and AKEL in particular, has an anti-racist stance, but there is ambivalence in the broader 'popular movement', which consist of all Left-wing groups allied to AKEL. Different groups on the Left emphasise different aspects and at times contradict each other. AKEL, at its 18th Congress, pledges that it 'will work so that foreign workers employed in Cyprus get the same treatment as their Cypriot colleagues and will decisively fight against possible phenomena of racism and xenophobia' (AKEL 1995: 40). This clearly sets AKEL against racism; however the reference to 'possible phenomena' and not 'actual phenomena' implies that racism and xenophobia are something to guard against in some distant future. Also AKEL does not refer to the ways in which it will fight racism and little initiative has been taken by the Party to support migrant workers. Furthermore, 'illegal foreign workers' are referred to as a problem and AKEL calls upon the Government to take 'drastic measures to put an end to the illegal employment of foreign workers'. (AKEL 1995: 40) This phrase 'drastic measures' may well mean, in practice, violation of the fundamental human rights of undocumented workers, as well as other migrant workers, who may come under any heavy handed Police action. However, recent initiatives by some of AKEL's MPs, such as those in the Human Rights Parliamentary Commission (House of Representatives 1997b) illustrate that AKEL is taking up the issue of racism more seriously and that the debates over racism in Europe are beginning to influence AKEL policy makers.[38] Furthermore, AKELists, in alliances with others, are in the process of setting up an anti-racist organisation and a network for the rights of immigrants.[39] Nonetheless, for AKEL (AKEL 1995: 40) and PEO the shortage of labour could be met with the employment of Turkish Cypriots rather than 'foreign' labour. Again we see the connection of the treatment of migrant labour with the vision of solution to the Cyprus problem.[40]

Activists and leaders of PEO refer to the need to guarantee the rights of migrant workers (*I Simerini* 18.8.96, Papaefstathiou Executive Secretary of PEO). However, their reference to 'social problems' that allegedly derive from the arrival of 'alien cultures' undermines this. Under the heading 'The Problem of Foreign workers' the Report by the outgoing General Council of PEO suggests that 'the foreign workers are importing new customs (hqh kai eqima) and social problems' (PEO 1995: 64). To quote once more the PEO report 'the alien workers are carriers of different attitudes, principles and values, who have the potential to influence on social institutions. Furthermore problems are created either as a result of extra-marital relations or when the upbringing of children is given to foreign domestic helpers etc' (PEO 1995: 64). Also it calls upon the government to take all necessary measures to put an end 'illegal employment of aliens' (PEO 1995: 64; 66). In its newspaper PEO regularly blames unemployment on the presence of migrant workers (*Ergatiko Vima* 8.9.93; 17.7.96) as does *Haravyi* (1.3.97; 9.7.96; 25.6.95). They do not see the connection with calling for 'harsher measures' against undocumented migrant workers and a repression which may violate the rights of all migrant workers.

In contrast to the above however, PEO officials speak of 'defending the rights of "foreign" workers, whenever there are problems, which goes to show that PEO are not against foreign workers' (*Ergatiko Vima* 8.9.93). PEO favours the re-negotiation of the conditions for employment of migrant workers in such a way that it guarantees their own rights, but also that they do not undercut the wages of Cypriots (Interview with Michalis Papaefstathiou the Executive Secretary of PEO, *I Simerini* 18.8.96).

From the evidence above, it is apparent that both major trade unions are united in striking against the presence of migrant workers, both are concerned about the so called 'alien cultures' they 'bring in' with them and both fail to properly organise migrant workers. This supports Paul Gilroy's suggestion that racism unites the indigenous working class (1987). Race is here just as important in class structuration as class is to race (Anthias 1990; 1992b). In Cyprus all unions are remarkably united on this, whilst there are significant differences on other subjects. Furthermore, the common trade union actions against migrant workers illustrate that race consciousness and mobilisation can be an alternative to class.

Towards a multi-ethnic, multi-cultural Cyprus?

In some versions of Greek Cypriot nationalism, 'foreigners' are seen as 'contaminating', undermining and 'estranging' (αλλοτριωυουν) Cypriots from Hellenism, by 'de-Hellenising' Cyprus (Шαφελληνισμος της Κυπρου), which is according to nationalists the 'strength' of the nation (cited in the section dealing with trade unions). A recorded incident involving severe beating of, and racial violence against, eleven Bangladeshi students by a group of young Greek Cypriots, in the immediate aftermath of the murder of two Greek

Cypriots by Turkish fascists in the buffer zone in August 1996, illustrates this.[41] This discourse does not relate intrinsically to the attempts to resolve the Cyprus problem, but the existence of the problem creates the conditions of 'national emergency' that make it conducive to chauvinistic nationalism and racism.

There is no singular anti-racist recipe or strategy for eliminating racism since there are different loci of racialisation. Structural changes, changes in policies and their administration, educational programs, trade union and political activities all have a very important role to play in defending the rights of migrant workers. Structural changes would alter the 'material bases' that generate racism and the kinds of policies that systematically, intentionally or by default produce racial effects. Educational programs and populist discourse could deal with the level of ideas and attitudes (see Anthias and Yuval-Davis 1992). A more open public debate would lead to a greater awareness to issues of racism and give the opportunity for migrant workers to participate. Migrant workers need to be incorporated in the trade unions and be involved in struggles for improving workers lives.

On a wider scale a serious attempt to disconnect and disentangle the presumptions in the idea that 'migrants equals social problems' must be undertaken. In the context of Cyprus a major breakthrough for anti-racism would be to disentangle the national problem from an alleged need to be 'strict' on migration and migrants. In fact 'patriotism' could be redefined to include a call for the protection of rights and well-being of all people resident in Cyprus. The existence of the Cyprus problem and the perceived need to 'internationalise' the Cyprus problem by Cyprus could be invoked for treating migrants more equally. The maintenance of the rule of law and protection rights is indeed a requisite for accession to the EU, an argument already invoked by some Cypriot politicians in very recent debates.[42]

The fact that Cyprus is host to migrant workers may well have longer term social implications on the question of identity, as identity is very much a contextual and shifting phenomenon. Matsis and Charalambous believe that the presence of 'foreign workers' has had profound effect on the economy, but also 'on the social fabric of a small society that has already been altered by the presence of foreign tourists on a massive scale and on the democratic profile of the country' (1993: 41). There are debates over identity in Cyprus among Greek Cypriots over 'Helleno-centrism' and 'Cypro-centrism' (Papadakis 1993; Mavratsas 1997) and among Turkish Cypriots over Turko-cetrism and Cypro-centrism (Adiloglou 1989; Mehmet Ali 1989). The cultural aspect of the 'national' issue between Greek Cypriots and Turkish Cypriots needs to be reconsidered in the light of the presence of migrant workers. Although historically 4 per cent or less than 30,000 of the population consisted of ethnic groups, other than Greek Cypriots or Turkish Cypriots, there has never been such a large number of 'others' in Cyprus; not just tourists but more permanent residents. Perhaps more significantly the fact that there is such variety of ethnic groups, much more visible, interacting in a new way, creates the conditions for a new epoch in Cyprus, at least demographically speaking.

The presence of migrant workers may affect the debate on Cypriot identity. The ongoing debate over Greek Cypriot identity, on the relationship of Greek Cypriots to their ethnic background as Greeks and their geographical location and in their capacity as Cypriot citizens (Papadakis 1993; Mavratsas 1997; Panayiotou 1997) needs to take account of the existence of migrants in Cyprus. For the Turkish Cypriots, who live in the occupied territories matters are quite different as the conditions are very different; nonetheless a similar debate is taking place, but in a different setting[43] (Mehmet Ali 1989; Kilziyurek 1990; 1993).

'Cypriotists' or 'Cypro-centrists' are more open to diversity than the Greek Cypriots nationalists or 'Helleno-centrics' (Panayiotou 1997). However, localisms, such as 'Cypriotism', could also become hostile to migrant workers as the collusion of the Trade unions (who are Cypro-centred) against migrant workers indicates. Nonetheless, those who are more sympathetic to Cyprocentrism are generally less concerned with 'purity'. They range from the cosmopolitan centre-liberals, to social democrats and to those on the Left of the political spectrum. It is from these ranks that anti-racists are primarily drawn from. This is because the Left has an 'internationalist' tradition, as does 'cosmopolitan' liberalism, and generally speaking the Left is closer to the 'Cypro-centrist' side (Papadakis 1993). 'Cypriotism' or 'Cypro-centrism' already entails some elements of tolerance and diversity within it, as it allows for the peaceful and creative co-existence of Greek Cypriots and Turkish Cypriots. Notions of the 'purity' of the 'nation' are more the exclusivity of the Right and nationalists.

A new paradigm of an open and plural Cypriot identity, irrespective of ethnic origin could emerge allowing for difference but retaining a sense of geographical location. The consciousness of 'mother-Cyprus' which entails both Greek Cypriots and Turkish Cypriots as proposed by Kizilyurek (1990) must now extend to incorporating migrants residing in Cyprus. However, a move towards Cypriotness, even if both communities follow it, may not be strong enough as an ideology. More importantly, material processes (such as organisations, institutions) which actually work towards materialising this (see Attalides 1979), are today weaker than they were before the election of the Right wing administration in 1993. There are forces (media, state) which are strongly opposed to this. With the re-election of Mr Clerides as President in the 1998 Presidential elections this is set to continue.

There is the additional factor, that Cyprus is heading towards joining the EU, which is already changing attitudes. For example, the scheduled change in the law on homosexuality following a decision by the European Court for Human Rights, is partly the result of anticipation of entry in the EU. The principle of tolerance and respect for difference is increasingly invoked in anticipation of Cypriot entry to the EU. There may be another even more important factor within the process of accession: the fact that Cypriots would be exposed more and more to the anti-racist movements of Europe and a regime for rights of migrants and minorities in Europe.

However, accession to the EU may also bring Cyprus into a 'fortress Europe', through the imposition of regimes such as Shengen. The rise of racist and neo-fascist groups and the increasing rate of violence and prejudice against migrants and ethnic minorities movements in Europe, do not create a good precedent for Cypriots to follow. Furthermore, the failure of the anti-racist movement to combat racism in Europe does not provide an inspiration (Lloyd 1983), whilst the conditions of antagonism and the hierarchical relations in the EU are conducive to the exacerbation of racial prejudice and intolerance, rather than combating them. Europeanisation is no magic formula, but learning from the European experience is certainly likely to be beneficial for Cypriots.

Conclusion

To understand better the migration processes in Cyprus a fuller picture of the processes of migration of labour must be provided. Global factors need to be born in mind, as they underpin the migration changes taking place in Cyprus. As Castles point out, the world has entered a 'new phase of mass population movement' and 'migration in Europe and the situation of ethnic minorities in Europe can fully understood in a global context' (1993: 17). According to Castles, these processes have become 'increasingly contradictory and complex' because 'governments sought to address irreconcilable goals' (1993: 23).[44]

In Cyprus the policies governing the rights of migrant workers are not properly thought through, nor are they well implemented and administered. There is a lack of a proper legislative framework governing the rights of migrant workers. The media, in their sensationalist and alarmist drive, have contributed to creating a climate that racialises migrant workers by presenting them as 'a problem' for Cypriot society.

The discourse analysis of the terms employed about with migrant workers illustrates that the denial of any support for citizenship rights may be linked to the idea of an alleged 'inability to integrate' in Cypriot society of alleged 'alien cultures'. Ideas about the boundaries of the 'nation' may explain the decision to allow indefinite stay for all Greek nationals, whilst all others have permits with expiry dates (*I Simerini* 2.3.97). Furthermore, the calls for allowing Greek origin workers from Eastern Europe, such as Greeks from Pontos, by those on those on the nationalist Right[45] and the Right wing trade unions, corroborate this. Trade unions and the labour movement have not played their role in organising and including migrant workers in their struggles. Their collusion against migrant workers has contributed further to the marginalisation and racialisation of migrant workers, and has done no favours to Cypriot workers, whose wages are undercut further.

Anti-racism is beginning to appear in Cyprus but there is much scope for developing this further in order to enhance the position and rights of migrant workers there. After all, migrants provide new challenges for the small Republic. Accession to the EU may provide scope for co-operation and utilisation of the experience of the anti-racist movement in Europe, but at the same time expose Cyprus to all the negative aspects of 'Europeanism'.

At the turn of the century, Cyprus, a small divided island is in the process of accession the EU and seeks to overcome the current de facto partition. The last UN initiative, in Switzerland in August 1997, failed to provide a breakthrough, but the year 1998 is thought to be critical in the history of the Cyprus problem (Kyle 1997). A new initiative is said to be unfolding in anticipation of the start of accession negotiations, following the Presidential elections in February 1998. Working towards a Cyprus that is plural, open and tolerant is the best way for greeting the next century, with the hope for building a Cyprus without divisions and barbed wires, where diverse ethnic background will mean cultural richness, not conflict and prejudice.

Acknowledgements

Many thanks to Professor Floya Anthias and Gabriella Lazaridis for their comments. I especially appreciate the invaluable advice, guidance and help of Floya Anthias in writing this paper.

Bibliography

Adiloglou, M. (1989) in Mehmet Ali, A. (ed.) *Turkish Cypriot Identity in Literature*, FATAL Publications: London, pp.23-34.

AKEL (1995) *18th Congress, Material and Other Documents*, 16-19 November 1995, (official translation), Nicosia, Cyprus.

AKEL (1996) *The Class Structure of the Cypriot Society and the Economic and Social Changes*, CC AKEL, Nicosia, Cyprus.

Anthias, F. (1987) 'Cyprus' in Clark, C. and Payne, T. (eds.) in *Politics, Security and Development in small states*, London, pp.184-200.

Anthias, F. (1990) 'Race and Class revisited - Conceptualising Race and Racisms', *Sociological Review*, February, Vol. 38, pp.19-42.

Anthias, F. (1992a) *Ethnicity, Class, Gender and Migration- Greek Cypriots in Britain*, Avebury: Aldershot.

Anthias, F. (1992b) 'Connecting "Race" and Ethnic Phenomena', in *Sociology*, Vol. 26, No. 3, pp.421-438.

Anthias, F., and Ayres, R. (1983) 'Ethnicity and Class in Cyprus', *Race and Class*, XXV, (1983), pp.59-76.

Anthias, F. and Yuval-Davies, N. (1983) 'Contextualising Feminism-Gender, Ethnic and Class Divisions', *Feminist Review*, No. 15, pp.62-76.

Anthias, F. and Yuval-Davies, N. (1992) *Racialised Boundaries*, Routledge: London.

Antoniou, A. (1996) 'Attention, Racism is Awaiting...' in *O Phileleftheros* 26.10.96.

Attalides, M. (1979) *Cyprus: Nationalism and International Politics*, Q Press: Edinburgh.

Balibar, E. (1991) 'Racism and Nationalism' in Balibar, E. & Wallestein, I. *Race, Nation, Class: Ambiguous Identities*, Verso: London.

Castles, S. (1993) 'Migration and Minorities in Europe. Perspectives for the 1990s Twelve Hypotheses' Wrench, J. and Solomos, J. (eds.) *Racism and Migration in Western Europe*, Berg: Oxford, pp.17-34.

Charalambous, J., Sarafis, M. and Timini, E. (eds.) (1996) *Cyprus and the European Union: A Challenge*, University of North London Press: London.

Christodoulou, D. (1992) *Inside the Cyprus Miracle - The Labours of an Embattled Mini-Economy*, University of Minnesota.

Daniel, W. W. (1968) *Racial Discrimination in England*, Penguin: London.
Droussiotis, M. (1994) *Apo to Ethniko Metopo stin EOKA B* (From the National Front to EOKA B), Nicosia.
Gilroy, P. (1987) *There ain't no Black in the Union Jack*, Routlege: London.
Hall, S. et al (1978) *Policing the Crisis*, Macmillan: London.
Hitchens, C. (1997) *Hostage to History, Cyprus from the Ottomans to Kissinger*, Third Edition, Verso: London.
House of Representatives (1997a) *Report of the Parliamentary Commission on Employment and Social Insurance*, 1) 'The Uncontrolled Presence of foreign Workers in Cyprus and the problems that are created as a result of the absence of a relevant legal framework which must regulate their presence in our country'; 2) 'The cultural and social needs of foreigners, men and women, who are working in Cyprus' and 3) 'Foreign workers'.
House of Representatives (1997b) *Report of the Parliamentary Commission on Human Rights* titled: 'The Observing of the Human Rights of Aliens who Arrive Illegally to Cyprus to seek Employment or with the intention of Seeking Political Asylum'.
Kizilyurek, N. (1990) *Oliki Kypros*, Nicosia.
Kizilyurek, N. (1993) *Kypros Peran tou Ethnous*, Nicosia.
Kitromilides (1979) 'The Dialectic of Intolerance', in Worsley, P. and Kitromilides, P. (eds.) *Small States in the Modern World: Conditions for their Survival*, Revised Edition, New Cyprus Association and Cyprus Geographical Association, Nicosia, Cyprus pp.143-186.
Kitromilides, P. (1981), 'The Ideological Framework of Political Life in Cyprus', in Tenekides G. and Kranidiotis I. (eds.), *Cyprus: History, Problems and Struggles of its People*, (in Greek) Hestia: Athens, pp.449-474.
Kranidiotis, Y. (1993) 'Cyprus and the European Community', Conference Paper, *Cyprus: From Ottoman Province to European State*, organised by the Cyprus Research Centre and the Institute of Commonwealth Studies, 20-21 September 1993.
Kyle, K. (1997) 'Cyprus: In Search for Peace', *Minority Rights Group International Report*, Minority Rights Group: UK.
Lloyd, C. (1993) 'Universalism and Difference: The Crisis of Anti-Racism in the UK and France' in Rattansi, A. and Westwood, S. (eds.) *Racism, Modern and Identity*, Polity Press: Cambridge, pp.222-243.
Loukaides, G. L. (1982) 'Can Foreign National Married to a Cypriot Citizen be Deported for Security Reasons?', *Matters of Cyprus Law*, Vol. I, Nicosia, Cyprus, pp.171-178.
LSE and The Hellenic Centre Conference (1996) *Cyprus and the EU*, organised by the LSE in association with the Hellenic Centre, 31.10.96.
Matsis, S. and Charalambous, A. (1993) 'The Demand and Supply Dimensions of the Labour Marker: The Issue of Foreign Labour' in Demetriades, E.I., Khoury,

N.F., Matsis, S. (eds.) (1996) *Labour Utilization and Income Distribution in Cyprus*, Department of Statistics and Research, Ministry of Finance, Nicosia, Cyprus, pp.23-54.

Mavratsas, C. (1997) 'The Ideological Contest between Greek-Cypriot Nationalism and Cypriotism 1974-1995: Politics, Social Memory and Identity' *Ethnic and Racial Studies*, Vol. 20, 20 November 1997, pp.717-737

Mehmet Ali, A. (ed.) (1989) *Turkish Cypriot Identity in Literature*, FATAL Publications: London.

Miles, R. (1989) *Racism*, Routledge: London.

Moore, R. (1975) *Racism and Black Resistance in Britain*, Pluto Press: London.

Panayiotopoulos, P. I. (1995) 'Cyprus: The Developmental State in Crisis', *Capital and Class*, No. 57, Autumn 1995, pp.13-54.

Panayiotopoulos, P. I. (1996) 'End of Empire and the Emergent Post-Colonial State: The Case of Cyprus', paper presented at the *Third International Congress of Cypriot Studies* Nicosia, 16-20 April, 1996.

Panayiotou, A. (1997) 'Cypriotism', Unpublished paper.

Papadakis, Y. (1993) *Perceptions of History and Collective: a Study of Contemporary Greek Cypriot and Turkish Cypriot Nationalism*, PhD. D Thesis.

Peck, J. (ed.) (1988) *The Chomsky Reader*, Serpent's Tail: London.

PEO (1995) *Theses of 1995 Congress*, Nicosia, Cyprus.

PEO (1996) [Pan-Cyprian Labour Federation] *Labour Statistics*, Nicosia, Cyprus.

PIO (1993) *The Cyprus Problem*, Nicosia, Cyprus.

PIO (1996) Press and Information Office Press Release 30.12.96.

PIO (1997a) *The ALMANAC of Cyprus 1996*, P.I.O., Nicosia, Cyprus.

PIO (1997b) [Press and Information Office] *The Republic of Cyprus - An Overview*, Nicosia, Cyprus.

Planning Bureau (1989) *Study on Labour Shortage. A Note on Importing Labour from Abroad*, September 1989, Nicosia.

Planning Bureau (1993) *Strategic Development Plan*, Nicosia.

Protopapas, A. (1996) 'Foreign Workers and the Ten Nos' *O Phileftheros* 31.12.96-1.1.1997

Schlesinger, P. written with Elliot, P. (1991a) 'Some Aspects of Communism as a Cultural Category' in Schlesinger, P. *Media, State and Nation, Political Violence and Collective Identities*, Sage: London, pp.92-110.

Schlesinger, P. written with Elliot, P. (1991b) 'The Rise and Fall of a Political Slogan: The Case of "Eurocommunism"' in Schlesinger, P. (ed.) *Media, State and Nation, Political Violence and Collective Identities*, Sage: London, pp.11-136.

Solomos, J. and Wrench, J. (1993) 'Introduction' in J Wrench, J. and Solomos, J. (eds.) *Racism Migration in Western Europe*, Berg: Oxford, pp.1-23.

Solomos, J. and Back, L. (1995) *Race, Politics and Social Change*, Routledge: London.

Tornaritis, C.G. (1980) *Cyprus and its Constitutional and Other Legal Problems*, Second Edition, Nicosia, Cyprus.

Vasta, E. (1993) 'Rights and Racism in a New Country of Migration: the Italian Case' in Wrench, J. and Solomos, J. (eds.) *Racism Migration in Western Europe*, Berg: Oxford, pp.83-98.

Wilson, R. (1994) *Cyprus and the International Economy*, Macmillan: London.

Notes

1. 'Foreign' is placed in inverted commas as the word 'foreign' in Greek (and the Cypriot dialect in particular) has the dual meaning. It means 'guest' but it may also mean 'alien,' as the word 'xenos' derives from the first word of xenophobia. 'Εχουμε ξευους' means we have guests; but at the same time it means 'αλλοδαπος' or 'alien.'

2. This was an illegal terrorist organisation led by a former Nazi collaborator and former General, George Grivas. It was allegedly launched to campaign for *Enosis*, union with Greece, and carried out bombings, murders of civilians and tried several times to assassinate President Makarios (See Droussiotis 1994).

3. I am grateful to Kypros Pefkos for his archiving and AKEL for providing me with access to their newspaper archives. Also I am grateful to Eleni Mavrou and Pavlos Kalosynatos for their assistance and comments.

4. From January 1996 to March 1997 there have been 189 articles/news reports that referred to migrant workers. 86 which were from *O Phileleftheros*, 28 from *I Simerini* and 22 from *Haravyi* and 11 from *Alitheia*, and 6 from *I Machi*, 9 from *Ergatiki Foni* and 6 from *Ergatiko Vima*, which are the main newspapers of Cyprus and *To Periodiko* 1, which is a magazine and others (See also Political Orientation of Press in Appendix I).

5. Other, international and conjectural factors were crucial: The collapse of Beirut as the Middle Eastern commercial centre meant that the nearest regional centre Cyprus gradually took that role. Also the collapse of the Eastern European regimes allowed the pouring in of investment by the newly emergent bourgeoisie from these countries, in the light of accessibility (off shore companies, professional and trained personnel, linguistic and religious ties etc.). By and large offset the immediate consequences of the Gulf war, which threatened to dampen economic development, at the time.

6. Economic growth of the island during the years 1981-86, averaged around 6 per cent, for 1987-88; it was 5 per cent, whilst for 1989-93 it was 5 per cent. Since 1993 it slowed down to an average of about 3 per cent. (PIO 1997a) In the immediate post 1974 period, 1975-80, with an average growth was 10 per cent per annum manufacturing and construction became the leading sectors, as a result of the reconstruction efforts and the booming Arab markets. However,

this has been drastically altered in the 80s and 90s where it is the tertiary sector and tourism that are the main driving force of the economy (Matsis and Charalambous 1993).

7. Reported in *To Periodiko* 29.11.96.
8. This is on the basis that the total economically active population in 1995 as 301,000 (PIO 1997a). Antoniou (1996) on the same figure of 40000 speaks of over 16 per cent of the economically active population.
9. Figures to illustrate these are not available in this paper, but an obvious example is that of machinists in the garment industry that consists entirely of women.
10. It would be misleading to assume that absolutely all of these people classified as 'artists and musicians' are necessarily in the sex industry. There is a sizeable wealthy Russian minority residing in Cyprus, but the vast majority must be assumed to be so.
11. OEV is acronyms for Organisation of Employers and Manufacturers and KEVE is acronym for Centre for Scientific Manufacturers Chambers.
12. PEO is the Left wing union. It stands for Pan-Cyprian Federation of Labour and is the largest trade union; SEK is the Right-wing Confederation of Cypriot Labour; and DEOK is a small Democratic Labour Federation of Cyprus, connected to the small Socialist party EDEK.
13. All matters to do with immigration are primarily the responsibility of the Immigration Department, of the Interior Ministry, but this department works in collaboration with the Ministry of Labour. The ultimate responsibility lies with the Interior Minister (see *Report of the Labour and Social Insurance Parliamentary Commission*, House of Representatives 1997a) The procedure is that the Immigration Department provides the permit with the consent of the Labour Ministry, which considers the matter from labour point of view (1997b:3). The procedure is also set out in the Report of the Labour and Social Insurance Parliamentary Commission (1997) and have been also made public by the immigration authorities in reply to a questionnaire by *To Ergatiko Vima* 8.9.93 and another in *To Periodiko* 29.11.96.
14. As above.
15. Undocumented workers are those migrant workers, who do not have the necessary permits granted to their employers by the Immigration Department and thus become the 'responsibility' of the Police to deport them as 'illegal immigrants'.
16. These are the following conditions:
    (a) During strikes, the foreign worker would not be allowed to be strike breakers.

(b) In case of redundancies the first to be sacked would be 'foreign' workers.
(c) The employer would provide basic, but acceptable, facilities and would cut up to 10 per cent from wages for accommodation and another 15 per cent for food, if provided.
(d) No other wage cut to be allowed other than those provided by legislation or on the basis of employment conditions.
(e) No part of pay to go to any intermediary, agent or middleman or 'agent'.
(f) Foreign workers would enjoy the full rights of all workers, save for that of changing employer/place of work/type of work, that requires permit firm the authorities.
(g) Foreign workers may or may not join one of the trade unions and must fulfil their financial obligations and the employer to make allowances and deduct up to 1 per cent of their income for subscription (*Ergatiko Vima* 27.9.95).

17 See Report of the Employment and Social Insurance Parliamentary Commission 1997 and Report of the Human Rights Parliamentary Commission 1997.

18 'Agents' here refers to those intermediaries, who exploit the fact that in some countries there is poverty and/or repression to extract sums of money to for illegally transporting these people to another country.

19 These provide for heavy punishment, such as imprisonment of and imposition of heavy fines, against those who employ undocumented workers.

20 Only two paragraphs are devoted on the position of migrant workers, where it is noted that there are no social services specialising on migrant workers. It is also noted that at times financial assistance was provided but the attempts to create a centre for the recreation of migrants failed. (1997a:8).

21 There is little research to illustrate this. However, it can be drawn out of other studies which note the nature of the state of Cyprus as 'pot-colonial state' (Panayiotopoulos 1995), the ideological content of post independent Cyprus (Kitromilides 1979; 1981), the political structures and institutions (Attalides 1979; Anthias and Ayres 1983; Anthias 1987).

22 It has to be pointed out that although there is no report of any problems or issues raised about the kind of procedures and checks upon entry to Cyprus by migrant workers, these are worth studying, as discrimination may be exercised and unfair treatment may be practised. However it falls outside the scope of this paper. Such a study ought to examine on the ground the whole treatment of foreign workers at ports and airports, the role of immigration officers, the police and officials as well as the role of employers and others in the process.

23. The Cyprus constitution, it was described by the famous constitutional commentator de Smith as 'tragic' and 'absurd' and 'perhaps the most rigid constitution in the world' de Smith S.A. (1964), *The New Commonwealth and its Constitutions*, pp.282-285. In fact the rigidity of the British-made constitution meant that a Greek Cypriot could not marry a Turkish Cypriot without one denying his/her own 'communal citizenship' For more on the Cyprus Constitution see Tornaritis (1980).
24. Even then the wife is considered to be a denizen and apparently can be deported in cases of national security on the basis of the Act *On Aliens and Migration* as she can still be classified as an 'illegal immigrant' (Loukaides 1982: 172).
25. This was put forward on the 25.5.97. It was justified on the basis of bringing the law in compliance with Basic Articles 6 and 28 of the Constitution and the relevant international Treaties, presumably the European Convention of Human Rights and Fundamental Principles included, which Cyprus has incorporated as part of its' domestic law.
26. Only minute Leftist groupings, such as the Troskyists Ergatiki Democratia and Aristeri Pteriga, do so but they are very marginal.
27. There are articles and reports that fall outside this period that are quoted and analysed but the bulk of analysis is within this period.
28. This paper may be open to the accusation of replaying the 'number game' earlier in this paper. However, the difference in this paper is it attempts to analyse and interrogate the assumptions behind news coverage and articles in a disciplined and methodical manner, thus a look at the various reports of figures is a necessary part of the paper.
29. These very words were used by Margaret Thatcher in a 1978 interview, before her election as British Prime Minister.
30. The party is led by Vasos Lyssarides and proclaim itself as a socialist party, but appears today as one of the most vociferous nationalistic ones, although on many social issues, particularly class issues it retains to follow a 'socialistic' approach. This may be changing as the party is now part of the Government coalition since the elections in 1998. The party seems now to be moving more to the neo-liberal direction.
31. The extract from that letter reads: 'I have been in Cyprus for one and a half years and what has happened is too much for a person like me, when I cannot sit on my own balcony without getting verbal abuse from Cypriot people, who call me "mavro" or shout other bad words...'. Lanitis, in the same paper the following week suggests that he has received many letters by migrant workers complaining about their plight (*The Cyprus Weekly* 7-13.10.97).

32   The other newspapers are the marginal papers of the Leftist groupings, referred to in note 14 *Ergatiki Democratia* (their newspaper has the same name) and Aristeri Pteriga (their paper is called *Sosialistiki Ekfrasi*).
33   Pavlos Kalosynatos 'The "audacity" of the Filipino Workers', *Neolea* 4.10.97.
34   As Anthias and Yuval-Davies illustrate the discourses of racism and sexism can be separated, even though there is close interconnection between the two discourses in practice 'as experienced by the groups of subjects are intermeshed' (1992:131).
35   This pamphlet/study happens to be the most up to date and detailed study of class in Cyprus by AKEL. For 1992, the pamphlet/study suggests that 60.7 per cent of the economically active population belong to the working class, as employees, but there is a reduction of the industrial working class in comparison to 1980 and 1985.
36   Cy£ means Cyprus Pounds.
37   Interview with Andreas Vasiliou, SEK Regional Secretary for Famagusta.
38   In the deliberations of the Human Rights Commission the AKEL MP Doros Christodoulides and others showed sensitivity and seem to be advancing arguments from the anti-racist discourse in Europe (House of Parliament 1997b).
39   A Conference to launch this is scheduled for May 1998.
40   AKEL's proposals for the solution of the Cyprus problem lie in the restoration of the unity of the Cyprus Republic which is to be independent. There would be a single sovereignty, international personality and citizenship, but internally it is to be organised along federal lines, with a Turkish Cypriot and Greek Cypriot region and a strong central government, as agreed in the High Level Agreements of 1977 and 1979 and as provided in the UN resolutions. (AKEL 1995).
41   The incident refers to violent attacks on 11 Bangladeshi students at Ayia Napa, on the 29th of August, last week (See *I Alitheia* 31.8.96). The students were brutally beaten with sticks and other instruments by a group of Greek Cypriot racists threatening to kill them if don't leave the country within 24 hours; their motive was that the students are Muslims like the Turks.
42   AKEL MP Christodoulides during the deliberations of the Human Rights Commission (House of Parliament 1997b).
43   On the question of Turkish Cypriot identity issues such as the position of Turkish Cypriot position, vis-à-vis the settlers from Turkey, as Turkish policy is to colonise the occupied territories and where occupation troops are the real power holders.
44   Castles lists seven such goals: (1) Provision of labour supply; (2) Differentiation and control of migrant labour; (3) Immigration control and

repatriation; (4) Management of the urban problem; (5) Maintenance of public order; (6) Reduction in public expenditure; (7) Integration of minorities into social and political institutions; (8) Construction of national identity and maintenance of nation state.

45 Such as MP Rikkos Erotocritou of the Right wing DESY party (*O Phileleftheros* 4.10.96).

Appendix 1: The Political Orientation of the Cypriot Press

(*I Simerini*)	Nationalist Right / extreme Right Expresses those on the Right of the Governing party DESY and beyond (supported the 'anti-presidential fraction')
(*I Alitheia*)	Conservative Right / loyal to the Governing party DESY and particular President Clerides group (Third most popular paper)
(*O Phileleftheros*)	Establishment paper/ mainly mildly nationalist/ critical support to Governments (Most popular paper)
(*Haravyi*)	Left wing / AKEL newspaper (Second most popular paper)
(*Neolea*)	Left wing / EDON newspaper (circulated as a pull-out of Haravyi
(*O Agon*)	conservative centre Right/ nationalist / loyal to the Right wing parties, mainly DEKO
(*Ta NEA*)	Centre Left/ Nationalist controlled by EDEK, small circulation
(*Ergatiko Vima*)	Left wing / PEO newspaper, largest trade union paper.
(*Ergatiki Foni*)	conservative Right / SEK newspaper, second largest Trade Union paper.
(*I Machi*)	Very Right-wing, paper of the 1974 Coupist N. Samson; very small circulation
(*To Periodiko*)	Cypriot magazine

Appendix 2: Tables 1-7

Table 1: Per cent of the economically active population employed in each Sector of the economy

Year	Primary	Secondary	Tertiary
1961	46.0	22.7	31.3
1973	38.4	25.8	35.8
1975	27.5	25.6	46.9
1978	22.8	32.5	44.7
1993	13.2	26.3	60.5
1996	12.6	25.0	62.4

Source: Economic and Social indicators, Planning Bureau 1995, Nicosia.

Table 2: Per cent of the GDP in each sector of the economy, in current market prices

Year	Primary	Secondary	Tertiary
1961	27.9	20.5	51.6
1973	17.0	25.0	58.0
1975	19.2	21.8	59.0
1978	13.1	32.7	54.2
1993	6.3	26.0	67.6
1996	5.5	24.9	69.6

Source: Economic and Social indicators, Planning Bureau 1995, Nicosia.

Table 3: The workers requiring reference granted by the Ministry of Labour

Steel industry	400
Agriculture/farming	1450
Industry/conversion (metapoihsh)	1400
Construction	1200
Commerce	1600
Hotels/restaurants	1470
Transport	400
Banks /insurance	180
Other services	2400

Source: Report of the Labour and Social Insurance Parliamentary Commission 1997. Also available in *To Periodiko* 29.11.96.

Table 4: The 'foreign' workers that do not need reference

Greece (mainland)	3500
'Foreigners' married to Cypriot women	2000
Domestic Helpers	6200
'Artists' (female dancers in 'clubs' and caparets)	1100
Managers in off shore companies*	3700
Tourist Agents	500
Total:	17000

Source: Report of the Labour and Social Insurance Parliamentary Commission 1997. Also available in *To Periodiko* 29.11.96.

* According to figures from Press Conference of Minister of the Interior, Off shore Companies 5200 (*I Alitheia* 18.1.97).

Table 5: Countries of origin of immigrants (as available from 1994)

Bulgaria	2400
Sri Lanka	1854
Philippines	1500
Syria	1281
Romania	800
Britain	1000
Russia	800
Egypt	820
Yugoslavia	700
Lebanon	656
Greece	2403
Total	14400

Source: *To Periodiko* 29.11.96.

Table 6: 'Foreign' workers by occupation and country of origin on 31.12.1994

Country	[1]	[2]	[3]	[4]	[5]	[6]	[7]	[8]	[9]
Greece	336	338	188	175	859	53	454	0	2,403
Bulgaria	45	27	0	3	325	166	1671	163	2,400
Sri Lanka	3	3	0	0	1424	255	69	0	1,854
Philippines	11	9	6	12	1015	0	219	228	1,500
Syria	37	90	13	4	142	278	717	0	1,281
Romania	2	3	6	6	199	229	273	482	1,200
UK	250	250	100	47	202	20	131	0	1,000
Egypt	21	49	18	2	158	394	178	0	820
Russia	6	6	12	26	423	23	252	52	800
Yugoslavia	7	60	1	0	17	221	394	0	700
Lebanon	92	245	57	17	82	0	163	0	656
Poland	6	9	5	5	96	40	51	52	280
Georgia	0	0	0	0	90	90	80	0	260
Thailand	4	2	0	0	98	0	34	88	226
Sweden	13	15	8	1	129	0	39	0	205
Jordan	29	48	3	0	22	98	0	0	200
India	5	10	4	0	47	95	39	0	200
USA	40	74	17	0	0	0	19	0	150
Germany	9	51	4	0	23	0	38	0	125
Other	122	131	58	2	49	217	42	119	740
Total	1,038	1,420	500	300	5,500	2,179	4,863	1,200	17,000

[Note from Editor: The total number of foreign workers was given the Immigration Office but the distribution was based on facts from the stay permits given by the Ministry of Labour as well as estimations on working people who do not require reference by the Ministry of Labour such as artists, domestic workers, Greeks married with Cypriot women and foreigners who work for Off Shore companies.]
Source: PEO (1996).

[1] Qualified & Technicians
[2] Managerial
[3] Secretarial
[4] Sales
[5] Services
[6] Farming
[7] Production
[8] Artists & Musicians
[9] All Occupations

Table 7: Total number of foreign workers

Year	Matsis & Charalambous (1993)	Report of the Labour and Social Insurance Parliamentary Commission 1997
1980	1500 (1%)	-------
1989	4000 (2%)	-------
1990	-------	6,000
1991	7900 (3.1)	7,100
1992	1600 (6%)	13,700
1993	------	13,300
1994	------	14,400
1995	-------	22,039
1996	----------	27,000

9 European Union Citizenship: Exclusion, Inclusion and the Social Dimension

Dora Kostakopoulou

Citizenship may have historically been linked to the emergence and crystallisation of national-statist communities, but can no longer be confined within them. Citizenship rights can be granted by other levels of jurisdiction, and duties need not be reduced to those which individuals owe the state (Steenbergen 1994). The introduction of the supranational institution of Union citizenship by the Treaty on the European Union (1 November 1993), as a supplement to national citizenship, has shown that individuals can be members of multiple, diverse, overlapping and interacting political communities (Meehan 1993). More importantly, Union citizens have the right to enter the territory of another Member State, to reside there and take up activities as employed or self-employed persons without requiring the host state's consent. At the infranational level too, the mobilisation of ethnic migrant groups in Western Europe has called into question traditional assumptions about the unity and homogeneity of national publics, thereby prompting several states to reconsider their responses to demands for respect for unassimilated otherness (i.e., the challenge of diversity) and for political inclusion (i.e., the challenge of membership).

Although the past decade has witnessed a flurry of new scholarship on citizenship, it was not until the 1990s that theorists became fully aware of the challenges facing citizenship theory; namely, the challenges of diversity, membership and the emergent supra and transnational dynamics. There are two important reasons for this. First, traditional accounts of citizenship, be they liberal, participatory, communitarian or sociological, assumed that political community is an undifferentiated collectivity, in which the image of the rational, male, white citizen often tends to be the norm for all. Second, that literature took for granted that citizenship has traditionally relied upon and regulated legal bonds within sharply bounded national communities. In this respect, theorists proceeded to analyse the meaning of citizenship and examine its role in promoting civic engagement or justifying social policy and welfare within bounded national frameworks.

As regards the former assumption, feminist and anti-subordination literature has exposed the structures of inequality and the oppression belying the liberal ideal of universal citizenships and has outlined a transformative framework for sociopolitical inclusion and cultural recognition (see Young 1990; Fraser 1995; 1997; Minnow 1990). It is true to say that the social context of mutliculturalism is something that even liberal theorists can no longer afford to ignore (see John Rawl's Political Liberalism (1993)). In *Multicultural Citizenship,* Kymlicka (1995) seeks to reconcile the values of liberalism with group-based minority rights - albeit at the risk of defending a rather essentialist conception of single, coherent and secure national-societal cultures. The nationally bounded character of citizenship, however, has led to limited access from outside and state-induced cultural homogenisation inside (Brubaker 1992; Baubock 1992; Anthias and Yuval-Davis 1992).

With respect to latter assumption, an increasing number of scholars has taken issue with 'citizenship's rootedness' within the nation-state paradigm, and a debate has begun to emerge concerning the possibility of its 'uprootedness'. This research has culminated in conceptions, such as, transnational citizenship (Baubock 1994), postnational citizenship (Soysal 1994) or cosmopolitan public law (Held 1995) - conceptions that seem to serve better the contemporary global as well as internally differentiated environments. Evidently, the introduction of the supranational institution of Union citizenship has fuelled this debate.

Although there is hardly any doubt that the institution of Union citizenship is a novel development, opinions diverge over its value and its impact. For sceptics, Union citizenship is a mere exercise in public relations, a 'symbolic plaything without substantive content' (d' Oliveira 1995; Lyons 1996; Guild 1996: 30-54). Other theorists are more prepared to cede Union citizenship a positive institutional role, even though this may be a future one (Preuss 1996; Weiler 1995; 1996).

It is certainly the case that the personal scope of Union citizenship is restrictive as it inappropriately transplants the logic and the language of the nation-state onto the European level.[1] True also, the material scope of Union citizenship is, at present, quite limited: with the exception of political rights, Union citizenship has not added much to existing Community law and it does not contain any duties. However, these shortcomings should not overshadow the fruitful possibilities entailed by this institution. Union citizenship signals the prospect of a post-national political arrangement based on a redefinition of community and rearticulation of citizenship. To put it differently, Union citizenship entails the promise of uncovering new ways of conceiving community, membership, citizenship, and enhancing democratic initiative by enabling multiple membership, by both natural and legal persons, in various overlapping and strategically interacting political communities formed at various levels.

In this paper, I shall attempt to tease out the promise of Union. In what follows I will first address the limitations and shortcomings of the present institution of Union citizenship, then, I will discuss the deficiencies of the European migration regime. Finally, I will proceed to outline alternative framework of citizenship beyond the nation-state and by so doing, to flesh out some ideas for further institutional reform.

Citizenship and multifaceted exclusion in the European Union

The institution of Union citizenship may have laid the foundations for the formation of a European polity, but it has conditioned belonging to this polity upon tenure or acquisition of the nationality of one of the Member States (MS)(Article 8(1) EC). The restrictive personal scope of Union citizenship results in relegating over ten million third country nationals to the periphery of the emerging European civil society. This exclusionary form of citizenship is hard to justify from a normative point of view, since third country nationals have been residing, living and working for several years in the territories of the Union and contributing in many ways to the development and flourishing of the European societies. Their exclusion from full membership to the European political community has to be understood with reference to national conceptions about 'who should or should not belong to the community' which have been transferred to the European level.

It is interesting to note here that although Article 48 EEC refers to the free movement of workers within the Community, secondary legislation has made it clear that only workers who are nationals of the Member states can benefit from the free movement provisions (articles 48-51 EC). The restrictive interpretation of the term 'workers', which was introduced by Council Regulation 1612/68 and Council Directive 68/360,[2] constitutes an unwarranted restriction on the Founding Treaty, given that its draftsmen were primarily concerned with enhancing labour mobility - and not with circumscribing labour mobility by nationality. Nevertheless, the free movement provisions created an 'incipient form of European citizenship' for Community nationals.

The 1973 Declaration on European identity (Annex 2 to chapter II, 7th Gen. Rep. EC 1973) set pointers for the development of special rights for citizens in the EU,[3] and the idea of 'Passport Union' gave considerable boost to European citizenship (Bull. EC Suppl. 7/1975). The Adonnino Committee on 'a people's Europe', which was set up by the Council of Ministers in 1984 in order to make the EC a tangible reality for its citizens, took for granted the exclusion of non-EC nationals from the protection against discrimination that EC law affords to EC nationals, in the fields of free movement and residence, access to employment, social security, housing and so on.

The Commission has been aware of the problems created by the exclusion of a group of persons from Community law who are involved in the economic process of the Community either as consumers or service providers. Despite the underdeveloped nature of European citizenship in the 1980s, for example, in 1985, the Commission drafted a background report recommending the extension of social and political rights to third country nationals resident in the EU (ISEC/B12/85, Luxembourg 1985). But the Council ignored these proposals as national governments opposed this extension. Interestingly, when the Commission used its powers under Article 118 to establish a prior communication and consultation procedure on migration policies in relation to third country migrant workers, several Member States filed complaints with the European Court of Justice arguing that the Commission had exceeded its competence and impinged on the Member states' sovereign power in the field of immigration rules (Decision 85/381, OJ 1985 L 215/25). The Court of Justice ruled that the Commission had exceeded its procedural powers to the extent that its consultation procedure aimed at securing conformity between national measures and Community policies and actions on the other (Joined Cases 281/85, 285/85, Germany v Commission [1987] ECR 3203). As regards the question as to whether migration policies could be seen to fall within the ambit of Article 118 which provides for co-operation among the Member states, the Court ruled positively on the grounds that state policies towards third country nationals have an impact upon employment and, more generally, the improvement of living and working conditions within the Community.

The European Parliament and the Economic and Social Committee have also taken issue with the unjust exclusion of third country nationals, and have highlighted the need for a more inclusive European identity. More specifically, these institutions have recommended that free movement should apply to all resident workers irrespective of nationality, and that third country nationals should have the same rights to family unification as EC national workers (OJ EC 183, 15/7/91). It has also been suggested that non-EC migrants should enjoy protection from discrimination on the same footing as EC nationals and the right to vote in local elections (OJ EC No. C 360, 15/10/90: 173). In a Communication issued on 23 February 1994, the Commission announced its intention to draw up a proposal for a Council directive on the right of third country nationals to travel in the Community without a visa (COM(94) 23 Final). The Commission's initiative was welcomed by the Economic and Social Committee and the European Parliament as an important step both for the completion of the internal market and to counter discrimination against non-EU citizens. Both institutions endorsed the proposed directive (COM(95) 0346), despite the fact that the right to travel concerned only short stays (OJ C 153/38 28.5.96; A4-0218/96, OJ C 347/62 18.11.96).

The 1996 Intergovernmental Conference which culminated in the Treaty of Amsterdam (signed on 2 October 1997) conferred on third country nationals the right of intra-EU movement for three months (Articles 62(1), 62(3) EC). Measures defining the rights and conditions under which long-term resident third country nationals may reside in other MS will be adopted by the Council acting unanimously on a proposal from the Commission or on the initiative of a MS (Articles 63(4) EC). Although the creation of a Community law competence in matters relating to third country nationals is a welcome development (the Community has had competence in the conditions of employment of legally resident third country nationals), it falls short of treating third country nationals as full and respectful participants in the Europolity. Third country nationals have not been given access to European citizenship and will not able to move and reside within the Community as freely as EC nationals and European Economic Area nationals. Notably, in its proposals for the revision of the Treaty on European Union at the IGC, the Migrants' Forum had suggested the broadening of the concept of European citizenship by conditioning it on domicile, that is, by extending its personal scope to citizens of non-MS who have been legally resident for five years in the Community. The absence of political will for such an amendment is regrettable, not only as a matter of principle but also because of its practical impact on the position of third country nationals in the EU.

Conditioning European citizenship on domicile may be necessary for redressing the inequitable position of third country nationals, but it cannot be the sole determinant factor in alleviating this or any other form of inequality. Essential for inclusion and respectful belonging in the Euro-polity, as indeed in any other polity, are also policies aimed at combating structures of socio-economic inequality and practices of discrimination. Although Union citizenship has been presented as a 'degendered', 'de-raced' and 'classless' category, its personal scope, in reality, reflects gender, race and class differentials. It excludes long-term resident third country nationals and does not embrace non-active economic actors (-who are not self-sufficient), be they women engaging in domestic work and care for dependent relatives, unemployed people or persons who have not acquired the necessary skills due to institutionalised racial discrimination in education and labour markets. In addition, differential levels of protection against racial discrimination often posit obstacles to the mobility of ethnic migrant citizens. The Amsterdam Treaty lays emphasis on the protection of fundamental rights and the elimination of discrimination of all kinds especially based on 'sex and ethnic origin, religion or belief, disability, age or sexual orientation' (Article 13 EC). This requires Community legislation. However, the fact that decisions in this area will be taken by unanimity weakens the impact of this provision.

Equally important is the development of a form of 'European social citizenship'. Promoting the 'citizen dimension' of the Union requires concern over the long-term effects of unemployment, of poorly-rewarded part-time work and sporadic or low employment of various sorts. Unemployed people, women, old people, ethnic communities, religious minorities, disabled people, young people, informal carers, homeless people, travellers, people with mental illnesses and disabilities, all are at risk of social and economic exclusion. Tackling social exclusion requires an understanding of why vulnerable groups fall into poverty as well as an examination of other issues associated with poverty, such as, problems of low pay, part-time working, child care facilities, sex, race, disability discrimination within the labour market, and regional disparities within the EU.

True, a strategy for growth and job creation is vital. But vital too is the recognition that the problem of unemployment will not be automatically solved by economic growth. The Commission's White Paper on *Growth, Competitiveness and Employment* recognised that employment, especially employment generation, is important for the future of European integration, but failed to identify specific political initiatives in this area (COM(93) 700). Similarly, the 1994 White Paper on *European Social Policy* stressed the importance of the preservation of the 'European social model', but, at the same time, failed to discuss the impact of rising unemployment upon the social security systems of the Member States (COM(94) 333). Along very similar lines, the European Parliament has argued that deregulation of working conditions and reductions in minimum wages may not be the best way for achieving greater competitiveness and discouraging the shift of investment towards the low-wage producer countries (A3-0079/94, No C 91/224, 10/4/94). According to the European Parliament, economic prosperity, competitiveness, increased productivity and social progress are not conflicting ideals; instead, they are 'two sides of the same coin'. In this respect, it has criticised attempts to dismantle the European social model under the pretext of seeking to promote employment and has re-affirmed its commitment to fundamental rights to social protection as a constitutional element in the EU (A4-0122/94, OJ No C43/63, 19/1/95). The Intergovernmental Conference offered a good opportunity for the Commission to promote the principles of a European social model and to place social policy onto the IGC agenda. Instead of articulating an ambitious programme of legislative provisions and social policy measures at the European level, however, the Commission concentrated on consolidating and improving social policy measures: the promotion of 'civil dialogue' and the Cupertino with the social partners; the acceptance of the *acquis communautaire* in the social field by all the MS; the monitoring of the transposition and implementation of existing Community social legislation; the development of heterogeneous and flexible policies within given financial constraints, and the encouragement of responsible partnership at all levels in line with the principle of subsidiarity; the co-ordination of the employment policies of the Member States. The Member States consented to the insertion of a new Title on Employment in the Treaties (it creates a mechanism for co-ordinating national employment policies and the possibility for certain Community measures in this area), and the 1997 UK General election brought an end to the UK's social policy opt-out.

The Amsterdam Treaty has incorporated the Social Agreement, which previously applied only to fourteen states, in the Treaty. As such, it has laid the foundations for a coherent European social policy. Although the provisions of the Agreement have been strengthened to ensure equal opportunities and equal treatment for men and women in the workplace, the new common social policy is still limited. This is because important issues such as social security, redundancies, and worker representation still require unanimity. In addition, the common social policy needs to incorporate the right to work and rights in employment as well as to provide effective protection for vulnerable groups, such as, the elderly, children, the unemployed an so on.

The institutionalisation of a European social citizenship would help transform European citizenship from a 'virtual quality' to a status which is meaningful to those citizens who do not avail themselves of the rights to free movement. In this way, the circle of membership would gradually expand to encompass a wider range of people and embrace them as valuable and full-fledged members of the European political community. Tackling the internal boundaries of membership, however, requires also an examination of the external dimension of membership, that is to say, of the processes by which boundaries are drawn and redrawn around the European political community. This is because a political community's immigration policy reveals the type of society to which its citizens aspire and the value of citizenship.

Boundaries, borders and the rhetoric of exclusion: towards a European immigration policy

A characteristic feature of the European migration regime is the lack of systematic thinking about the kind of immigration policy that the creation of 'an area without internal frontiers' would require and the form this policy should take. At first sight, this may seem understandable; immigration policy has principally been a matter of unilateral state action and, naturally, the Member States have been reluctant to relinquish their sovereign control over the admission and treatment of 'aliens'. In the 1980s, the prospect of the establishment of an internal market by the end of December 1992, coupled with mounting fears that the abolition of checks at internal borders will render any control of immigration impossible, necessitated a common approach to migration. But the MS were determined to resist pressures for Community competence in this area. They opted, instead, for an informal, intergovernmental form of co-operation. Intergovernmental co-operation in visas, immigration and asylum policy may thus be viewed as the 'spill over' effect of the establishment of a single market without internal border controls.

The functional link between internal mobility of labour and external border controls may help us to understand why the MS agreed to co-operate in this area, but it cannot account for the restrictive and law enforcement character of the migration policy which has emerged from this pattern of co-operation.

Indeed, rigorous regulation of workers' mobility at the external frontiers and the tightening of visa policies have been presented as a logical and a functional prerequisite of the internal market. In reality, however, these have been political choices. As such, they may be better understood with reference to the broader context of national restrictive immigration policies operating since late 1960s - early 1970s in several Western European countries (Cesarani and Fulbrook (eds.) 1996; Baldwin-Edwards and Schain 1994). By situating EU-wide migration policies within the wider political and ideological climate which has construed immigration and asylum policy as part of the 'law and order' problem of the Member States, one can understand why third country nationals have been excluded from full-membership in the Euro-polity as well as why intergovernmental co-operation has resulted in restrictive migration policies.

Prior to the setting up of the Group of Co-ordinators which compiled the Palma document (1988),[4] inter-governmental co-operation in immigration and asylum matters had been ad hoc and uncoordinated. A number of ad hoc bodies and agencies, such as the TREVI Group, the Ad hoc Group on immigration and the Schengen Group, set up under the aegis of the EC Interior and Justice Ministers, were charged with devising policies in immigration and asylum matters. The emphasis was on restricting the entry of non-EU nationals by tightening visa policies, tightening external border controls, intensifying internal surveillance and reducing the number of asylum seekers. State cooperation in these areas provided the means of improving the effectiveness of national restrictive immigration policies and consolidating the process of policy alignment which had commenced in the 1980s, despite existing differences in administrative rules and procedures.

As these bodies were outside the competence of Community law, the secretive and unaccountable manner in which they operated gave rise to many complaints. The complaints were compounded with criticisms about the content of the legal instruments that emerged from this pattern of intergovernmental co-operation. Both the Schengen Accord (14 June 1985) and the Supplementary Agreement for the execution of the Accord (19 June 1990) have been criticised for lacking adequate protection of human rights and the principle of equality of treatment; for the uneasy relationship with the

Geneva Refugees Convention of 1951; for failing to protect personal data, and for the extensive powers of the Schengen Executive Committee (Schutte 1991; Spencer 1995; Wallace 1996). Many institutional actors have expressed their dismay at the prospect of an authoritarian 'Fortress Europe'; that is, a Europe with a hard outer shell against Third World immigrants and refugees.[5] Attention has also been drawn to the fact that such legislation could only engender hostility towards Europe's ethnic migrant population and legitimise in a way anti-immigration sentiment and xenophobic speech.

The tightening of asylum rules under the Schengen (1990) and Dublin Convention (15 June 1990, in force as per 1 November 1996), which has now superseded the Schengen's chapter on asylum, has also been criticised for failing to observe the Geneva Convention, as amended by the 1967 New York Protocol, and the European Convention of Human Rights. The Dublin Convention sets out criteria for determining which Member State is responsible for examining an asylum claim, and institutionalises the 'one chance' principle; that is to say, a decision on asylum made by the first country in which an application for asylum is lodged is binding upon the rest signatories. This means that rejection of an application by one state precludes a further application to any other Member state of the Union. The UNHCR criticised the unfairness of the 'one chance' rule, especially since there are neither harmonised asylum procedures nor uniformity in the interpretation of the Geneva Convention. In addition, it has been observed that the new regime does not obviate the risk of refoulement given that asylum seekers have been returned to 'third countries' which are, by no means, safe.[6] The impositions of sanctions on air and sea carriers (Article 26, Schengen II) has also been subject to criticisms for impeding unfettered access to status determination procedures and to asylum from persecution.

The Treaty on European Union institutionalised the pattern of intergovernmental co-operation in immigration matters, the crossing of external borders, asylum policy, police and customs co-operation, albeit in a more diluted form by providing for links with Community institutions (Title VI on co-operation in the fields of justice and home affairs - the so called 'Third Pillar'). Although this was an advance on the previous ad hoc and uncoordinated pattern of co-operation and Article K9 introduced the possibility for the Communitarisation of the matters listed in K1 to K6, that is, their transfer to Community competence (Article 100c EC),[7] the Third Pillar failed to establish a coherent, integrated, principled and justiciable Union immigration policy. Decision-making under the Third Pillar continued to remain secretive and the Commission had a limited role in this process. In addition, consultation with the EP was confined to reports submitted to it ex post facto (O'Keeffe 1995: 916-919). More importantly, the absence of national parliamentary involvement and judicial supervision (judicial review by the European Court of Justice was optionally provided only for Conventions under Article K3(2)) exacerbated the democratic deficit of the Community.

Concerned about the lack of effective judicial guarantees concerning the protection of individual rights in the fields of immigration and asylum, the Commission proposed that the ECHR should have precedence over the External Frontiers Convention[8] and that the European Court of Justice should be able to give preliminary rulings on its interpretation (COM (94), 23 Final, February 23, 1994, Article 29). However, certain MS were not prepared to agree on the proposed jurisdiction of the European Court of Justice. Indeed, it is due to disagreements among the MS over this issue and to a dispute between the UK and Spain over the status of Gibraltar, that the External Frontiers Convention has still not been signed. Lack of progress in this area, however, did not prevent agreement in initiatives governing the admission of asylum seekers. The Commission Communication on Immigration and Asylum policies (COM(94) 23 Final), the Resolution on Minimum Guarantees for Asylum Procedures (OJ C 274, 19 October 1996), the joint position on the Harmonised Application of the term 'refugee' in Article 1 of the Geneva Convention (adopted on 23 November 1995, Bull. EU 11-1995), all have confirmed fears that future harmonisation of asylum policy will contain restrictive asylum regulations.

The IGC introduced some crucial reforms to the framework of Intergovernmental co-operation in Justice and Home Affairs. It transferred from the Third Pillar to the First the areas of immigration and asylum, the rights of third country nationals, external border controls and judicial co-operation in civil matters. The transfer means that the principles and institutional rules of the Community will now apply to decision-making in these areas and that discussion by the Council and COREPER (the committee of permanent representatives) will replace multi-level negotiations conducted under the aegis of the K4 Committee. More specifically, the new Title on 'Progressive Establishment of an area of Freedom, Security and Justice' (which also entails special arrangements for Ireland, the UK and Denmark) sets out a five year transitional period from the entry of the Amsterdam Treaty into force, during which the Council will take decisions by unanimity and the

Commission will share the right of initiative with the MS, before a possible decision at the end of that period to move to qualified majority voting and co-decision with the European Parliament (Article 67 EC). In addition, the Amsterdam Treaty incorporates the much criticised Schengen acquis into the framework of the Union, but leaves the Council to decide the legal basis for each of the provisions, declarations and decisions which constitute the acquis (i.e., either the First or Third Pillar). Until such determination has been made, the Schengen measures will be regarded as act adopted on the basis of the Third Pillar (see Article B of the Protocol on integrating the Schengen acquis).

It is certainly the case that this positive, albeit initially limited, extension of accountability in immigration and asylum matters will please the critics of the Third Pillar. However, progress in this comes at a price. The ECJ has no jurisdiction to review operations relating to the maintenance of law and order and the safeguarding of internal security (Article 68(2) EC), but the interpretation of these restrictive provisions will be a matter for the Court itself. In addition, national executives have decided to circumscribe the role of the ECJ and prune its integrative dynamic by restricting requests for preliminary reference rulings to courts of the last instance (Article 68(1) EC). Moreover, requests for reference by national courts of last instance are discretionary -not mandatory. These inhibitions on the ECJ's jurisdiction are likely to undermine legal certainty, the consistent interpretation of Community law across the MS, and will have undesirable implications for individuals who will now have to pursue their cases through the successive ties of national jurisdiction. This suggests that the MS are determined to maintain as much control as possible over the shape of the new legal and institutional framework on immigration and asylum.

If this is the case, the question that arises here is whether the new arrangements and possibly increasing gains in democratic and judicial accountability will result in substantive changes in European immigration and asylum policy. Will they lead, for example, to a questioning of the restrictive focus of the European migration policy and of the Schengen Convention as the model for the development of a Common Migration Policy? Admittedly, the fact that the Schengen acquis will be incorporated into the Union without any further discussion over the substantive content of its provisions and decisions does not leave much room for optimism. After all, it is the MS who have designed the previous migration regime and have chosen to replicate their national restrictive immigration policies at the European level. More importantly, the provisions of agreements and decisions taken at the European level, have been progressively incorporated in the Member states' national legislation, thereby reinforcing the rhetoric of exclusion. In this respect, it might be unrealistic to expect a questioning of the European 'overlapping consensus' on restricting the admission of migrants and asylum seekers and the articulation of a principled immigration policy which pushes forward the logic of membership- citizenship.

It is worth mentioning here that Southern European states have also been forced to adopt immigration policies congruent with those operating in Western Europe, even though these were countries of emigration rather than immigration until the 1980s. In Spain, for instance, Law 9/94 (19 May 1994) diluted the rights of asylum seekers provided for under the 1978 Constitution for asilados (the right to stay on humanitarian grounds and protection against refoulement). In Portugal, (General) Decree-Law no. 59/93 (March 3) has speeded up the expulsion process for immigrants and made the assisting of illegal immigration a criminal offence (European Current Law Yearbook, 1993: 34). Following this Decree-Law, Law no. 34/94 on Defining the Regime of Receiving Foreigners or Refugees at Temporary Installation Centres, stipulates that installation centres are used for humanitarian or security reasons or in cases of entry into Portugal without the necessary visa (European Current Law Yearbook, 1994: 733). In addition, Decree Law No. 292/94 (on Creating the National Cabinet of supplementary Information Required at National entries (SIRENE)), has established the national SIRENE Cabinet. It may be interesting to note here that Decree-Law No. 253/94 concerning the Portuguese Nationality Regulation amended Decree Law no. 322/84 (12 August 1994), thereby increasing the necessary period of residence in Portugal in order to acquire Portuguese nationality by naturalisation from 6 years to 10 years (European Current Law Yearbook, 1995, p.706). Incidentally, there has been a progressive convergence in restrictive residency requirements for naturalisation in Southern Europe in the 1990s. Greece raised the residence requirement from eight years to ten in 1993, whilst in Italy, the 1992 Law on Citizenship n. 91 (5 February) has increased the period of residence required for naturalisation from five to ten years. In addition to the longer period of residence, the acquisition of Italian nationality for non-EC nationals has been conditioned upon the fulfilment of a greater number of conditions than in the past. Given the legacy of exclusion, the question that needs to be addressed here is whether Union citizenship, as a new form of citizenship beyond the nation-state, can provide any helpful insights towards disrupting the exclusionary focus of the present migration regime by promoting flexible internal and liberal external membership rules.

The promise entailed by Union citizenship

Unearthing the radical potential of Union citizenship requires a rethinking of the appropriateness of using the category of the nation-state as the lens through which to view developments in the European Union (Wessels 1997). Tempting as it may be to model the emerging community in the European Union and European identity on the basis of patterns set by the 19th century process of national community and national identity building, notions of the past may not be the best key in order to explain developments in the future (Koopmans 1992: 1047-1052). This is due to inherent weaknesses within the nation-state paradigm as well as to the undesirable political implications that a possible transfer of state or nation related concepts at the European level may yield for both Europe's ethnic population and the nature of the emerging polity in Europe.

For example, Smith has sought to apply his ethno-national approach to nationalism to the question of European identity (Smith 1992: 55-76). Observing that the European Union lacks the shared symbols, myths, memories, common history, cultural heritage and ethnic pedigree required for national community building, Smith proceeds to argue that a European collective identity can, nevertheless, be created out of an 'eclectic patchwork'; that is, on the basis of a 'family of cultures'. The latter term refers to partially shared historical traditions, such as Roman law, parliamentarism, democracy as well as heritages, such as humanism, rationalism, romanticism and classicism (Smith 1992: 70-74). According to Smith, a pan-Europeanist nationalist movement could possibly forge common myths and symbols out of the common European heritage and, in the process lay the foundations for a new type of collective identity which overarches, but does not abolish individual nations.

Admittedly, such an approach to European identity formation is consonant with Smith's overall essentialist approach to nationalism, that is, with his suspicion against 'artificial' political identities (i.e., 'state-manufactured political culture') as well as his belief that supranationalist ventures turn out to parallel, step by step, nationalist goals and assumptions (Smith 1991: 183, 194-195). However, Smith offers no convincing justification as to why the project of the uniting of Europe should be the mirror image of nationalist projects. In arguing that a European collective cultural identity may be forged on the basis of 'families of culture', Smith overlooks that the latter are crossed by the most diverse and often contradictory currents. Furthermore, why should the theme of shared heritages and traditions be the only repository of the myths and symbols required by community building? Arguably, there exist subversive memories of suffering due to wars, slavery, colonialism, which could enhance identification with the European project and foster a sense of commitment to the future of Europe.

Smith insists on the importance of retrospective narratives of shared heritages and common origins for community-building in the EU, because he models the emerging community in the EU on the basis of patterns and assumptions derived from the processes of national community building. Moreover, Smith tends to view the nation as the political reflection of necessary essences and relations (i.e., the common myths and memories of a territorial home) which, in a way, predetermine the outcome of their articulation. Such an essentialist approach, however, is bound to yield exclusionary results, especially for those who are perceived as 'not belonging to the same community' (Kostakopoulou 1997; Howe 1997). Smith himself admits this by saying that 'the forging of a deep continental cultural identity to support political unification may well require an ideology of European cultural exclusiveness' (Smith 1992: 76). Clearly, by viewing European identity as the 'mirror image' of an essentialist conception of national identity, Smith ends up projecting the deficiencies of the latter onto the former.

Equally inappropriate might be essentialist narratives which ground European identity on mythical essences and the fictitious commonalities that the various national, ethnic collectivities might possess. Arguably, 'Europe' does not need to be filled with Euro-centric myths based on the conception of Europe as a 'unique culture area' in order to function as an integrating device. Such narratives can only ignite European racism and xenophobia by culture-baiting ethnic minorities as aliens and essentialising differences between Europe and non-European worlds (Pieterse 1991: 3-10).

An alternative approach to community building in European Union and European identity would have thus to conceptualise European Union as a political community based on principles which transcend the particularistic framework of nationality. True, Union citizenship has been conditioned upon possession of state nationality. But the project of the uniting of Europe has also given an unprecedented expression to multiple identifications and attachments. More specifically, it has shown that citizens' interests, concerns and loyalties are no longer tied to the national level but they are extended both upwards (the supranational level) and downwards (the sub-national level). This dispersal of political allegiance over various units highlights the plural and flexible character of one's commitments and, in effect, undermines the nation-states' ability to monopolise the terms of collective identity and to compel unqualified allegiance. National identification can no longer be propounded as the identification which should always override other allegiances in scope and power. This has implications for the way we think about community.

Unlike communities based on ascriptive membership, that is, on thick communal attachments,[9] or liberal consensual communities (i.e., 'communities of shared values', 'communities of shared final ends'), the notion of community suited to the EU is one in which the various constituent units display their commitment to the future of the Union, in the sense of working together towards creating 'an ever closer union among the peoples of Europe' while preserving and respecting the distinctive identities of its members.[10] In this process, there is neither consensus nor indeed certainty over the juridico-political shape of the outcome. There is only an active concern and a willingness on behalf of its units to participate in the collective shaping of this process by designing appropriate institutions. What unites, therefore, the various political units together in the Union is less their agreement on some final shape of the Union or some common set of determinate values, than their shared concern and a willingness to participate in the 'adventure' of European integration. In such a 'community of concern and engagement', all its corporate and individual members, associated by virtue of their differences from one another, share a concern over the nature and the future of the polity and are engaged in the common experience of shaping this future.

Communities of concern and engagement are 'heterogeneous' democratic publics in which individuals can participate both as citizens and members of communities which have equal status in the public sphere (i.e. to take action both as citizens and as black citizens, or gay citizens, or old age pensioners citizens). This, in turn, requires the transcendence of the nationality model of citizenship and the articulation of an alternative conception of citizenship based on domicile.

As a formal legal criterion for understanding membership to a community, domicile is based on certain factual requirements from which an intention on the part of the prospective member to make that particular territory the hub of ones' interests and life can be deduced. It is considerably less exclusionary than the nationality principle since it would include all those residents who have made a particular territory their home, the centre of their economic life, who pay taxes and are affected by state policies, and participate in a whole web of social interactions which undoubtedly generate expectations. If Union citizenship were conditioned on domicile, long-term resident third country nationals would enjoy citizenship rights on an equal footing with Community nationals. At another level, domicile could easily be propounded as a Community law concept, thereby providing fairness and uniformity in its interpretation across the Member States.

Domicile as the legal criterion for membership to the European political community could foster the creation of a civic and inclusive European identity. That is to say, of an identity which does not exhibit the homogenising logic that has accompanied the formation of national and cultural identities, but values, instead, diversity. Recognition of the dynamic and supplementing inter-relationship of European identity with other forms of identification, in turn, facilitates the creation of complex and multifaceted inter-relationships of individuals, interest groups and voluntary associations, subnational authorities with multiple and strategically interacting tiers of government (Meehan 1993: 1-35, 185).

Such interactions can only be empowering if, in addition to extending the personal scope of Union citizenship, more differentiated forms of citizenship could be institutionalised (Young 1989: 252-258; 1990). The latter would aim at combating the various structures of inequality and social exclusion in the European Union. Feminist and anti-subordination scholarship have provided fruitful insights in this respect by exposing the tendency of liberal ideal of universal citizenship to neglect the structures of sex, race inequality as well as the wider socio-political effects of such blindness to difference.

True, differentiated citizenship has been criticised for contradicting the orthodox conception of citizenship as a matter of isonomia (i.e. legal equality) and equity (i.e. those who are similarly situated be similarly treated) (Miller 1995: 432-450). However, the crucial point that needs to be emphasised here is that certain groups may need differential treatment not because they are 'essentially' different, but because they live in a discriminatory society which turns differences which are irrelevant from a moral point of view into disadvantages. In addition, it may be argued that possible application of Young's schema of differentiated citizenship to the EU may lead to underscoring redistributive issues in the EU, given Young's emphasis on the cultural politics of recognition (Frazer 1995). If this line of criticism is correct, then one should either move beyond the redistribution/cultural recognition dilemma or achieve some sort of synthesis of the two by devising another model. However, it seems to me that the distinction between 'political economy' and 'culture' is entirely theoretical. The politics of 'difference' is a response to multifaceted structures of domination and oppression and a means to achieve socio-economic equality. Indeed, Frazer herself concedes that the split between redistribution and recognition does not reflect a genuine antinomy, and that it is possible to combine an egalitarian politics of distribution with an emancipatory politics of recognition (Frazer 1997: 127). In keeping within my discussion, a form of European social citizenship is necessary for the creation of an inclusionary European polity.

The differentiated means that could be employed to combat inequality and social exclusion in the European Union include: i) group rights, along the lines suggested by Young (1989: 259-261; 1990: 175-183) in the context of her theorisation of justice as the project of enpowerment of historically oppressed groups. Group rights as 'institutionalised means for the explicit recognition and representation of oppressed groups', apply to certain categories of people by virtue of their specific circumstances and they supplement the general tier of rights applicable to all. They include guaranteed representation in political bodies, public funds for advocacy groups, veto rights over specific policies that affect the group directly, language rights, cultural rights, reproductive rights for women and so on. In the EU, initiatives such as the formation of a Committee of the Regions (1992), the Migrants Forum, the European Liaison Committee of Non-governmental organisations involved in the fight against poverty could be seen as positive steps towards enabling expression of these actors' viewpoints as well as of encouraging policy initiatives by the groups themselves. In addition, Article 2(4) of Directive 76/207, which provides for equal treatment of men and women in the context of employment, leaves room for measures which promote equal opportunities for men and women by removing existing inequalities which affect women's opportunities in the areas referred to in art. 1(1). Although much depends on the scope that the Court of Justice will give to art. 2(4), it is true to say that the European Court of Justice has been instrumental in enhancing the rights of pregnant and birthing mothers (another example of group rights). The Commission, backed up by the European Parliament, has introduced Positive Action Programmes aiming at tackling sex discrimination beyond the workplace and promoting equal opportunities for women. A crucial feature of these programmes is the recognition that women's educational and employment opportunities are closely linked with the sharing of family responsibilities. ii) Regional rights of increasing opportunities for self-governance. The enshrining of the principle of subsidiarity has given a new impetus to this, but, as I argue below, a lot depends on whether the full potential of subsidiarity as a decentralist principle will be realised. iii) Socio-economic rights aiming at targeting the various facets of economic inequality. The latter may range from specific polices aiming at eliminating regional disparities in development and improving the structural adjustment of Europe's poor regions to measures designed to combat homelessness, child poverty and so on. By seeking to tackle economic inequality, the aim of structural rights is to ensure that membership in the community is not denuded of meaning as a result of abject poverty. For this reason, the forging of a partnership between all those involved in the fight against poverty, in both public and private sectors and at local, national and Community levels is instrumental for effective action against poverty (OJ No C281/5, 28/10/91). In addition to the principle of partnership, the Community's action programmes (1989-1994 and 1994-1999) espouse the principles of multidimensionality and participation. The principle of multi-dimensionality reflects two things: first, the realisation that social exclusion is a multidimensional phenomenon; second, it can only be tackled by multi-objective policies and strategies. The principle of participation, on the other hand, aims at encouraging effective participation by the least privileged groups, promoting solidarity and active citizenship. Finally, another important feature of structural rights is that they encapsulate a mixed (both individual and corporate) approach to welfare as they recognise that groups and regions could have legitimate claims for economic development and assistance.

Furthermore, a 'heterogeneous European public' could only be inclusive and empowering if it encourages political participation, by all those who share a desire to 'participate in a common experiences and not in a common life' (Wolin 1993: 472). This requires the strengthening of the democratic legitimacy of the EU by: i) increasing the powers of the European Parliament (from assembly to co-legislature), ii) creating institutional links between the European Parliament and national parliaments, establishing partnerships between the two and, generally speaking, strengthening of the role of national parliaments in the project of European integration, iii) promoting transparency, openness and accountability at all levels of decision-making (Williams 1990; Lodge 1994). The Amsterdam Treaty has introduced some significant reforms in this area, which have put the European Parliament on an equal footing with the Council in the legislative process; namely, it has extended significantly the scope of the co-decision procedure and simplified it by removing the third reading. In addition, the Amsterdam Treaty has introduced closer ties with national parliaments. Under a protocol annexed to the Treaty, national parliaments will have a six week period to scrutinise and debate legislative proposals or proposals for a measure to be adopted in the context of the Third Pillar before these are placed on the Council's agenda. Moreover, the institutionalisation of a new right of information (Article 255 EC) commits the EU to greater openness into its institutional decision-making processes.

More openness and democratic accountability has also been introduced in immigration and asylum related matters as a result of the partial Communitarisation of the Third Pillar (section 3 above). This has remedied some important deficiencies of the old intergovernmental structure, thereby laying the foundations for a coherent Community immigration policy which respects the rule of law and international human rights standards. However, it must also be borne in mind that the transfer of immigration and asylum policy within the Community's competence may not be such a 'leap forward', if the emphasis continues to be on controlling and restricting migration flows, by seeking to tackle their 'root causes', to curb illegal immigration, and even to facilitate the repatriation of qualified African nationals residing in Europe.

Institutionalising forms of better management of immigration and of more democratic control may fall short of a principled response to immigration, in so far these policies do not lead to the questioning of the legitimacy of a 'Schengenland' vision of Europe and to a re-examination of the meaning, terms and conditions of membership in the EU. After all, alienage distinctions are produced with respect to certain conceptions of what constitutes membership - conceptions which are reflected in the ways in which states respond to immigration and ethnic diversity. The 'Communitarisation' of immigration and asylum policy needs thus to be accompanied by a radical rethinking of the issues of immigration, citizenship and community in the EU. I hope the discussion hitherto has furnished some ideas towards this direction by placing these issues within a conceptual framework which examines the politics of inclusion/exclusion and the drawing of boundaries in the EU, but, at the same time, refuses to view those boundaries as limits to the scope of justice.

Bibliography

Anthias, F. and Yuval-Davis, N. (1992) *Racialized Boundaries; Race, Nation, Gender, Colour and Class and the Anti-racist Struggle*, London: Routledge.
Baldwin-Edwards, M. and Schain, M. (1994) 'The Politics of Immigration', *West European Politics: Special Issue*, 17, No.2.
Baubock, R. (1992) *Immigration and the Boundaries of Citizenship*, Warwick: Centre for Research in Ethnic Relations.
Baubock, R. (1994) *Transnational Citizenship: Membership and Rights in International Migration*, Aldershot: Edward Elgar.
Brubaker, R. (1992) *Citizenship and Nationhood in France and Germany*, Cambridge, Ma.: Harvard University Press.
Cesarani, D. and Fulbrook, M (eds.) (1996) *Citizenship, Nationality and Migration in Europe*, London: Routledge.
Commission of the European Communities (1985a) Report on *A People's Europe*, ISEC/B12/85, Luxembourg.
Commission of the European Communities (1985b) Decision 85/381, O. J. 1985 L 217/25.
Commission of the European Communities (1991) Opinion on the *amendment of the Treaty*, 21/10/90, Bull. EC Suppl. Brussels: CEC.
Commission of the European Communities (1993) White Paper on *Growth, Competitiveness and Employment*, COM(93)700, Bulletin of the European Communities, Supplement 8, Brussels: CEC.
Commission of the European Communities (1994a) White Paper on European Social Policy - A Way forward for the Union, COM(94)333 final.
Commission of the European Communities (1994b) Communication to the Council and the European Parliament on Immigration and Asylum Policies, COM (94), 23 Final, February 23.
Commission of the European Communities (1994c) Proposal for a Council Directive on the right of third-country nationals to travel in the Community, COM(95) 0346,OJ C 306, 17.11.95.
Commission of the European Communities (1995) Report on the *Functioning of the Treaty on European Union*, Bulletin of the European Union, 5/95, Brussels: CEC.
Commission of the European Communities (1996) Communication on *Racism, xenophobia and anti-Semitism*, COM (95) 653 -C4-0250/96, 13.12.95.
Conference of the Representatives of the Governments of the Member States (1997) Draft Treaty of Amsterdam, Document CONF/4001/97, 19 June 1997 and the subsequent version (http://ue.eu.int/Amsterdam/en Treaty/treaty.htm).
d'Oliveira, J. (1995) 'Union Citizenship: pie in the sky?', in A. Rosas and E. Anatola (eds.) *A Citizens' Europe: In Search of a New Order*, London: Sage, 58-84.

Economic and Social Committee (1996) Opinion on the Proposal for a Council Directive on the right of third-country nationals to travel in the Community, 96/C 153/08, OJ C 153/38.

European Council (1995) Joint Position concerning the Harmonized application of the definition of term 'refugee' in Article 1 of the Geneva Convention European Parliament, Bull. EU 11-1995.

European Council (1996) Resolution on Minimum Guarantees for Asylum Procedures, OJ C274, 19 October.

European Parliament (1990a) Resolution on *Freedom of Movement for non-EEC nationals*, Doc. 12A3-175/90. O.J. No. C360, 15.10.90, 173.

European Parliament (1990b) Resolution on *Union Citizenship*, O. J. 183, 15.7/91.

European Parliament (1994) Resolution on *Employment in Europe*, Doc. A3-0079/94, No C 91/224, Thursday, 10 March 1994.

European Parliament (1995) Resolution on *The White Paper on European Social Policy - A Way Forward for the Union* A4-0122/94, O.J. No C/43/63, Thursday, 19 January 1995.

European Parliament (1996a) Legislative Resolution embodying Parliament's opinion on the proposal for a Council Directive on the right of third-country nationals to travel in the Community, A4-0218/96, OJ C 347/62, 18.11.96.

European Parliament (1996b) *Resolution on the convening of the IGC*, A4-0068/96, Art. 4.5.

Frazer, N. (1995) 'From Redistribution to Recognition? Dilemmas of Justice in a 'Post-Socialist Age', 212 *New Left Review*, 68-93.

Frazer, N. (1997) 'A Rejoinder to Iris Young', *New Left Review*, 126-129.

Friedman, M. (1989) 'Feminism and Modern Friendship: Dislocating the Community', *Ethics*, 99, 275-290.

Guild, E. (1996) 'The Legal Framework of Citizenship of the European Union' in *Citizenship, Nationality and Migration in Europe*, D. Cesarani and M. Fulbrook (eds.), London: Routledge, 30-54.

Held, D. (1995) *Democracy and the Global Order*, Cambridge: Polity Press.

Howe, P. (1997) 'Insiders and Outsiders in a Community of Europeans: A Reply to Kostakopoulou', *Journal of Common Market Studies*, Vol.35, No.2, June, 309-314.

Koopmans, T. (1992) 'Federalism: The Wrong Debate', Guest Editorial, *Common Market Law Review*, 29, 1047-1052.

Kostakopoulou, T. (1997) 'Why a Community of Europeans Could be a Community of Exclusion: A Reply to Paul Howe', *Journal of Common Market Studies*, Vol.35, No.2, June, 300-308.

Kymlicka, W. (1995) *Multicultural Citizenship*, Oxford: Oxford University Press.

Lodge, J. (1994) 'Transparency and Democratic Legitimacy', *Journal of Common Market Studies*, 32, 3, 343-368.

Lyons, C. (1996) 'Citizenship in the Constitution of the European Union: rhetoric or reality?' in R. Bellamy (ed.), *Constitutionalism, Democracy and Sovereignty: American and European Perspectives*, Aldershot: Avebury.

Meehan, E. (1993) *Citizenship and the European Community*, London: Sage.

Miller, D. (1995) 'Citizenship and Pluralism', *Political Studies*, Vol. 43 (Special Issue), 432-450.

Minnow, M. (1990) *Making All the Difference: Inclusion, Exclusion and American Law*, Ithaca, NY: Cornell University Press.

O'Keeffe, D. (1995) 'The Emergence of a European Immigration Policy', *European Law Review*, 20, 1, 20-36.

Pieterse. N. (1991) 'Fictions of Europe', *Race and Class*, 32, 3, January-March, 3-10.

Preuss, U.K. (1996) 'Two Challenges to European Citizenship', *Political Studies*, XLIV, 534-552.

Schutte, J.J.E. (1991) 'Schengen: Its Meaning for the Free Movement of Persons in Europe', *Common Market Law Review*, 28, 549-570.

Smith, A.D. (1991) *National Identity*, London: Penguin Books.

Smith, A.D. (1992) 'National Identity and the Idea of European Unity', *International Affairs*, 68, January, 55-76.

Soysal, Y. (1994) *Limits of Citizenship: Migrants and Postnational Membership in Europe*, Chicago: Chicago University Press.

Spencer, M. (1995) *States of Injustice*, London: Pluto Press.

Steenbergen, van B. (1994) *The Condition of Citizenship*, London: Sage.

Wallace, R. (1996) *Refugees and Asylum: A Community Perspective*, London: Butterworths.

Weiler, J.H.H. (1995) 'Does Europe need a Constitution? Reflections on Demos, Telos and the German Maastricht Decision', *European Law Journal*, Vol. 1, 3, 219-258.

Weiler, J.H.H. (1996) 'European Neo-Constitutionalism: In Search of Foundations for the European Constitutional Order', *Political Studies*, XLIV, 517-533.

Wessels, W. (1997) 'An Ever Closer Fusion? A Dynamic Macropolitical View on Integration Processes', *Journal of Common Market Studies*, Vol. 35, No.2, June, 267-299.

Williams, S. (1990) 'Sovereignty and Accountability in the European Community', *The Political Quarterly*, Vol. 61, 3, 299-327.

Wolin, S. (1993) 'Democracy, Difference and Re-cognition', *Political Theory*, 21, 3, 464-483.

Young, I.M (1989) 'Polity and Group difference: A Critique of the ideal of Universal Citizenship', *Ethics*, 99, 250-274.

Young, I. M (1990) *Justice and the Politics of Difference*, Princeton: Princeton University Press.

Notes

1. Article 8(1) of the Treaty on European Union (TEU) states: Citizenship of the Union is hereby established. Every person holding the nationality of a Member State shall be a citizen of the Union.
2. See Council Regulation 1612/68 on *Freedom of Movement for Workers within the Community* (OJ 1968 L 217/2), as amended by Council Regulation 2434/92 (OJ 1992 L 245/1); Council Directive 68/360 on *the Abolition of Restrictions of Movement and Residence within the Community for Workers of Member states and their Families* (OJ 1968 L 257/13; OJ Special Edition 1968-69, 485).
3. The Copenhagen Summit contrived the Declaration on European Identity - a text which set out, for the first time, the basic principles for the internal development of the Community and furnished a framework for the formation of a civic European identity on the basis of the principles of rule of law, social justice and respect for human rights and democracy; Annex 2 to chapter II, 7th Cen. Rep. EC, 1973.
4. The Palma document highlighted both the 'essential' and 'desirable' measures required for the abolition of internal controls and proposed their implementation before the end of 1992.
5. In Britain, the Refugee Council, the Joint Council for the Welfare of Immigrants, Amnesty International, Justice, all have deplored the current trends in immigration and refugee policy.
6. See the UNHCR's position on Conventions recently concluded in Europe (on the Dublin and Schengen Conventions), Geneva: UNHCR, 1991 cited in Spencer, *States of Injustice*, :.94.
7. In November 1993, the Commission suggested the possibility of applying Article K9 of the treaty on European Union to asylum policy (Bull. EU 11-1993 point 1.5.5). Although the Commission listed the advantages of applying Article 100c EC in terms of the participation of the European Parliament and the ECJ in decision-making in this field, legal certainty, transparency, and the speed of the decision-making procedure, it, nevertheless, went on to add that the most appropriate forum for pressing the case would be the 1996 Intergovernmental Conference (COM(95) 566). It may noted here that the Community has had competence over visas: Article 100c EC requires the Council to determine the third countries whose nationals must be in possession of a visa when crossing the external borders of the Member States. Based on Article 100c EC, Council Regulation No 2317/95 lays laid down a common list of 101 countries and territorial entities whose natonals must be in possession of a visa. However, the Court has annulled this Regulation because the Council made modifications to it after the European Parliament had given its opinion (Parliament v Council [1997] ECR I-3213).

8 The External Frontiers Convention has superseded the parts of Schengen that deal with external borders; see COM(93) 684 Final.
9 I am referring here to nativist narratives of community and to the communitarian emphasis on the 'family-neighbourhood-nation' complex. Marylin Friedman (1989) has criticised the latter for harbouring oppressive structures for women.
10 The discussion here draws upon my essay 'Towards a Theory of Constructive Citizenship in Europe', *The Journal of Political Philosophy*, 4, 4 (December 1996) 337-358.

Index

A

Africans, 8, 21, 37, 39, 47, 52, 55, 59, 60-1, 64, 67, 83, 120, 197
Age, 51, 62, 72, 80, 85, 89, 92, 96, 98, 100, 102, 110, 184, 194, 200
Albanians, 9, 10, 50, 105-20, 130
Aliens, 114, 131, 140, 146, 148, 152, 157-9, 162, 164, 168, 186, 193
Anti-immigration, 8, 63, 187
Anti-racism, 153, 160, 163
Assimilation, 74, 76, 97, 118, 130, 152
Asylum, 3, 4, 19, 42, 105, 164, 186-9, 190, 197-202

B

Belonging, 90, 113, 116, 181, 184, 192
Black, 11, 21, 60-1, 129, 154, 164-5
Border, 2-3, 10, 20, 31, 39, 41, 57, 64-5, 105-6, 108, 113, 117, 120, 123, 131, 134-5, 137, 186-9, 202
Boundaries, 1, 2, 4-5, 10, 14, 22, 51, 116, 118, 123, 138, 162, 164, 186, 198-9
British, 8-9, 31-2, 52, 59, 83, 85-103, 119, 141, 169

C

Catalonia, 8, 55-6, 60, 67-79

Citizenship, 1, 2, 8, 10, 17-8, 21, 23-4, 31, 46, 49, 50, 52, 75, 85, 98, 102, 116, 118, 145, 149, 162, 168, 170, 179, 180-5, 190-1, 193-6, 198-202
Citizenship, 8, 49, 52, 149, 179, 180-1, 191, 199-202
Class, 2, 8, 10, 51, 63, 75, 80, 111, 113, 139, 149, 151, 154-6, 159, 163-5, 169, 184, 199, 201
Collective identity, 192-3
Collective Identity, 192-3
Colonialism, 4, 52, 68, 152, 192
Colour, 10, 51, 154, 199
Community, 1, 7, 9-10, 14, 30-2, 35, 38, 43, 45, 48-9, 52, 59, 63, 65, 71-2, 75, 79-81, 85-7, 89, 92, 94-8, 100-3, 108, 110, 114, 116-9, 130, 137-8, 145, 148, 152, 155, 161, 164, 179-94, 196-202
Consciousness, 159, 161
Criminal, 26, 67, 105-6, 116, 119, 130, 190
Culture, 7, 9, 11, 22, 30, 40, 45, 47, 62, 75-6, 81, 91, 96-7, 114, 127-8, 130, 138, 148, 152, 157, 192-3, 195
Custom, 39, 61, 91, 113, 131, 148, 158, 188
Cyprus, 6, 9, 139, 141-3, 145-6, 148-57, 159-70

205

D

Data, 6-7, 13-16, 18-27, 29, 31-3, 56, 58, 60, 62, 72, 83, 106, 109-10, 120, 126, 141, 144, 187

Democracy, 28, 88, 103, 123, 125, 192, 200-2Development, 3, 4, 9-10, 13, 16, 31-2, 35, 38, 40, 43-4, 49, 52, 70-2, 74, 78-81, 86, 93, 95, 101-2, 125, 131, 139, 141-3, 148, 153, 163, 165-6, 180-5, 190-1, 196, 202Difference, 5, 6, 8-9, 18, 25, 28, 40, 46-7, 75, 85-6, 89, 95, 105-7, 113, 118, 151, 157, 159, 161, 165, 169, 187, 193-5, 201

Differential exclusion, 8, 56, 75

Differentiation, 22, 59, 118, 170

Diversity, 10, 15, 75, 80, 112, 117, 119, 161, 179, 194, 198

Division of labour, 81, 135, 144, 154

Domestic workers, 45, 60, 153-5, 175

Domination, 195

E

Eastern Europe, 119, 120, 123, 125, 134-5, 138, 144-5, 162, 166

Economic migrants, 3, 8, 59, 64, 72, 105, 126-7, 132, 135, 138

Economy, 4, 7, 9, 13, 19, 35, 37-40, 42, 44, 50, 52, 56-9, 62, 64-5, 69-71, 73, 77-9, 106, 108, 110, 119, 125, 127, 131-2, 134, 137, 141-2, 156, 160, 166, 172, 195

Emigration, 38, 51-2, 56, 60, 69, 78, 81, 118, 137, 190Employment, 3, 11, 19-20, 27, 44-6, 51-2, 56, 59, 62-3, 65-6, 71-3, 81, 96, 106, 110-11, 114, 117-8, 127, 130, 133, 135, 137-8, 141, 143, 146-8, 150, 153, 155, 158-9, 164, 167-8, 182-5, 196, 199-200

Equality, 74, 149, 187, 195

Equity, 195

Ethnic, 1, 2, 4-6, 8-10, 21, 30-2, 47, 50-1, 59, 61, 68, 75-6, 80, 98, 101, 108, 110, 113, 117-20, 137, 144, 151, 153, 155, 160-3, 165, 179, 184, 187, 191-3, 198-9

Ethnic group, 2, 5, 61, 101, 160

Ethnic minority, 75, 110, 120, 151, 155, 162, 193

Ethnicity, 1, 5, 17, 21, 24, 29, 47, 163

Ethnocentrism, 3, 5

Europe, 1, 2, 4-8, 10-11, 13-15, 18, 20, 31-3, 35, 37-9, 41-2, 44, 46, 48-52, 55-7, 59-60, 62-3, 67, 69-70, 76, 78-81, 83, 85, 87-8, 96, 98-9, 101-3, 105-6, 108, 119-20, 123, 125-6, 130, 132-5, 137-9, 143-5, 148, 153-4, 157-8, 161-4, 166, 168-9, 179-95, 197, 199-202

European Union, 18, 42, 50, 85, 97-9, 132, 134-5, 164, 179, 181, 183, 188, 191-3, 195, 199-202

Exclusion, 1, 2, 4-6, 8-11, 35, 37, 45-6, 56, 65, 67, 73-5, 78, 92, 98, 101-2, 107, 109-10, 114, 118, 120, 132, 135, 138, 179, 181-2, 184, 186, 190-1, 194-5, 198, 200-1

Expatriates, 8, 9, 83, 85-8, 91-4, 103

G

Gender, 2, 6, 10, 51, 59, 113, 119, 152, 154-5, 163, 184, 199

Generation, 75, 79, 184

Global, 1, 10-11, 13, 25, 54, 78-80, 97, 125, 137, 143, 162, 180, 200

Globalisation, 1, 8, 56, 78

Greece, 6, 9, 11, 56, 64, 105-11, 113-20, 123, 125-8, 130-5, 137-8, 140, 173-5, 191

Guest worker, 2, 123

H

Health, 8, 24-5, 65-6, 83, 85, 88-90, 92-8, 100, 102-3, 110, 132

H

History, 2, 27, 35, 37, 56, 62, 69, 119-20, 128, 139, 142-3, 163-5, 192

I

Identity, 2, 4, 9-10, 42, 74-5, 92, 97, 102, 107, 116, 118-9, 138, 160-1, 163-6, 170, 182, 191-4, 201-2
Ideology, 1, 5, 10, 16, 79, 114, 149, 151, 161, 192
Illegal immigrants, 41-2, 118, 130-2, 146, 151, 167-8
Immigrants, 3, 8, 21, 23, 25, 31, 41-2, 47, 57-9, 61, 75, 80, 118-9, 123, 126, 129-33, 137-8, 141, 146, 151, 158, 167-8, 174, 187, 190, 202
Immigration, 2, 4, 7-8, 10, 23-5, 27, 29, 31, 39, 41-3, 45-8, 50-2, 55-66, 70-1, 74-6, 78-81, 106, 118-9, 123, 125-7, 130-2, 135-8, 146, 148, 167-8, 170, 175, 182, 186-90, 197, 199, 201-2
Inclusion, 2, 5, 11, 35, 43, 83, 85, 102, 110, 118, 125, 130-1, 148, 179-80, 184, 198, 201
Indigenous, 44, 72, 74-6, 132, 142, 159
Informal economy, 13, 19, 44, 60, 64-5, 71, 77, 110, 119
Integration, 2, 7, 9, 11, 22-4, 28-30, 33, 37, 45-6 48-50, 61, 65-8, 71, 73-6, 79, 85, 98-9, 102, 110, 118, 131, 134, 138, 152, 170, 184, 194, 197, 201
International division of labour, 81, 135
Italy, 2, 4, 6-7, 14, 24, 29, 31, 33, 35, 37-42, 44-52, 56, 70, 107-8, 126, 132, 134, 137-8, 152, 191

K

Knowledge production, 14, 19, 31

L

Labour force, 4, 39, 43-4, 96, 110-11, 118, 132
Labour market, 4, 7, 8, 11, 24-5, 27-8, 40-1, 43-4, 46-7, 51, 56-9, 73, 75, 77, 79-81, 101, 109, 111, 113-15, 131-3, 143-4, 153, 155, 184
Labour migration, 123, 125, 131-2
Law, 21, 23-4, 26, 41-2, 48-9, 54, 63-5, 71, 76, 91, 93, 106-7, 110, 130, 133, 136-7, 145-6, 148-9, 160-1, 165, 168, 180-3, 186-7, 189-90, 192, 194, 197, 200-2
legal, 3, 9, 19-20, 23, 42, 44-6, 59, 63-4, 66, 71, 73, 75-6, 85, 113, 118, 125, 129-33, 135, 145, 147, 150, 164, 180-1, 187, 189-90, 194-5, 202
Legal, 3, 9, 19-20, 23, 42, 44-6, 54, 59, 63-4, 66, 71, 73, 75-6, 85, 113, 118, 125, 129-33, 135, 137, 145, 147, 150, 164, 166, 180-1, 187, 189-90, 194-5, 200, 202

M

Marginalisation, 8, 48, 64-5, 74, 114, 162
Media, 1, 8-11, 25, 31, 38, 40, 56, 68, 77, 98, 105-6, 108, 116-7, 141, 144-5, 147, 150-3, 155, 161-2, 165-6
Migrant, 1, 2-4, 6-10, 13-15, 17, 19, 20, 22, 25, 29-32, 35, 37, 39, 41-5, 47-50, 52, 55-68, 70-7, 79, 83, 85-95, 97-102, 105-10, 114-5, 117-20, 125-7, 129-36, 138-9, 141-63, 166-70, 179, 182-4, 187, 190, 195, 201
Migration, 1, 2-4, 6-11, 13-25, 28, 29, 31-3, 35, 37-46, 49, 51-2, 54-6, 59-60, 62-3, 65, 68, 70-1, 74, 77-81, 83, 102-3, 105-8, 113-4, 117,

119-20, 123, 125, 128, 130-2, 134-5, 137, 138-9, 142-3, 145-6, 150, 152, 154, 160, 162-4, 166, 168, 181-2, 186-7, 190-1, 197, 199-200
Minorities, 2, 58, 72, 74-5, 77, 107-10, 114, 120, 137-8, 142, 151, 155, 157, 161-2, 164, 167, 170, 180, 184, 193
Moroccans, 8, 39, 47, 55-6, 58-60, 62, 64, 67- 74, 76-9
Multiculturalism, 2
Multiple identities, 10
Muslims, 8, 48, 68, 108, 170

N

Nation, 1, 2, 7, 10, 16, 18, 35, 51, 62, 92, 138, 159, 161-2, 164-6, 170, 191-2, 199
National identity, 170, 191, 193
Nationalism, 1, 76, 118-9, 159, 164-5, 191-2
Nationality, 17, 19, 21, 27, 29, 58-9, 62, 91, 118, 135, 181-3, 191, 193-4, 199-201
Native, 9, 93, 98, 114
Networks, 11, 22-3, 25, 29, 40, 77, 83, 91, 94, 99, 100, 125, 130, 147, 150, 158
New racism, 2, 4
New right, 197
Newspapers, 10, 83, 97, 116, 141, 143, 145, 151, 153-5, 158, 166, 169, 171

O

Oppression, 120, 123, 151, 155, 180, 195
Origin, 5, 17-19, 32, 61, 64, 68, 75, 79, 86, 107, 109, 113, 116, 118, 148-9, 152, 161-2, 174-5, 184, 192
Other, 2, 5-9, 15-17, 19-22, 25, 27-9, 31, 41, 45, 48, 50, 55, 56-63, 65-6, 68-71, 73-7, 79, 85-6, 89, 91, 95, 100-1, 105-7, 109-16, 118, 123, 125-35, 137, 139, 141, 144-51, 153-4, 156-7, 159-60, 163, 166-70, 173, 175, 179-80, 182-4, 188, 193-4, 196
Otherness, 6, 179

P

Parallel economy, 125, 127, 131
Participation, 8-9, 48, 62, 75, 92, 196-7, 202
Patriarchal, 45
Political parties, 8, 45, 48, 142, 149
Politics, 2, 11, 52, 90, 103, 118, 131, 137-8, 163-6, 195, 198-9, 201
Polity, 2, 165, 181, 184, 191, 194-5, 200-1
Poverty, 38, 46, 78, 108, 120, 123, 141-2, 147, 168, 184, 196
Power, 5, 8, 31, 35, 38, 44, 52, 76, 108, 112, 114, 147, 150, 170, 182, 193
Public, 7, 10, 14, 18, 24, 29, 31, 41, 46, 52, 58, 61, 66, 68, 73, 76, 78, 95, 106, 108, 111, 112, 116, 131, 141, 148, 153, 160, 167, 170, 180, 194-5, 197

R

Race, 4, 8, 10, 11, 47-9, 51-2, 62, 76, 139, 151, 155, 159, 163-4, 166, 184, 195, 199, 201
Race discrimination, 81
Racialisation, 6, 9, 139, 150-1, 153, 155, 159, 162
Racism, 2-7, 9-11, 31, 37, 46-8, 52, 61-2, 75, 77, 113, 119, 137, 139, 141, 149, 150-1, 153-5, 158-9, 162-6, 169, 193, 199
Refugees, 3, 23, 29, 31-2, 42, 50, 105, 107-8, 120, 137-9, 142, 187, 189, 190, 200-2

Regularisation, 3, 6-7, 43, 58-60, 109, 119
Religion, 24, 29, 62, 76, 108-9, 148, 184

S

Schengen, 3, 41-2, 55, 105-6, 108, 134, 187, 189-90, 201-2
social security, 3, 24, 29, 65, 98-9, 106, 120, 146, 182, 184-5
Social security, 3, 24, 29, 65, 98-9, 106, 120, 146, 182, 184-5
Society, 2, 4, 7, 9, 11, 16, 21, 32, 35, 37, 42, 45, 47, 49-0, 56, 60-4, 66, 68, 74-7, 79, 85, 96, 103, 105, 107, 110, 116, 118, 120, 127-8, 130-3, 137-8, 141, 148, 150-3, 155, 160, 162-3, 181, 186, 195
Southern Europe, 1-6, 10-11, 31, 51, 60, 70, 73, 75, 79-81, 87, 102, 120, 125-6, 134, 190
Spain, 2, 6, 8-9, 55-66, 68-72, 75-81, 83, 86-96, 98-103, 126, 132, 134, 137-8, 189-90
State, 1-3, 6-8, 10, 14, 17-19, 21, 22, 24-5, 29, 31-3, 35, 41, 52, 58, 63-4, 66, 70, 74-5, 80, 85, 89, 93-6, 98-102, 106, 108, 111, 117, 120, 125, 133-35, 138-9, 141, 146, 148-9, 152, 161, 163-6, 168, 170, 179, 181-2, 184-8, 190-1, 193-4, 198-9, 201-2
Stereotype, 7, 47, 62, 69, 72, 77, 115-6, 119, 128, 139, 150, 154
Subordination, 5, 74

T

Trade Unions, 42, 66, 132, 139, 141-3, 145, 147, 151-2, 155-7, 159, 162, 167-8, 171
Tunisians, 7, 35, 37-9, 40-51, 54

U

Undocumented, 7, 9, 19, 25, 56, 72, 105-6, 109, 111, 119, 123, 125-33, 135, 138-9, 143-4, 146, 148, 151, 153, 156, 158, 167-8
Unemployment, 38-40, 58, 61, 65, 69, 78-9, 108, 114, 131, 141-2, 153, 156-8, 184

V

Violence, 3, 5, 46-7, 138, 152, 159, 161, 165-6

W

Welfare, 8, 29, 40-2, 47, 49, 58, 75, 78, 95, 100-03, 132-3, 135, 153, 180, 196, 202
Women, 1, 2, 8-10, 13, 43, 45-6, 49, 55, 67, 69, 71-3, 75, 90, 93, 95-6, 101-2, 112-13, 115, 119, 127-8, 144-5, 149, 153-5, 164, 167, 173, 175, 184-5, 195, 202